# The European *Roman d'Analyse*

# The European *Roman d'Analyse*

## Unconsummated Love Stories from Boccaccio to Stendhal

Adele Kudish

BLOOMSBURY ACADEMIC
NEW YORK • LONDON • OXFORD • NEW DELHI • SYDNEY

BLOOMSBURY ACADEMIC
Bloomsbury Publishing Inc
1385 Broadway, New York, NY 10018, USA
50 Bedford Square, London, WC1B 3DP, UK
29 Earlsfort Terrace, Dublin 2, Ireland

BLOOMSBURY, BLOOMSBURY ACADEMIC and the Diana logo are trademarks
of Bloomsbury Publishing Plc

First published in the United States of America 2020
This paperback edition published in 2021

Copyright © Adele Kudish, 2020

Cover design by Eleanor Rose
Cover image: Psyche entering Cupid's Garden, 1903 (oil on canvas), Waterhouse, John William (1849-1917) / Harris Museum and Art Gallery, Preston, Lancashire, UK / Bridgeman Images

All rights reserved. No part of this publication may be reproduced or transmitted in any form or by any means, electronic or mechanical, including photocopying, recording, or any information storage or retrieval system, without prior permission in writing from the publishers.

Bloomsbury Publishing Inc does not have any control over, or responsibility for, any third-party websites referred to or in this book. All internet addresses given in this book were correct at the time of going to press. The author and publisher regret any inconvenience caused if addresses have changed or sites have ceased to exist, but can accept no responsibility for any such changes.

Library of Congress Cataloging-in-Publication Data

Names: Kudish, Adele, author.
Title: The European Roman d'analyse: unconsummated love stories from Boccaccio to Stendhal / Adele Kudish.
Description: New York: Bloomsbury Academic, 2020. | Includes bibliographical references and index.
Identifiers: LCCN 2019025894 (print) | LCCN 2019025895 (ebook) | ISBN 9781501352225 (hardback) | ISBN 9781501352232 (epub) | ISBN 9781501352249 (pdf)
Subjects: LCSH: Psychological fiction, European—History and criticism. | Love in literature. | Man-woman relationships in literature.
Classification: LCC PN3448.P8 K77 2020 (print) | LCC PN3448.P8 (ebook) | DDC 809.3/9353—dc23
LC record available at https://lccn.loc.gov/2019025894
LC ebook record available at https://lccn.loc.gov/2019025895

ISBN: HB: 978-1-5013-5222-5
PB: 978-1-5013-7375-6
ePDF: 978-1-5013-5224-9
eBook: 978-1-5013-5223-2

Typeset by Integra Software Services Pvt. Ltd.

To find out more about our authors and books visit www.bloomsbury.com and sign up for our newsletters.

*To Austin, for everything*

# Contents

| | |
|---|---:|
| Acknowledgments | viii |
| An Introduction to Analytical Fiction | 1 |
| 1  The Unconsummated Life in Boccaccio's *Elegia di madonna Fiammetta* | 35 |
| 2  Link on Link: The "Chain of Dishonor" in Marguerite's *Novella 10* and Cervantes's "El curioso impertinente" | 63 |
| 3  Sign Seeing and Failures of Mind Reading in Lafayette's *La Princesse de Clèves* | 101 |
| 4  Self as the "Grand Misleader" in Richardson's *Clarissa* and *The History of Sir Charles Grandison* | 127 |
| 5  Silence and the Cruel Gaze of Society: Austen's *Persuasion* and Stendhal's *Armance* | 157 |
| Conclusion | 191 |
| Works Cited | 196 |
| Index | 209 |

# Acknowledgments

Writing this book has been an incredible education, and I am grateful for having had so many supporters, friends, and teachers who have helped it come together. I want to first thank my editor at Bloomsbury Academic, Katherine De Chant, whose enthusiasm and dedication have kept me going through this process, as well as the editorial staff at Bloomsbury without whose hard work this book would not be as beautiful as it is. I'd also like to thank the anonymous reviewers whose patient reading provided much encouragement as well as vital comments and suggestions.

In the last few years of writing, I have experienced the generous support of my chair at Borough of Manhattan Community College, Joyce Harte, who gave me confidence to persevere in this project and who ensured course release time and recommendations for fellowships. I was awarded two PSC-CUNY Grants and was fortunate to take part in the City University of New York's Faculty Fellowship Publication Program, directed by Shelley Eversley. My FFPP faculty mentor, Matt Brim, as well as the other fellows in my cohort, Álvaro Baquero-Pecino, Tara Bahl, Melissa Dinsman, Meghan Fox, Carly Gieseler, and Lara Kattekola, provided invaluable feedback and discussion for both the book proposal and the chapter on *La Princesse de Clèves*. At BMCC, a number of colleagues and friends provided input during our informal research workshop group. They are Tracy Bealer, Keridiana Chez, Leigh Claire La Berge, Rochelle Rives, and Jason Schneiderman. I also want to especially thank my good friend and office mate, Jungah Kim, for keeping me on track by making many library dates and for always offering me an intellectual challenge.

Over the years, many people have read or talked with me about chapters and different aspects of this work. Elizabeth Alsop, Anastassiya Andrianova, Rajeev and Tiffany Dehejia, Caroline Dezutter, Suzanne Farrell Smith, Lol Fow, Tal Gross, Trevor Jockims, Charlotte Kent, Jean-David LaFrance, Caitlin Leffel-Ostroy, Bettina Lerner, Anne McCarthy, Evelina Mendelevich, Nataša Milas, Pia Padukone, Sydney Schwartz, David Sharp, and Lori Yamato have provided much-needed support, insights, and most importantly, friendship.

Immeasurable thanks go to my mentors, André Aciman, Rachel Brownstein, Kimberlee Anne Campbell, Clare Carroll, Giancarlo Lombardi, John D. Lyons, and Lía Schwartz, as well as the late Jon-Christian Suggs and Kathryn Talarico, whose unwavering support and example of scholarliness and professionalism I aim to replicate for my students throughout my own career. Reid Barbour, Patrick McHenry, and Caroline Weber also very kindly took time out of their busy schedules to read this work when it was in draft form.

This book was written in a number of libraries around New York City, including at the Wertheim Study at the Steven A. Schwarzman Building of the New York Public Library and at other university libraries through the Manhattan Research Library Initiative (MaRLI), as well as at the Bibliothèque Nationale de France in Paris thanks to the support of a PSC-CUNY Grant, the CUNY Graduate Center's Renaissance Studies Travel and Research Grant, and a CUNY Writing Fellowship. I also would like to thank my research assistants Alsatia Ragusa and Damian Ruff for their editorial support and readiness to help in the final stages of this project.

A version of Chapter 4 was published in *Studies in Philology* as "Lost 'in a Sort of Wilderness': The Epistemology of Love in Richardson's *The History of Sir Charles Grandison*" (114:2 [2017], pp. 426–45) and it is with the kind permission of the editor that it appears in this book in a slightly modified form. In addition, parts of Chapters 3 and 5 appeared in *The French Review* and *The Explicator* as "'[La] plus Jolie [de] Toutes Celles Qui Avaient Jamais Été Écrites': Madame de Thémines' Letter as Proto-Psychological Fiction in *La Princesse de Clèves*," *The French Review* (91–3 [2018], pp. 56–69), and "'Emotions so Compounded of Pleasure and Pain': Affective Contradiction in Austen's *Persuasion*," *The Explicator* (74:2 [2016], pp. 120–24), and I appreciate the permission to include them here.

I wish to thank my parents, Deniza and Samuel Kudish, for their constant support, and my daughter Rosalind for her remarkable patience (and the occasional, much-welcomed distraction) while I was writing this book. Most of all, I would like to thank my husband, Austin Brown, for always listening and reading, and for providing the kind of real love and understanding that only exist *outside* of fairy tales.

# An Introduction to Analytical Fiction

> *And these very tricks that the senses play on our understanding are played back on them in return. Our soul disturbs the senses, they lie and deceive each other at will.*[1]

## Our "Soul Error": Self-Deception and Self-Doubt

"Que sçay-je?" "What do I know?" This motto, rooted in both introspection and self-doubt, steers Montaigne through his magnum opus, the *Essais* (1580). Like Descartes decades later, Montaigne grapples with a fundamental question: how do we know that we are not being deceived by our senses? But unlike Descartes, who manages to wrestle himself from the grasp of the evil genius through rationalism, and arrives at his famous *cogito*, Montaigne not only does not see a way out of self-doubt, he practically embraces it.[2] The essayist remains fixed within his paradox, resigned to being deceived. Presumption—the cousin of self-deception—Montaigne tells us, in his "Apology for Raymond Sebond," "is our natural and original disease."[3] In another essay dedicated entirely to presumption, Montaigne elaborates on this inherently flawed judgment:

---

[1] "Et cette même piperie, que les sens apportent à notre entendement, ils la reçoivent à leur tour. Notre âme parfois s'en revanche de même, ils mentent et se trompent à l'envi" (Montaigne II, 386). Unless otherwise stated, translations from the French are my own.
[2] That is not to say that Descartes fundamentally reconciles self-knowledge in his rationalist philosophy. While the *cogito* indubitably demonstrates that the thinking thing thinks, other kinds of knowledge, including sensory knowledge, remain relatively opaque, and the problem of radical skepticism remains comparatively unresolved.
[3] "est notre maladie naturelle et originelle" (II, 178-9). *Une présomption* indicates "[un] jugement fondé sur des apparences, sur des indices," that is, a judgment based on evidence, particularly sensory evidence, according to the first edition of the dictionary of the Académie française (1694) (ARTFL Project, University of Chicago).

I feel harassed by an error in my soul which displeases me, since it is both unjust and inconvenient. [...] It is because I underestimate the value of things that I already own, and the things that I own, I lower their value, so that they become foreign, absent, and not mine.[4]

In Montaigne's reading of human nature, which dissects behavior and exposes our motivational rudderlessness, the senses and the passions always strive to triumph over reason. This is our "soul error,"[5] which devalues what we already have and overvalues what we do not. One's insight is seldom trustworthy, since our insights often go too far and then miss their mark: "the greatest fault of insight is not that it does not pursue its course to the end, but that it goes beyond it,"[6] writes La Rochefoucauld a century after Montaigne.

This pessimistic worldview has been exemplified since the biblical author's aphorism— "the heart is deceitful above all things" (Jeremiah 17:9)—and the Greek imperative to "know yourself" ("γνῶθι σαυτόν" [gnothi seauton]), which was born out of a paradox; the ancient Greeks were keenly aware that "self-searching is most commonly the offspring of self-distrust and misgivings" (Lovejoy 1). And the fathers of history, Herodotus and Thucydides, "[press] to the fore in various ways [...] the *limited* nature of access to others' minds" (Baragwanath 36, referring specifically to Herodotus) and alert readers "to important epistemological truths about the limits of historical knowledge" (Baragwanath 37). These philosophers, historians, and religious writers depict the order of things as an ironic *mise en abyme*,[7] which certain

---

[4] "Je me sens pressé d'un'erreur d'âme qui me déplaît, et comme inique et encore plus comme importune. [...] C'est que je diminue du juste prix les choses que je possède, de ce que je les possède: et hausse le prix aux choses, d'autant qu'elles sont estrangères, absentes [et] non miennes" (II, 441). Almost identically, two hundred years earlier, Boccaccio, appropriating the voice of a fictional woman abandoned by her lover, laments that "solamente le cose liberamente possedute sogliono essere reputate vili, quantunque elle siene molto care, e quelle che con malavvolezza s'hanno, ancora che vilissime sieno, sono carissime reputate" (*Elegia di madonna Fiammetta* 175) ["new things are more appealing than those one often sees, and men always desire more intensely what they do not possess than what they do possess" (*The Elegy of Lady Fiammetta* 56)]. Montaigne did read Boccaccio, whose *Decameron* he lists with other works as "simplement plaisants [...] dignes qu'on s'y amuse" (II, 121) ["simply pleasant { ... } worthy {of being read} for amusement"], although it is unclear whether he had read the *Elegia*. More likely his maxim was derived independently or from a different or even shared source.

[5] The way in which Roger Shattuck translates Montaigne's "erreur d'âme" (*Proust's Way* 84).

[6] "Le plus grand défaut de la pénétration n'est pas de n'aller point jusqu'au but, c'est de le passer" (*Maximes* 78).

[7] A term coined by André Gide to describe the effect of infinite regression. According to Lucien Dällenbach, *mise en abyme* foremost has to do with reflexivity (42), a form that we will see quite often in the *roman d'analyse* in ironic and meaningful tensions between the metaphors of and allusions to mirroring and distorting.

fiction authors, in their turn, populate with tragicomic characters who are poor readers of themselves, of each other, of their environments, and of signs from the gods. We are lost, as two of Samuel Richardson's heroines claim, "in a wilderness of doubt and error" (Richardson, *Clarissa* 565) or, as Madame de Clèves' mother warns her about the French court in Marie-Madeleine de Lafayette's *La Princesse de Clèves*, "if you judge from appearances here, [...] you will often be deceived; truth and appearances seldom go together."[8] We cannot know what others are thinking, nor be sure of our own desires. "The passions of the soul," as Pascal puts it, quoting Montaigne, "lie and deceive themselves at will" (20).

This book examines eight canonical novels and novellas that both predate and follow Montaigne, La Rochefoucauld, and Pascal in their widespread distrust of the self's motivations from a new perspective that I call "analytical fiction," vis-à-vis comparative and transhistorical literature. *The European Roman d'Analyse: Unconsummated Love Stories from Boccaccio to Stendhal* defines the sub-genre of analytical fiction—an adaptation of the French term in the book's title—whose works, I argue, can be interpreted together as a tradition that anatomizes the epistemology of troubled or failed love.[9] This sub-genre stands in contrast to other, more widely recognized novelistic sub-species such as, for example, the picaresque, the bildungsroman, the realist novel, the gothic novel, the novel of adventure, or the marriage plot novel. The texts analyzed in this study, a selection of novels and novellas written between 1343 and 1827, namely Boccaccio's *Elegia di madonna Fiammetta* (1343–44), Marguerite de Navarre's tenth *nouvelle* from the *Heptaméron* (1558), Cervantes's interpolated novella, "El curioso impertinente" (in *Don Quixote* Part I [1605]), Lafayette's *La Princesse de Clèves* (1678), Richardson's *Clarissa* (1748) and *The History of Sir Charles Grandison* (1753), Jane Austen's *Persuasion* (1817), and Stendhal's

---

[8] "si vous jugez sur les apparences en ce lieu-ci, [...] vous serez souvent trompée: ce qui paraît n'est presque jamais la vérité" (*La Princesse de Clèves et Autres Romans* 157).
[9] The term I employ here, "sub-genre," is more or less my own. What I designate "sub-genre," Northrop Frye calls throughout *Anatomy of Criticism* a "mixed form" of fiction, and he also employs the term "species." Seymour Chatman designates these as "generic subclasses" (*Coming to Terms* 10) (a term which seems to have been more recently utilized by computer scientists) of the narrative text type; I use the terms "subclass," "form," "sub-genre," and "sub-species" interchangeably. As a point of interest, Michael McKeon points out that "Frye's usage is unusual in that he employs the term 'genre' to refer to what we would call the 'mode' of narrative (or 'prose fiction')" (*Theory of the Novel* 2).

*Armance* (1827), are here compared all together for the first time.[10] I argue that these texts are linked through a shared pessimistic philosophy that questions the validity of every kind of communicative sign (i.e., representation itself) and denies the legitimacy of introspection. These particular eight novels and novellas (and the philosophy that circumscribes them) may be best classified as anti-humanist works, in Michael Moriarty's terminology, as a rather Augustinian philosophical and quasi-religious revolt against Renaissance humanism, revealing "a certain disenchantment, a sense of disenfranchisement that could not be expressed through available political channels or discourses" (*Early Modern French Thought* 37). In their distrust of motivation, these novels and novellas reveal some of the darkest human impulses, including betrayal, self-harm, and rape; acts that defy representation.[11] Through close readings, and through the conceptual frameworks of genre theory and narratology, I argue that the *roman d'analyse*'s damning epistemology of love constitutes a previously uncatalogued and under-theorized sub-genre in the history of the novel. At the same time I demonstrate how this type of fiction enacts a larger philosophical

---

[10] Although I am delineating a central interpretation that links these texts as *romans d'analyse*, at the same time, I am in no way discounting other readings. John Campbell, for example, takes issue with Jean Fabre's statement in *L'Art d'analyse dans la Princesse de Clèves* that "lorsqu'un roman fait place à l'analyse il faut que cette place soit la première, sinon la seule, et qu'elle se subordonne ou qu'elle élimine tout le reste" (Fabre 19) ["when a novel makes use of analysis, analysis must be the central, if not the only concern, and it must subordinate or even eliminate everything else"]. Campbell reminds his readers that there always exist simultaneously a number of interpretive approaches that can and should be pursued, or at least acknowledged. This book takes a middle road; instead of arguing, like Fabre does, that analysis subordinates all other ways of reading these texts, I make the analysis of motivation, feeling, and doubt the central foci of my study, which I acknowledge is only one particular interpretive project, though one that I find meaningful and rewarding.

[11] The subject of sexual violence must be discussed in this book because attempted rapes occur in both Marguerite's tenth *nouvelle* and Richardson's *Grandison*, there is a reported rape in the *Elegia*, and of course, an actual rape in *Clarissa*. To commit rape is an act of dehumanization, clearly for the victim, but also for the rapist; the act of violence alone strips the perpetrator of a defense on the basis of mental state. In the middle ages, according to Mary J. Baker, "both the degree of violence and the intentions of the perpetrator were critical factors in determining whether or not rape occurred. In his *Decretum* (c. 1140) Gratian distinguished between rape, where violence was a necessary condition, and seduction, where guile might be applied and promises made. [...] The idea that beguiling speeches [that led to what we would call rape] did not constitute violence was upheld into the sixteenth century" (272). Today, the act of violence is sufficient for establishing guilt, regardless of motivation. However, our idea of "rape culture" in some ways functions as the beginnings of the exploration of the mindset of the rapist and how rapists are socialized to commit rape. This opens the terrifying possibility of endowing the rapist with rationalization, whereas previously we considered the failure to exercise control over the self as demonstrating the collapse of reason. Nevertheless, the gendered cultural prejudices and assumptions that underlie this guilty act must be revealed. The acts of sexual violence discussed in this text are historicized within their own cultural understanding of rape, and are treated seriously as literary representations of a real act that affects real women.

project for its various authors: an anatomy of the psyche wherein we are unable, or unwilling, to know ourselves.

Whereas in various cultures, the consummation of physical love or a promise to marry can act as metaphors for self-knowledge, *romans d'analyse* (henceforth also called analytical fiction, novels of analysis, analytical novels, and, sometimes, proto-psychological fiction) have the reverse effect. Here, the metaphor of unconsummated love is deployed to illustrate a fundamental lack of insight regarding the self, while characters are driven by their irrational passions, including lust, fear, jealousy, and anger. I will discuss the question of what love is in analytical fiction in more detail shortly, but for the moment, suffice to say that the sort of love evidenced in these texts is, more often than not, self-love in the sense that La Rochefoucauld uses it in his *Maximes* (1665), "unpredictable and essentially mysterious" (de Mourgues 89):

> Self-love is the love of oneself, and of all things for the sake of oneself. [...] Nothing is so impetuous as its desires, nothing is as secret as its plans, nothing is as clever as its desires. [...] Its convolutions are beyond imagining; its transformations surpass those of any metamorphosis, and its subtleties those of chemistry. [...] It twists and turns in a thousand perceptible ways (*Collected Maxims and Other Reflections* 147–49).[12]

Cunning, labyrinthian, all-powerful, capable of defying every other force—this is self-love, and as we will see, it rules the *roman d'analyse*. It is why, as Christopher Tilmouth puts it, "the humanists' dream of rational self-governance and moral autonomy is [...] doomed to failure" (33).[13] The redoubling, cyclical turns and returns of doubt in characters' psyches remind us that, in analytical

---

[12] "L'amour-propre est l'amour de soi-même, et de toutes choses pour soi [...] Rien n'est si impétueux que ses désirs, rien ne si caché que ses desseins, rien de si habile que ses conduites [...] Ses transformations passent celles des métamorphoses, et ses raffinements ceux de la chimie [...] Iiest à couvert des yeux les plus pénétrants; il y fait mille insensibles tours et retours" (*Maximes* 91).

[13] The idea of self-love is evidenced at least as early as Augustine, who echoes the pessimistic biblical belief about our inability to know ourselves. His theology preached that human knowledge is limited and incomplete, that our behavior tends to be self-serving and flawed, and that the will naturally strives toward the *wrong*, except through God's grace. In *The City of God* Augustine outlines his precept of the "separate cities of love:" "two cities have been formed by two loves: the earthly by the love of self [*amor sui*], even to the contempt of God; the heavenly by the love of God, even to the contempt of self" (477). The Augustinian and, later, the Calvinist precepts regarding moral psychology and governance influenced what is usually called Jansenist theology (the Augustinian theology of Jansenius), which directly shaped the particularly fatalistic ethos for many literary figures including Pascal, La Rochefoucauld, and Lafayette. For an excellent summary of these religious texts that contextualize self-governance, see Tilmouth 1–26.

fiction, "the all-pervading presence of self-love is not a theory, but a biological fact" (de Mourgues 91). The seemingly endless frustrations and anguish of love, the pessimism inherent in its renunciation, and, in these principally secular literary works, the lack of a divine being to provide any alternative model for self-governance, all function as the mainsprings of analytical fiction.

Rather than depicting "transparent minds," as in Dorrit Cohn's famous formulation, novels of analysis deal in the *opacity* of the human mind.[14,15] Analytical fiction is ultimately about characters reading and guessing at each other's and their own hidden motivations and assumptions; it is concerned with depicting the relationship—often lacking or destabilized—between knowledge and feeling in characters, and the networks of understanding between narrators and characters and between authors and readers. Affairs in which the would-be lovers miscommunicate through spying and misread signs, scenes of protracted, frustrating, and ultimately inconsequential physical contact (such as hand-holding), and on the other extreme, the full-scale collapse of reason resulting in acts of dehumanizing violence, depict narrators and characters who are constantly faced with false, incomplete, or withheld information, deception, misprision, doubt, and confusion, leading to self-deception, jealousy, and crises of self. These are read in this study as symptoms of a more fundamental preoccupation with the human psyche as incomprehensible.

Yet, analytical fiction attempts to engage in epistemological and psychological problems that it cannot resolve on the terms of either epistemology or psychology. An examination of narrative temperament and motifs, on the other hand, helps to elucidate the way in which narrators, characters, and readers interact and cope with the inhibition (to use a Freudian term) of knowledge in pre-Freudian literature. Analytical fiction, then, cannot bring a reader closer to a better understanding of the human heart and mind, per se, but it can illustrate the often winding and incomplete aesthetic journey that such a search entails.

The remainder of this introduction leads the reader through my methodology, the history of the term "*roman d'analyse*," and the attributes and motifs of analytical fiction, before situating this sub-genre into the history of the novel.

---

[14] Cohn's introduction enumerates a number of authors and critics who have illustrated "the importance of the mimesis of consciousness for the history of the novel" (9).

[15] This is a reference to Peter Caruthers's cognitive science study *The Opacity of Mind: An Integrative Theory of Self-Knowledge*, in which the author does not engage with any literary texts. Caruthers finds that "we never have either authoritative or privileged knowledge of most kinds of propositional attitude [including our own motivations]. On the contrary, our access to almost all such attitudes is interpretive rather than transparent" (14).

The following five chapters then provide close readings of eight representative texts, and examine the interrelationships between narrative properties, such as cyclicality, ellipsis, indescribability, silence, and epistemological failures embodied by jealousy and self-doubt.[16] At first, these features may appear to belong to different categories. On further examination, however, the distinctions between them collapse, and the interrelations become more apparent. Jealousy begins with a character's misreading of a sign (often rendered as an ellipsis); then come doubt about the veracity of that (mis)reading, the attendant silence that accompanies such doubt, and the eventual resolution of the doubt. Then, cyclically, a new doubt arises from a fresh misreading of another sign. The narrators of analytical fiction become complicit and often fall victim to this same scheme, which, ultimately, derives from the authors' extreme skepticism. While there is variation in each text examined, the blueprint of analytical fiction remains stable.

Chapter 1, "The Unconsummated Life in Boccaccio's *Elegia di madonna Fiammetta*," contrasts the representation of action versus language in Boccaccio's novel against that in Guilliaume de Lorris and Jean de Meun's *Le Roman de la rose* (1230–75) and Apuleius's Cupid and Psyche story from *The Golden Ass* (late second century CE). This first substantive chapter also defines the way in which the concept of the unreliable narrator functions in analytical fiction using Fiammetta as an example. Throughout the *Elegia*, Fiammetta weighs her own anguish against a variety of exempla and finds that the exempla come up short in comparison to her personal trauma. In many ways, Chapter 1 scaffolds the subsequent ones by both framing analytical fiction against a background of non-analytical texts as well as illustrating more of the key features of the sub-genre (the cyclical-but-dilated narrative durée, dissimulation and deception, the trope of indescribability, and lack of self-knowledge among them).

Chapter 2, "Link on Link: The 'Chain of Dishonor' in Marguerite's *Novella 10* and Cervantes's 'El curioso impertinente,'" focuses on two early modern

---

[16] While "rejecting close reading has sometimes appeared to be progressive" (J. Peterson 47), the practice of close reading (what Barbara Johnson calls "a careful teasing out of the warring forces of signification that are at work within the text itself" [cited in Culler's "The Closeness of Reading" 11]) is enjoying renewed attention. Culler affirms that the skill of "examining closely the language of a literary work or a section of it, has been [...] a sine qua non of literary study" ("The Closeness of Close Reading" 8), but that "the work of close reading is not primarily to resolve difficulties but [...] to describe them, to elucidate their source and implications. [...] It involves poetics as much as hermeneutics" (10). To me, close reading involves a sustained focus on a text's structures and language, combined with the deployment of a vocabulary and critical framework for literary analysis. It requires a back-and-forth between deductive and inductive reasoning, in that the reader both has to know what she is looking for in the text, as well as letting the text be the guide.

analytical novellas that are themselves embedded in non-analytical frames (The *Heptaméron* and *Don Quixote* Part 1, respectively). These texts represent the madness of a male protagonist and the extremes that he will go to when afflicted by the "disease" of irrational love. And both novellas illustrate the use of counterintuitive approaches to coping with desire, but in which deliberation always proves inconsequential. But Cervantes's text follows the route of seduction, while Marguerite's character attempts to rape his would-be lover. Neither affair ends well for the protagonists, as both women end up in convents and the men die in war or of a broken heart. However, as is typical in analytical fiction, love is never fully extinguished in any of the characters.

Chapter 3, "Sign Seeing and Mind Reading in Lafayette's *La Princesse de Clèves*," is central to this book in its elucidation of the use of narrative indescribability and the vocabulary of interpretation, reading, and spying that undercut a simple progression forward in the narrative, creating an affective environment of anxiety, shame, and distrust. The chapter argues that Lafayette employs an ironic recurring structure throughout her text that centralizes, simultaneously, a kind of plumbing of the psyche and an almost systematic drive toward self-deception by juxtaposing scenes of sagacious mind-reading with ones of abject lack of self-knowledge. The princess, in rejecting life, also rejects a world in which all endings are arbitrary and relationships can be capriciously terminated and revived, and in which we must all learn to live with our own self-deception.

Chapter 4, "Self as the 'Grand Misleader' in Richardson's *Clarissa* and *The History of Sir Charles Grandison*," illustrates that characters in analytical fiction are visibly self-deceived even in the epistolary mode. First, the chapter compares Richardson's last two novels with *La Princesse de Clèves*, pointing out the strong links between the pessimistic view of love taken in Lafayette's work and the anti-romantic stance regarding marriage evidenced in Richardson's last two novels. The following two sections focus on *Clarissa* and *Grandison* separately. The *Clarissa* section concentrates on analytical scenes in which Lovelace and Clarissa mirror each other in their mutual self-deceptions. The last part of the chapter demonstrates how *Grandison* remains unresolved by re-opening doubt and indecision at the end through a direct reference to Lafayette's novel, and because of Clementina's abstention from love. The chapter ends with a brief defense of the comparative approach used in this book.

Chapter 5, "The Cruel Gaze of Society: Austen's *Persuasion* and Stendhal's *Armance*," takes us to the early part of the nineteenth century, where the analysis swings outward (only to be drawn right back in) to examine the role that familial and societal setting—always closed, suspicious, and judgmental—plays in understanding analytical fiction and how it generates silence in the main characters as well as in an analytical narrative more generally. Although one ends tragically and the other happily, *Armance* and *Persuasion*, I argue, both hinge on troubling and loaded silences that undermine almost every intimate scene involving the main characters. Just as in *Persuasion*, in which Anne's fear of war and her lack of family recast the ending of the supposed marriage-plot novel as far less optimistic than a fairy-tale ending, the silence that overwhelms the characters of *Armance* surpasses public fear, and becomes internalized.

Finally, the book's conclusion takes stock of the arguments made throughout about unconsummated love acting as a metaphor for the impossibility of self-knowledge. The conclusion is also more personal in that it interrogates the positionality of the critic interested in questions of irony, insight, and self-knowledge through the reading and interpretation of painful and sometimes violent stories that herald the unfeasibility of love. The conclusion further confronts the issue of violence against women—including rape and attempted rape—that are touched upon throughout the book. The violence against the characters in the novels and novellas is enumerated, and another brief example, from Austen's *Emma* and Amy Heckerling's adaptation *Clueless*, is re-introduced from the introduction, where it serves as an illustration of an (ultimately false) cataleptic impression.

## Narrating a Sub-Genre: Frame and Method

This book does not seek to identify the first author to have written a work of analytical fiction,[17] which I will begin to define below, but rather describes the underlying motifs and narrative techniques of the sub-genre, as well as some

---

[17] Although many others have claimed to do so, at least for the "psychological novel." The *Elegia*, *La Princesse de Clèves*, *Clarissa*, Daniel Defoe's *Robinson Crusoe* (1719), Jean-Jacques Rousseau's *Julie or The New Heloise* (1761), Choderlos de Laclos's *Dangerous Liaisons* (1782), as well as novels of Johann Wolfgang von Goethe and Nathaniel Hawthorne have each been called the "first psychological novel" because they are all concerned with representing interiority. Frances Ferguson, whose article "Rape and the Rise of the Novel" situates *Pamela* and *Clarissa* as "first full examples of the psychological novel" (98), particularly well defines what this term actually means in her analysis on pp. 99–109, though it differs from analytical fiction, which I define here as a separate tradition from psychological fiction.

of the historical, social, philosophical, and religious contexts for the small selection of individual works discussed. I do not intend analytical fiction to indicate a prescriptive designation, but rather a descriptive one (Chapman 620). Moreover, my project, which assembles, as Anne-Lise François writes of her own work on the theory of recessive action, what seems to be "an odd assortment of primary texts" (xvii), is aided by assuming an implicit methodology that relies on intertextuality. Analytical fiction is found across the ages and across geographical boundaries (certainly, Proust's *À la recherche du temps perdu* [1913–27] is a novel of analysis, and various accounts indicate that Murasaki Shikibu's eleventh-century *Tale of Genji* is one, too), but direct connections of influence through translation and adaptation are easily found as well. Some examples include Lafayette's borrowings from Marguerite de Navarre in *La Princesse de Clèves* (and the tenth novella's inclusion in English in the schoolmaster and clerk William Painter's popular collection known as *The Palace of Pleasure*, containing ninety-four tales from around Europe in two volumes[18]). Richardson's and Stendhal's references to Lafayette's *The Princess of Clèves*, or Jane Austen's admiration and imitation of Richardson's novels, especially *Grandison*, are other examples of translations and borrowings, some of which predate the eighteenth-century ones that Mary Helen McMurran (whose work in trans-channel studies I discuss more below) examines. These elective affinities (to appropriate a term from another quasi-analytical novel), while not strictly necessary for a critical comparison, in my view, reveal correspondences that make tracing the line of analytical fiction even more valuable for students and scholars of the European novel.

Genre is notoriously tricky to pin down, and its variety and methods of categorization have proliferated so much since Aristotle's classification of lyric, epic, and drama in the *Poetics* that genre analysis can occasionally seem fruitless to pursue. There is the objection that Jonathan Culler raises, that genres "are simply taxonomic categories in which we place works that share certain features. […] If a text seems not to fit, this means only that a new category must be postulated" (*Theory of the Novel* 52), thus rendering "our taxonomic classes [as] […] artifices of description" (52). Indeed, the critique of genre as an artificial teleology, from Shakespeare's lampooning of Polonius's catalogue of genres, to Friedrich

---

[18] According to Dora Polachek, *The Palace of Pleasure* "would become a treasure trove for Elizabethan authors to plunder" (32), particularly Shakespeare and his contemporary dramatists. For scholars of translation history today, it represents one of the most important collections of early modern novellas.

Schlegel's theory of the transcendence of genre by the mixing of its forms in romantic literature (Hamlin 6, 13), to Benedetto Croce, to Jacques Derrida's "The Law of Genre" is, as Gérard Genette points out, "itself a subgenre" (*Introduction à l'architexte*, quoted in Castelvecchi 3).[19] But then again, Culler's description of genre in *Structuralist Poetics* is quite useful, as "a conventional function of language, a particular relation to the world which serves as norm or expectation to guide the reader in his encounter with the text" (*Structuralist Poetics* 136), and is loose enough to assuage concerns about artificiality and "making something fit." As Raymond Chapman argues regarding genre studies, "the emphasis now is not on the prescriptions which may guide and constrain the author, but on the expectations of the reader, whose approach to a text can be helped in recognition and discrimination. [...] If genre is regarded as semiotic and indicative rather than predetermined, the reader is both liberated and given new responsibility" (623). In this book I also follow Frye's somewhat impressionistic description of genre in *Anatomy of Criticism* as "based on analogies in form" (95) whereby "poetry can only be made out of other poems; novels out of other novels" (97). Moreover, Frye writes, "the purpose of criticism by genres is not so much to classify as to clarify such traditions and affinities, thereby bringing out a large number of literary relationships that would not be noticed as long as there were no context established for them" (247). This book establishes a context for the European *roman d'analyse*.

Frye's study of forms of fiction also provides the critical terminology of *romance, novel, satire, history,* and *anatomy* for this book, although the sincerity of his method has been questioned and his own internal, intentional ironies have been cited.[20] Nevertheless, the closest we can come to categorizing the *roman d'analyse* is under Frye's umbrella of the "anatomy" form, that which "has baffled critics, and there is hardly any fiction writer deeply influenced by it who has not been accused of disorderly conduct" (313). Of this form, which, in its pure configuration, he associates with Menippean satire, Frye writes, "it eventually begins to merge with the novel, producing various hybrids including the *roman à these* and novels in which the characters are symbols of social or other ideas" (312). He lists Boethius's *Consolation of Philosophy*, Burton's *Anatomy of Melancholy*, Sterne's *Tristram Shandy*, and Hogg's

---

[19] Stefano Castelvecchi provides an excellent summary of the debate about genre (1–12).
[20] Louis Mackey argues that "the relation between criticism and literature is, on [Frye's] own showing, ironic" (449).

*Confessions of a Justified Sinner* as examples. The Menippean satire, writes Frye, "deals less with people as such than with mental attitudes" (309) and "presents us with a vision of the world in terms of a single intellectual pattern" (310). We could say that this intellectualized species of fiction—skeptically presenting the world as unknowable—combines with the other forms that Frye delineates, the novel, the romance, and the history, to produce the sub-species that I call the analytical novel.

Narratology (a theory of narrative "dedicated to the study of the logic, principles, and practices of narrative representation" [Meister]) also serves as a frame for this study, beyond its generally understood function "as a set of descriptive terms and tools that allow us to break narratives down into their component parts in order to see how they fit together in ways that follow and sometimes transgress norms that generally govern the association of story and discourse" (Kent Puckett, "Narrative Theory's *Long Durée*," in *The Cambridge Companion to Narrative Theory* 16) (although the descriptive terms and tools of narratology, such as "narrator," "unreliability," "durée," etc., are also essential for constructing this argument). According to Puckett, narrative theory also, with its "powerful and seemingly universal methodological appeal" (16), allows us to see "one evocative expression of a longer intellectual history" that helps us to grasp "as a broadly philosophical effort [...] the nature and the production of social values" (16). The present book also provides a pan-European study, in a market where such books are relatively rare, that challenges the heuristic of discrete national literary traditions that maintains a mythology of separate Continental and English canons, exaggerates the artificial distinctions between them, and renders the two incompatible. April Alliston identifies this problem as "the exclusive boundary line that describes the national literary canon, and its linear transmission as a national patrimony" (2).[21] As McMurran puts it, the "rise" of the novel has been treated "as particular to a specific nation [...] with a special capacity to represent that nation. At the same time, the novel is recognized as an extraordinarily restless, heterogeneous, and supranational entity" (156). While McMurran places the reconciliation of these two visions of the novel historically,

---

[21] Alliston also convincingly disputes Peter Brooks's claim about social class, invoking a "separate female language within the male-dominated framework of aristocratic feudalism [ ... that] does in fact link [writers like Scudéry and Lafayette, i.e. those very authors Brooks identifies with the aristocracy] with the rise of the bourgeoisie" (24), and cites a number of critics, furthermore, who demonstrate that the "aristocratic" Lafayette in any case "had a far greater claim to a place at court in [her] much-admired [wit] than in [her] father's [name]" (24).

in the cross-Channel translations that emerged in the eighteenth century, I wish to situate that circulation even earlier, before the rise of the modern nation-state. In addition, as I hope to demonstrate here, the tools of narratology can help break down the mythology of entirely separate traditions by identifying ideological and stylistic commonalities between texts across historical as well as geographical boundaries.

Shared philosophical interests also help to explain the analogous as well as intertextual correspondences between novels produced in various European countries. The authors studied here as writers of analytical fiction are especially influenced by Pyrrhonean skepticism. While the early modern period's renewed interest in the skepticism of Sextus Empiricus is rooted in an amalgamation of factors outside of the scope of this study, it is in part embedded in what I earlier referred to as a rise in anti-humanist thought (or what Zachary S. Schiffman identifies in Montaigne as "the failure of the humanist program of education" [499]).[22] But at the same time, skepticism never really went away. As Richard Kuhns points out, Boccaccio, too, had read Sextus, even modeling a story in the *Decameron* (7.9) on Pyrrhonean skepticism (730). Francisco Sánchez's *That Nothing Is Known* (*Quod nihil scitur*) (1581), another example of Pyrrhonean skepticism,[23] likely influenced Cervantes's writing of *Don Quixote*. But while radical skepticism is omnipresent in analytical fiction, it does not serve as a mode of self-governance (a guide to living, as it were, that brings one ἀταραξία [ataraxia], or the Greek ideal of equanimity) in the same way as philosophical skepticism does. Instead, skepticism disrupts fiction even within fiction, paradoxically and elliptically challenging readers to submit to a denial of any community between appearances and reality, while simultaneously and necessarily suspending disbelief in the function of narrative.

Thus, it is the novel—a mode that can *narrate* skepticism—that remains the key object of study here, and the authors of the novels examined in this book (whether by analogy or intertextuality, or a combination of the two) develop their own cohesive idea of narrative skepticism. The novel, although not a late-developing genre as we have mostly now come to accept (since novels have been

---

[22] For more on the difference between Pyrrhonean (following the doctrine of the Greek physician Sextus (*c.* 200 CE) and Academic (popularized by Cicero in his *Academica*) skepticism, see Schiffman (499–516).

[23] In which the author "seek[s] the truth without ever having found it, and while he does not claim that it is impossible to find the truth, he is not certain that it will ever be found and cautions expectations accordingly" (Caluori 263).

written since antiquity), stands apart from the classical forms of lyric, epic, and drama as a mixed genre that performs both mimetically and diegetically, that is, both to show and to tell.[24] And the novel, as an inherently dialogical mode (even in the novels and novellas presented in this study, which often seem, at first glance, to favor a central character's voice and consciousness), can offer us, as Frye writes about Henry James, "an exhaustive analysis of human relationships" (311). It is possible that the *roman d'analyse* found its shape in the novel and novella because, while its narratives focalize a woman's mind (indeed, six of the eight primary texts studied in this book are either written by women or through the device of a fictitious female narrator, providing what Leon Edel calls in Modernist writing "the direct mental experience of the characters" [19–20]), its complex dialogism and ironic structure highlight an even stronger authorial voice.

## From "Roman d'analyse" to Analytical Fiction

The term *roman d'analyse* seems to have first been used only a few years after the publication of the last novel examined in this book (*Armance* in 1827), by Sainte-Beuve as a passing reference in his dedication of *Les Consolations* (1830) to Victor Hugo, in which he calls the *roman d'analyse*, along with the lyric poem, "a penetrating, exquisite, and luscious nourishment. It gets under your skin; it is enchanting."[25] The term then was resurrected at the end of that century by the novelist Paul Bourget, who defines the *roman d'analyse* as a type "which attempts to lay bare the various idiosyncrasies of such and such a person" (587).[26] Next, the twenty-year-old writer Raymond Radiguet described his own *Le Bal du comte d'Orgel* (1924), a reworking of *La Princesse de Clèves*, as "[a] novel in which it is the psychology that is novelistic. There, the only stretch of the imagination is applied not to external events, but to the analysis of the sentiments" (Aciman's translation,

---

[24] In writing about whether *La Princesse de Clèves* can be designated as an innovation of the novel, Nicholas D. Paige asserts that "Lafayette invented her princess, but she did not invent modern fiction, because *La Princesse de Clèves* becomes 'fiction' only in the rearview mirror of literary history. Instead, the novel was an isolated manipulation of longstanding conventions and local practices that changed precisely nothing" (36). In fact, Paige recalls that these "conventions and practices belonged to the Aristotelian tradition" (36) but in the sense that Aristotle's treatise on poetics privileged historical heroes and "the historical core of poetry [where] the object of imitation needed to be [...] real" (27).

[25] "Une nourriture exquise et pulpeuse. [...] On s'en pénètre; c'est un enchentement" (viii). Sainte-Beuve's own *Volupté* (1834) is an analytical novel.

[26] "qui se propose de mettre à nu les nuances individuelles de telle ou telle personnalité" (587).

"Passions of the Mind" 345 footnote).²⁷ Although he does not use the term *roman d'analyse*, it is very clear that it is to this type of novel that Radiguet is referring.

I rely for my definition of the French *roman d'analyse* primarily on two short books about Lafayette—Bernard Pingaud's, *Mme de La Fayette par elle-même* (1959) and Jean Fabre's *L'Art de l'analyse dans "La Princesse de Clèves"* (1970)—as well as on the critical writings of André Aciman. Aciman, who uses the term "psychological fiction" to refer to the *roman d'analyse*, notes that "the word *psychologique* [in French] suggests nothing remotely clinical or Freudian, but instead, the tireless [...] exercise of one faculty alone: insight—insight into the complex machinations of love and seduction and into the daily deceptions and vanities of social life" ("Passions of the Mind" 345). Aciman further theorizes this idea in seventeenth-century French fiction, focusing on the ways in which "the psyche is inconsequent, unchartable, *déréglé*, bizarre" ("L'Esprit de Pénétration" 107).

As I define them, works of analytical fiction integrate repetition and cyclicality of insight and counter-insight, discovery and reversal, self-deception followed by renewed doubt. As Robert Green points out about La Rochefoucauld's work, "for each maxim one likes, a countermaxim can be invented" (325), meaning that while there exist moments of satisfaction with knowledge or with self, there is no stable truth; all impressions ultimately prove to be equally false. Peter Brooks remarks in *The Novel of Worldliness* that the *Maximes* are similar to a *portrait morale* (a popular seventeenth-century genre) and are equally concerned with guessing at the state of mind of others: "placed under the emblem of penetration: the frontispiece [of La Rochefoucauld's *Maximes*], with its engraving of Seneca unmasked, is entitled 'L'Amour de la vérité,' and the liminary aphorism, 'Nos vertus ne sont le plus souvent que des vices déguisés,' ["Our virtues are often vices in disguise"] indicates the kind of search for truth La Rochefoucauld has in mind" (*The Novel of Worldliness* 63). Pierre Nicole, the *moraliste* and follower of Jansenius (who synthesized Augustinian theology with secular moral governance), whose work was admired by Madame de Sévigné and John Locke (who translated Nicole into English), for example, paints self-knowledge as a psychosocial phenomenon: "[man] does not only form his own portrait on what he knows about himself through himself, but also by seeing the portraits that he discovers in the minds of others."²⁸ Nicole's view of subjectivity as a

---

²⁷ "[un] roman où c'est la psychologie qui est romanesque. Le seul effort d'imagination est appliqué là, non aux événements extérieurs, mais à l'analyse des sentiments" (8).
²⁸ "[L'homme] ne forme pas seulement son portrait sur ce qu'il connait de soi par lui-même, mais aussi sur la vue des portraits qu'il en découvre dans l'esprit des autres" (12).

dialectic between self and others further underscores the instability of self-knowledge, and the fragile veil between one's own perceptions and those that one can glean from other people's apparent assessments. The same phenomenon is evidenced in each novel and novella discussed here. The interest in insights, proverbs, *pensées*, and maxims is evidenced in writers across Europe from Montaigne to Gracián (in *The Art of Worldly Wisdom*, 1647), to La Rochefoucauld, and to Mandeville (*The Fable of the Bees*, 1714), among others, but in the analytical novel, this interest is, of course, rendered in fiction.

Whereas in Aristotelian tragedy, *peripeteia* and *anagnorisis* enrich the intrigue and steer it toward a resolution, analytical fiction concentrates and reduplicates these devices in such a way that they take over the narrative. As characters go through cycles of recognition and reversal in their readings of other characters, the narrative itself obstructs any action-based plot. In this way, analytical fiction conceives of analysis and, ultimately, of the vacillation of non-action as plot itself. Characters in analytical fiction thus progress *not* from ignorance to knowledge, but jump elliptically from ignorance to passion, from indifference to love, from love to jealousy, or from love to madness and violence, and back again. Unlike the marriage plot novel, that is, another novelistic subclass concerned with the representation of love, analytical fiction's action rises and falls in a recursive plot until something, usually a death, *arbitrarily* breaks the pattern.

Even in Boccaccio's *Elegia* and Cervantes's "El curioso impertinente," although technically these are stories of love's abandonment, rather than unconsummated love, the love object's remoteness—be it in their glances, behavior, facial expression, or even overt lack of interest—provides cause for a would-be lover to misread these signals, or find them where they do not exist, and interpret them (usually erroneously) as a positive sign. This is a fairly simple paradigm. It becomes more complex when the love object inevitably gives in and ends up falling in love himself or herself, and the roles reverse: suddenly the love object becomes the lover, and the original lover loses interest because the former love object has become too available. In this way, because overt interest almost never yields the desired results, some characters learn that the best way to attract their love object is to feign indifference. This paradox in analytical fiction keeps characters apart: they believe an overt declaration of love will not yield as positive a result as will pretending not to care. If we define intimacy as the completion of knowledge or the transmission of what one truly thinks and feels to another character, analytical characters dissect desire, revealing how much it is inhibited by jealousy, self-doubt, and lack of self-knowledge. Analytical fiction demonstrates that it is difficult, if not impossible, to sustain intimacy.

As Pingaud points out, it is not necessary for a character in Lafayette to know for sure that his or her lover is a cheat; an imagined or possible infidelity is more than sufficient to cause a fit of jealousy because "the real obstacle between lovers is not destiny, or at least destiny is only its symbol. The obstacle is in their heart."[29] Similarly, Aciman refers to the phenomenon of falling in love, experiencing jealousy, and then searching for a cure, which merely launches the lover back into despair, as a "recursive matrix" in Baroque literature:

> The Baroque mind "wanders" in a world of deceptive appearances. [...] Things don and doff multiple disguises, and between mind and phenomena, stands an infinite layering of disguises among which, let us add, is the mind itself: self itself stands in its own way. Perception is constantly assailed by an unrepining transfer, dislodgment and destabilization of identities and, therefore, compelled to doubt everything because it sees everything as essentially shifty and multi-layered. [...] The Baroque mind gropes in the dark *fugally*, recursively. ("The Recursive Matrix" 99)

Since we can never trust our own understanding of the world, it is necessary to pretend, or to pretend to pretend, that we feel the opposite of what we think we feel, to respond to a constantly shifting world, and to protect ourselves from being over-exposed. The only moments in which we see a character's genuine feelings happens by accident and by a process that Martha Nussbaum terms "cataleptic impressions"—"blind, unbidden surge[s] of painful affect, [...] rather course and blunt instrument[s], lacking in responsiveness and discrimination" (269) or bouts of genuine and uncontrolled (and generally embarrassing) emotions that are triggered by a stimulus that catches the character entirely off-guard. But, of course, this insight is concomitant with jealousy, or fear, or both, and the lovers find fresh obstacles to consummating their love. Ultimately, it is not the Stoic interpretation of κατάληψις (catalepsis, or comprehension) that is privileged, but the skeptical critique of it, that no knowledge is truly graspable.[30]

---

[29] "[l]'obstacle véritable qui sépare les amants n'est pas la destinée, ou du moins cette destinée n'en est que le symbole. L'obstacle est dans leur cœur" (81).
[30] For more, see Martha Nussbaum's essay "Love's Knowledge" in the book by the same title about Proust and catalepsis (261–85).

I would like to illustrate how cataleptic impressions function in analytical fiction with a far lighter example from popular culture (although Austen or Proust would work here, too). This is the climax of Heckerling's film *Clueless* (1995), perhaps the best film adaptation of an Austen novel (*Emma*, one of the few comic *romans d'analyse*). Cher (Emma, played by Alicia Silverstone) is a handsome, clever, and rich Beverly Hills teenager whose highly self-curated image and seemingly-fixed worldview belie her fundamental self-deception. Toward the end of the film, Cher realizes, entirely against her intentions, that she is in love with her step-brother, Josh (the Knightly character, played by Paul Rudd). When she observes that Josh may be interested in her friend Tai (Harriet in *Emma*, played by Brittany Murphy), Cher, wracked with jealousy and confused feelings, is seen wandering dejectedly on Rodeo Drive. In voiceover, while Céline Dion's "All by Myself" plays in the background, Cher says:

> Everything I think and everything I do is wrong. I was wrong about Elton, I was wrong about Christian, and now Josh hated me. It all boiled down to one inevitable conclusion, I was just totally clueless … […] [here begins a fragmented montage of scenes from the film; interspersed with closeups of Cher, still walking] [Josh] dresses funny, he listens to complaint rock, he's not even cute in a conventional way … Ugh! And he's a hideous dancer, you couldn't take him anywhere. Wait a second, what am I stressing about? This is like, Josh. Okay, okay … so he's kind of a Baldwin. What would he want with Tai? She couldn't make him happy. Josh needs someone with imagination, someone to take care of him, someone to laugh at his jokes in case he ever makes any … then suddenly … [a pause, and a musical flourish along with a jet of water bursting out of a fountain behind Cher] Oh my god! *I* love Josh! I'm majorly, totally, butt-crazy in love with Josh! [The scene cuts to Cher now awkwardly sitting on the sofa with Josh] But now I don't know how to act around him. I mean, normally I'd strut around in my cutest little outfits, and send myself flowers and candy but I couldn't do that stuff with Josh …

There are a number of significant elements in this scene. First is Cher's sudden impression (the "one inevitable conclusion") that all of her previous ideas about matchmaking were false, which foreshadows the coming revelation about Josh (which, for all we know, might be false as well). Next, the series of fragmented camera cuts that alternate between close-ups of Cher and the montage of previous moments from the film, highlighting the character's consciousness splitting off in multiple directions. The build-up of a list of Josh's negative qualities (although she tempers some of these with a contingency: "he's not even cute *in a conventional way*") is immediately followed by the reversal ("okay, okay ... so he's kind of a Baldwin") and recognition of her love (humorously accompanied by trumpet fanfare and lit-up fountain feature), and finally, just as soon as the discovery of love happens, the realization that now her love is mixed with (albeit mild) pain. Now Cher feels that she no longer knows how to conduct herself around Josh when her typical feigned indifference (sending herself chocolates and dressing up, pretending it is for someone else) will not work. We laugh at this scene, as we do in the rest of the film, because of the ironies that Silverstone (through her acting) and Heckerling (through writing and direction) layer on. But what do Cher's multiple (and contradictory) revelations tell us about self-knowledge? Cher fails at putting together the right clues (just as Emma struggles with puzzles in Austen's novel) and she does not *have a clue* (in its Middle English usage, a "clue" or "clew" was a thread that could lead one out of a labyrinth) about her own mind and heart. Cher is able to find her way, but this is, ultimately, a romantic comedy (and again, the narrative trajectory so far would indicate that she is *still* mistaken). What about stories that cannot resolve as easily? Are we all totally "clueless" about what we want?

Before we go any further, it makes sense to pause for a moment and ask what does "love" refer to in analytical fiction? To what does it not? Certainly no one definition of erotic/romantic love serves to describe what a myriad different people may feel or agree to across various cultures, classes, and sexual identities and orientations, but the very general, modern idea of love, at least in cultures where one is permitted to choose one's lover freely, encompasses both physical desire as well as mutual caring and respect, and if that double commitment of physical and emotional attachment is transgressed or diminishes, it may hasten the end of love.[31] Certainly Cher in the example above would say that her love corresponds to this model (even if both the film and the novel it adapts suggest her brand of love is really self-love). But in analytical fiction, pain and pleasure are always merged.

For the most part, the kinds of love that form the subject of European analytical fiction are bifurcated: on the one hand, in marriage relationships (which even as late as Austen's time—even today—were subject to the dictates of the families of the partners) and, on the other hand, in romantic courtly love

---

[31] Erich Kahler puts it rather nostalgically: "Today it is forgotten that the most beautiful aspect of love is not its fulfillment—however intensely that is, naturally, desired—but its growth: the delays, aberrations, slow approaches, the sublime joys that can spring only from suffering. This whole process has been lost to us since the external obstacles have fallen away" (25).

(which ranges in definition from a platonic admiration and spiritual devotion of a man to a woman to an adulterous sexual affair). These two forces, which we can call, for convenience, marriage and love, are usually at odds (when they are treated as compatible—for example in *La Princesse de Clèves*, in which the husband claims he loves his wife as he would a mistress—a whole different set of problems arises). As we will see, while marriage is often (at least in the earlier works discussed) viewed with indifference, love is described as a disease or a dangerous affectation.[32] In other words, neither is pleasurable. In all kinds of poetry, fiction, and drama, the lovers' discourse is rendered in passionate, ambiguously braided opposites and representations of troubling affective states, one of the earliest examples of which is found in Sappho ("… tongue breaks and thin/fire is racing under skin/and in eyes no sight…" [63]). But it is interesting to note how much this type of poetry focuses on the lover, and how little on the love object. In the same realm of imaginative experience, in *Sodom and Gomorrah*, Proust's narrator explicates a pattern that afflicts

> those who have too little confidence in themselves to believe that a woman can ever fall in love with them, and also that they themselves can genuinely fall in love with her. They know themselves[33] well enough to have observed that in the presence of the most divergent types of woman they felt the same hopes, the same agonies, invented the same romances, uttered the same words, and to have realized therefore that their feelings, their actions, bear no close and necessary relation to the woman they love, but pass to one side of her (309).[34]

The Other/constructed love object becomes a function of the self, and as Pinguad and Aciman explain, the self stands in the way of comprehension and communication. This indirect path perhaps should not even be called "love," since the way that Marcel describes it is completely impersonal to the love object. This

---

[32] While today popular wisdom dictates that we "follow our hearts" and not be "so cerebral," the goal of early modern self-fashioning was to appear calm and indifferent. According to Alain Pons, writing in *The Dictionary of Untranslatables*, "when art, as a reflective and voluntary activity, allows itself to be too visible, the result is not attained, grace fails one, and one is dealing with 'affectation,' […] what [*sprezzatura*] risks lapsing into at every moment" (1050). This world is, in many ways, unknowable, in the context of Castiglione's concept of *sprezzatura* from *Il Cortegiano* and Nicolas Faret's *L'honnête homme, ou, L'art de plaire à la cour* (1630). Literary representations of burning, passionate love could then be seen as negative exempla of how not to behave.

[33] Ironically, Marcel does not really know himself well throughout the narrative.

[34] "doutent trop d'eux-mêmes pour croire qu'une femme puisse jamais les aimer, et aussi qu'eux-mêmes puissent l'aimer véritablement. Ils se connaissent assez pour savoir qu'auprès des plus différentes, ils éprouvaient les mêmes espoirs, les mêmes angoisses, inventaient les mêmes romans, prononçaient les mêmes paroles, pour s'être rendu ainsi compte que leurs sentiments, leurs actions, ne sont pas en rapport étroit et nécessaire avec la femme aimée, mais passent à côté d'elle" (223).

epistemology ultimately destroys love, not unlike in the depiction of the suffering lover in Sappho's poem. Neither representation of love can be consummated, since they are one-sided. Moriarty also points this out: "seventeenth-century moralists indebted to the Augustinian current (such as Pascal or La Rochefoucauld) will present human love as pure self-centered concupiscence, seeking sensuous or imaginary gratification, or both, and [are] incapable of any authentic union with or recognition of the other person" (Descartes xxviii). This is an affliction that goes even beyond Montaigne's principle that we overvalue the things we do not possess; it is rather what Shattuck describes as "the antithesis of the Midas touch; it turns the things we want, or want to know, into dross" (*Proust's Way* 89).

…

As we will see in the following two sections, analytical fiction is characterized by several key narrative elements which appear in all works of this type: first, a suspicion of language (both verbal and the language of the body), evidenced in a circular pattern of insights and the denial of those insights, what I call the trope of indescribability (defined and discussed below), and a particular internal narrative *durée* that dilates the time of coming to knowledge. Abstraction and reflection, as well as Fabre's word "*dédoublement*" (13) (which implies distancing and a splitting of the self, creating a sense of doubt, confusion, and self-deception), indicate vacillation and redoubling. The plot of the analytical novel does not unfold as we would expect: there is no progressive movement forward as there would be in what the French call *the roman d'apprentissage* (the bildungsroman) or the *roman d'aventures*. The passions, or emotions, which etymologically are linked to movement, agitation, and stirring, are centralized as in Longinus's treatise *On the Sublime* (Περί ὑψους—ὑψος means height or elevation, and as Emma Gilby has shown, "the most basic premise of *Peri hypsous* [is] the fact that language moves" [21]). But in analytical fiction, this movement is rendered recursive, cyclical, or circular.

For Longinus, "the effect of elevated language is, not to persuade the hearers, but to *entrance* them; and at times, and in every way, what *transports* us with wonder is more telling than what merely persuades or gratifies us. […] These sublime passages exert an irresistible force and mastery" (Aristotle-Horace-Longinus 100). As Gilby writes, the premise of Longinus's treatise is that "sublimity is characterized by the suddenness, and so often also the simplicity, with which it enmeshes the listener or reader in its arousal of emotion" (22). Edmund Burke's idea of the sublime takes "wonder" and "force" much farther, into the idea of terrifying pleasure mixed with pain that emanates from an aesthetic or bodily confrontation with expansiveness or death. As Jean-François Lyotard makes clear, Burke's aesthetic shows "that the sublime is kindled by the threat of nothing further happening. [...] In pain the body affects the soul. But the soul can also affect the body as though it were experiencing some externally induced pain. [...] Terrors are linked to privation: [...] privation of others, terror of solitude, privation of language, terror of silence" (Lyotard 537). Although analytical fiction tends to take place within closed spaces, rather than in soaring mountain landscapes that we have come to identify with Burke's idea of the sublime, the emotions that spring from a sudden confrontation with one's own lack of self-knowledge represent just this sort of terror. As we will see throughout the various interpretations of analytical fiction, characters who face the "privation" of others, of language, and of self, vacillate within the narrative and become immobilized by the terror of inaction.

## Analytical Fiction's Narrative Durée

For proof that we deceive ourselves, Montaigne reaches for Ovid: "how much do the poets support this idea, they who render Narcissus passionately in love with his own shadow. [...] And it is beyond belief that Pygmalion is so troubled by the sight of that ivory statue that he loves it and believes it is real?"[35] Ovid's pessimistic worldview is evidenced from the beginning of the *Metamorphoses* when the universe is described paradoxically as a *"discors concordia,"* or "inharmonious harmony" (Milowicki and Wilson 24).[36] For Ovid, "creation is merely the first stage in a process of universal devolution" (Milowikie and Wilson 24) on all levels of being: natural, human, and divine. As Cora Fox has noted while delineating the influence of Ovid's works in Elizabethan England, but which could equally serve for Montaigne's France, "Ovidianism served as a code for emotional expression in [that] period" (2). Most relevant for this study is the way in which Ovid's narrator prolongs the moment of un-knowing for his characters in an ironic way, so that the narrator and the reader witness the transformation while the character remains ignorant. Characters in Ovid hang *in ambiguo* and

---

[35] "combien donnent à la force des sens, les poètes, qui font Narcisse éperdu de l'amour de son ombre. [...] Et l'entendement de Pygmalion si troublé par l'impression de la vue de sa statue d'ivoire, qu'il l'aime et la serve pour vive" (II.384).

[36] We may be reminded of Lafayette's description of the sixteenth-century French court as "une sorte d'agitation sans désordre" (143) ["a sort of agitation without disorder"].

wonder—"*dum dubitant*" ("while [they stand] perplexed") (138–39). Indeed, *Metamorphoses* illustrates how even the most inherent attributes—species, gender, states of mind, family bonds—are not reliable signifiers of truth, and even the most inherent sources of authority and a sense of self are shifting and provisional.

Metamorphosis—the slide from one state to another—creates a moment before awareness, where a character's mind lags behind what has already occurred, or is in the process of occurring, to the body, in the same way that reason lags behind the passions. In this ambivalent, impotent state, where identity—to say nothing of body and desire—is suspended, death is also delayed. In Ovid's Pygmalion story, two interconnected layers of dramatic irony are at work: on the one hand, Pygmalion is a fool since he is kissing a statue, but on the other, he is not, because, as the reader knows, the statue will transform into a woman at the end of the story. Readers tend to see the central motif of the Pygmalion myth as that of the contrast between appearances and reality, but Ovid's representation of Pygmalion's speech and actions reveal a multi-layered misprision of the truth, and not merely a mistaking of X for Y. Pygmalion's error is ubiquitous and multidirectional. He conflates—not just mistakes—nature and artifice. Thus, for Pygmalion, illusion and the truth become one, in one of the most bizarre tales of technically (though only initially) unconsummated love. Before the transformation, Pygmalion strokes, speaks to, and adorns the statue he has created; he either truly believes that he is engaging in an act of reciprocal love, or is willing to entirely suspend his disbelief: "[he] kisses it and thinks his kisses are returned."[37] This false-and-yet-also-true belief is the key element of what makes this story an analytical one: Pygmalion's mistaking not only provides entry into the character's mind and allows us to see how it constructs the world, it also illustrates to us the fundamental opacity and volatility of that world.

Pygmalion's inner monologue travels back and forth between the real and the imagined until, in the transformation of the statue into a real woman, these two states fuse by an act of the goddess Venus. But even after this has happened, Pygmalion is not fully cognizant of the fact. Ovid's text endeavors to penetrate the character's inner thoughts in the language of the moment after the transformation as well, where Pygmalion is caught between ignorance and knowledge. The narrator seems to delight in Pygmalion's prolonged moment of unknowing and his ironic misprision of the truth: "the lover stands amazed,

---

[37] "oscula dat reddique putat loquiturque tenetque" (82–83).

rejoices still in doubt, fears he is mistaken, and tries his hopes again and yet again with his hand. Yes, it was a body!"[38] The three lines describing the sculptor suspended in doubt, hoping she is real, unable to speak, and afraid of the possibly unpleasant truth, do two things so typical of analytical writing: they dilate time and defer knowing.

Central to Pygmalion's significance is the paradox "ars adeo latet arte sua" ("with his art, he's hidden art") (82–3), which also indicates that the artist has hidden the illusion from himself.[39] The folly—through which we are able to read Pygmalion's mind—is the irony that Pygmalion accidentally deceives *himself* in an attempt to deceive others with his sculpture. *Ars adeo latet arte sua* becomes an Ovidian precept throughout the *Metamorphoses* to show not merely a contrast between appearances and reality, but a continuum between them, as well as the enduring vacillation between ignorance and self-knowledge. And it is not just suspension or dramatic irony that is at stake here; instead, the broader implication of this knowledge gulf is a persistent questioning of the capacity of human introspection. It is not only that the characters are foolish—although folly is certainly an element; rather, it is our folly and lack of insight into ourselves that drive us.

In Ovid, knowledge begins with questions of ontology: is Galatea flesh, or made of marble? Is Daphne caught, or is she still free? Has Diana transformed Actaeon into a stag or is he still a man? But on closer reading, these questions reveal themselves to be far more epistemological in nature: does Pygmalion know and understand that Galatea is not a real woman (or, later, that she is)? Does Daphne believe that she has already been caught by Apollo? Does Actaeon understand that he has become a beast? Ovid's characters, moved by the hands of fate, error, desire, or pride, are cyclically confronted with a force that subverts what was previously believed. *Metamorphoses* dilates the fictional space between error and truth and between ignorance and knowledge through the trope of transformation. In texts written later, there is no literal metamorphosis to signal changes in characters' epistemologies, and characters tend to be static rather than transforming.

Here, truth—although it purportedly remains at the center of every motivation—is a slippery ideal that ultimately is dwarfed by the search itself;

---

[38] "dum stupet et dubie gaudet fallique veretur,/rursus amans rursusque manu sua vota retractat./ corpus erat!" (84–5).

[39] This is very similar to the Roman aphorism "ars est celare artem" ("true art is to conceal art") whose origin is unknown.

the desire to know, to know what one should feel, what exactly is being felt, and ultimately whether it might be right to act on these perceived feelings becomes obsessive. Analytical fiction takes place in a closed society, which in Roland Barthes's definition, in an essay on La Bruyère, is "an enclosure" that "guarantees access to the psychological and the social without passing through the political" (*Critical Essays* 227). We can compare Barthes's definition of the closed society to Brooks's use of the term "worldliness," which he defines as "an arrest of the movement of human life in a stasis of words, the metaphorical expression of an essence rather than a narrative development" (*The Novel of Worldliness* 16). In analytical fiction, characters have little to do other than imagine and revise what they believe others think and feel, and whether what they themselves are thinking is correct. Their closed worlds are made up of, in large part, the confines of their own creation.

On the level of vocabulary, certain verbs, such as to think, to believe, and to dare, as well as verbs of seeing and seeming, illustrate that one character is attempting to produce knowledge about another, to read herself, or to do both. The trope of "love at first sight" is often exploited within analytical fiction both as the medium through which lovers become cognizant of each other and as a delaying device. In works like Boccaccio's *Elegia*, Marguerite's *Heptaméron* 10, and Lafayette's *La Princesse de Clèves*, the dilated first gaze melds pleasure and pain together from the beginning of a relationship, and anxiety and curiosity dilate the narrative *durée*. As Robin Valenza writes about *Clarissa*, which applies equally to many authors in this study, "Richardson seals off exits, denies Clarissa escape routes at every turn" (232); she is not permitted to move forward (and away from Lovelace). This very cutting-off of possibility also dilates it. Similarly, most duties to society and family, monetary considerations, and other mundane concerns are given secondary status, or, if anything, serve as another way to delay action, as excuses to cover up much deeper concerns about our ability to truly love, feel pleasure unmixed with pain, or even to live what we would call today a fulfilling life.

## In an Imagined State: The Trope of Indescribability

Analytical fiction also illustrates the difficulties of narrating passion. Characters in these works engage in compulsive over-reading, which highlights the tension between the emotions that characters feel and the difficulty the narrative has to express them. Throughout this book, we will also see narrators who openly insist on the insufficiency of literary language to express the deep and troubling passions felt by the characters (and even when characters narrate their own stories, the perception that they are confused, thwarted, or misled still dominates, as we saw in the example of *Clueless* and we will see in *Grandison* and other novels). In Marguerite and Lafayette, emotions are often alluded to in statements by the narrator that indicate it is the reader's responsibility to describe and understand. Marguerite's narrator in Novella 10, for example, claims "I cannot begin to tell you in detail what [the lovers] said to one another" (134), and later, "I will not try to describe […] [the] feelings. […] It would be impossible to set such anguish down in writing. It is difficult even for anyone to imagine such anguish" (143).[40] Similarly, Lafayette often employs the pronoun "on" (frequently translated in English by the passive voice) to suggest the emotions of her characters. The princess leaves the room of her dying mother "in a state that can be imagined."[41] The same turn of phrase is used when the princess realizes for the first time that she is in love, or when Clèves learns that his wife is in love with another man: "it is easy to imagine in which state they passed that night."[42] When an emotion is extremely strong, there is no visualizing it: "Madame de Clèves' embarrassment and distress were outside of what can be imagined."[43] It is perhaps surprising that works as focused on analysis as these should pass over emotion in a way that destabilizes the narrator's authority and confesses her inability to communicate the facts of her story (not to mention, in the case of Lafayette's text, such hyperbole existing in a work that is often praised for its classicism). And yet, we witness an almost compulsive use of this silencing device.

This problem, which I call the trope of indescribability, has been explained by previous critics in various ways. Cohn notes "the avoidance of psycho-narration" (21) in *Vanity Fair*, for example, where "the narrator is not much interested" (21) in characters' thoughts because "it would add little to the understanding of a fictional character or a fictional world that has already been amply explored" (21). But this is a different case, since the narrators that I examine in this study alternate between depicting characters' (sometimes

---

[40] "Je ne saurais entreprendre de vous conter […] les propos qu'ils eurent" (106); "je n'entreprends point vous dire la douleur […] car elle n'est seulement impossible à écrire mais à penser" (115).
[41] "en l'état que l'on peut s'imaginer" (173).
[42] "il est aisé de s'imaginer en quelle état ils passèrent la nuit" (260).
[43] "le trouble et l'embarras de Mme de Clèves était au-delà de tout ce que l'on peut s'imaginer" (255).

tortuous) interior deliberations and claiming that such feelings could not be expressed in words. There is no narrator's value judgment (Cohn 24) imposed on the character, as in Balzac or Thackeray, and in cases where the gnomic present is being used, as Cohn describes it, it comes from the characters themselves, rather than narrators. Instead, the narrative interjections of indescribability discussed here often privilege the "non-verbal quality of certain inner experiences" (Cohn 48). Other critics have viewed this phenomenon as a conceit that indicates shared cultural knowledge between writers and their contemporary readers. Lafayette, Culler writes, "displays [...] immense confidence in her readers" (*Structuralist Poetics* 134) to actually understand what *should* in fact be imagined. Seymour Chatman as well reads indescribability as a type of verisimilitude that "can only be read out at a deeper narrative level through familiarity with seventeenth-century mores" (*Story and Discourse* 50). And Barthes first theorized the idea of "écriture classique" as knowledge that, like the Sun King himself, is "unified and universal" (*Writing Degree Zero* 56). Maria Mäkelä offers a counter-reading to this accepted notion of cultural exemplarity, characterizing Lafayette's narrative interjections as the expression of "unprecedented experience" (19) and as "an attempt to imagine a character's state of mind through sociocultural exempla and maxims followed by a construction of a hypothetical courtly focalizer, a witness position (*témoin*) from which to attribute a mental state to the character" (20). For John D. Lyons (also writing about *La Princesse de Clèves*), the authorial interruptions represent a rumination on the experiential for the author: "it seems clear that [Lafayette] does not want to present imagination as being a way of thinking with a positive (helpful, constructive, edifying) use and as being within the control of the will" (*Before Imagination* 172).

Following Lyons, I read the refusal to narrate extreme emotions as inhibiting the power of imagination and, concomitantly, self-knowledge. This trope of indescribability can, furthermore, be connected to two other ideas: on the one hand, Kant's version of the sublime as "absolutely powerful, [...] which like all absolutes can only be thought [of], without any sensible/sensory intuition, as an Idea of reason, the faculty of presentation, the imagination, fails to provide a representation corresponding to this Idea" (Lyotard 537) and, on the other hand, to the idea of the *je ne sais quoi*, which, as Gilby points out, is "emblematic of the sublime experience, [and] can therefore be read only in its literal sense: that which cannot be known or guaranteed" (7). In other words, it follows that texts that incorporate the trope of indescribability underscore the unknowability of meaning, and the untrustworthiness of rhetoric, the power of ineffability and the "irretrievably periphrastic" (Gilby 7). They are not representable, but the sensations that would invoke the ineffable must be sublime (in the Burkean sense) in themselves, and as such, they produce both pleasure and pain simultaneously.

Juxtaposed with analytical fiction's distrust of rhetoric and the trope of indescribability, the sub-genre is very much entangled with the representation of sublime states in the sense described by Longinus. Affective reactions to literature have been documented in accounts of the sublime from Longinus to Lyotard, and even since Aristotle, whose theory of κάθαρσις [katharsis], or purgation (Aristotle-Horace-Longinus 39), is important here in the way it emphasizes the terror and pity aroused in a spectator of tragedy (less so than the spectator's sense of emotional release). But the even more paradoxical link between the emotive and the locomotive (emotions have to do with movement, but in analytical fiction they serve to arrest characters in indecision and self-doubt, just as sublimity both transports and renders immobile) is vividly realized when we pay attention to bodily reactions (including representations of blushing, paling, fainting, transports of rage—all of which are movements of the body that restrain metaphorical movement forward or the consummation of love). In analytical fiction, language is traumatic—what Sianne Ngai calls "noncarthartic feelings" (9)—not curative, as it is in Freudian psychoanalysis. As Lorna Mellon writes about *Hamlet*, invoking the affect theory of Cathy Caruth:

> Language is traumatic due to the fact that it tries to impart a truth that will never be fully recognized—every time we try to represent reality, we are only creating and indeed depending on a void that enables non-truths to perpetuate the trauma of misrepresentation. Because language is traumatic in its failure to create completely truthful representations of reality, not only is it hard to fully believe that it can solve any trauma, but furthermore, through testimony one is only repeating and recreating the traumatic event in words, the sense of which cannot be policed (117).[44]

---

[44] Regarding combatting the presentist "tilt" of affect theory, Wendy Anne Lee, whose book *Failures of Feeling: Insensibility and the Novel* was published just as the manuscript for this book was being completed (and thus I could not engage more with it, as I would have liked), writes that "every philosopher of the Enlightenment was also a theorist of affect" (4). Lee's book examines the psychological novel through what she calls "the Bartleby problem," and traces insensibility and refusal through eighteenth-century English fiction and philosophy.

Thus, we witness, in literature, "the trauma of language according to the logic of the double bind—language is traumatic, but without it, meaning would cease to exist" (Mellon 123). It is easy to see how the representation of life in fiction, poetry, and drama hinges on this fundamental paradox, and how the double-bind itself generates meaning.

## Situating Analytical Fiction in the History of the Novel

Although I deliberately bracket this study before the middle of the nineteenth century, before the advent of modern psychoanalysis, it is important to emphasize that just as analytical fiction does not serve as a forerunner to Freudianism, neither does it function as a precursor to the nineteenth-century type of novel frequently associated with "realism" or "psychological realism." Unlike realist fiction, the *roman d'analyse* is little concerned with the development of subjective identity. The "psychology" of novels like the *Elegia*, *La Princesse de Clèves*, or *Persuasion* is far different from that which, for example, Ian Watt describes in *The Rise of the Novel*, which deliberately contrasts Lafayette's novels with realist fiction, such as *Robinson Crusoe*, the work that to Watt represents the first psychological and modern novel. In doing so, Watt judges that "Defoe brought into the novel a treatment of the individual's psychological concerns that was a tremendous advance in the kind of forensic ratiocination which had previously passed for psychological description in even the best of the romances, such as those of Madame de Lafayette" (85). Earlier in *The Rise of the Novel*, Watt had already dismissed "French fiction from *La Princesse de Clèves* to *Les Liaisons dangereuses* [...] [as] too stylish to be authentic" (30), despite his admission that these novels are psychologically penetrating (Shattuck calls this a "lame explanation" [*Forbidden Knowledge* 11] and Olivier Delers describes Watt's assessment as "relegate[ing] the eighteenth-century French novel to the back row of literary history" [2]). Watt's limited circumscription of the modern novel is very much tied to a particular critical worldview. As Margaret Cohen puts it in her history of narratology in the novel in *The Cambridge Companion to Narrative*, "detail was [...] extremely important to Watt's account, which situated the novel in the context of the rise of science, a culture of quantification, and the takeoff of capitalism—in short, features of modernity isolated by German sociologist Max Weber, as well as by a Marxian lineage" (Garrett 253). Watt is so focused on "authenticity" that it leads him to claim that Defoe's mode of representing psychology through social and economic realism is far superior to anything that had been tried before.⁴⁵

But Watt is not the only critic who finds Lafayette's novel not quite "realistic" enough; Lydia Ginzburg, too, in *On Psychological Prose* criticizes *La Princesse de Clèves* as an inadequate precursor to the modern psychological novel because "however complex it may sometimes be, the psychological framework of Lafayette's book still takes its form from two basic and opposed elements. [...] Passion always comes up against another internal or external force that is opposed to it" (225). For Ginzburg, Lafayette's novel does not contain an "orientation towards authenticity" (201).⁴⁶ But this and Watt's description of novels that aspire to "a guarantee of the authenticity of [the author's] report, whose prose aims exclusively at what John Locke defined as the proper purpose of language, 'to convey the knowledge of things', and whose novels as a whole pretend to be no more than a transcription of real life" (Watt 30), sidestep a whole tradition in proto-psychological fiction in which verisimilitude, that is, a mimetic representation of "real life" as it is lived, is beside the point. The word "authentic," moreover, is an almost romantic, and certainly subjective, term that need not be conflated with the idea of "psychology." Nor should the idea of "realism." On the contrary, as Lyons notes, Lafayette's is "a text that [...] consistently transcends mundane and 'realistic' details of setting, personnel, and monetary transaction" ("Mlle de Chartres at the Jeweller's Shop" 117), while it is still rich in psychological insight. Similarly, Fabre writes, "the moral truth, as conceived by Madame de Lafayette, carefully excludes what we call realism."⁴⁷

---

⁴⁵ Another, much more recent, study that focuses on an account of economic and social factors in eighteenth-century French novels is Delers's *The Other Rise of the Novel in Eighteenth-Century French Fiction*, which problematizes "the myth of the French nobility [which] is just as pervasive and reductive as the myth of the French bourgeoisie" (Delers 7). Delers's fascinating interpretation of *La Princesse de Clèves* examines "the economic value of the body as commodity on the imperfect and nontransparent stock market of the court [that] clashes with the ontological value of the individual" (56), which has its roots in Lyons's depiction of the "environment of the novel" (Delers 55) as "a set of interlocking economies [...] of marriage, of physical objects such as jewels, of sexual desire, of information, and of wealth or money" ("Mlle de Chartres at the Jeweller's Shop" 118) from the moment the princess arrives at court "not so much a person but a *parti*" (Lyons 118).

⁴⁶ For Ginzburg, documentary texts offer a true psychological portrait of the writer, what she calls "intermediate prose [...]: memoirs, letters, maxims, and *caractères*. [...] The world of these genres was a concrete and sober one of penetrating observation and persistent analysis of the 'mainsprings' of behavior" (6) more than high poetry.

⁴⁷ "La vérité morale, telle que la conçoit Madame de Lafayette, exclut soigneusement ce que nous appelons le réalisme" (27).

Clearly, the novel is not a monolithic genre. As Paige writes in his preface to his English translation of Lafayette's *Zayde*:

> When most readers today think of "the" novel [...] it is in fact a certain type of novel that comes as if naturally to mind—the realist novel that, we have been taught, 'rose' triumphantly over the course of the eighteenth and nineteenth centuries. [...] This view is not so much wrong as incomplete: other vibrant fictional genres were practiced before and alongside the development of the realist novel. (1)

Similarly, Cohen posits, citing the incompleteness of Georg Lukács's *Theory of the Novel*, that "critics find increasingly problematic the project to write *the* or even *a* theory of the novel. It has become apparent that Lukács and his lineage have only been able to theorize 'the' novel by restricting their canon to a small subset of novels [...] most, moreover, adhering to a realist aesthetic" (Garrett 257). This long-perceived link between the "rise" of the novel and realism stems from realism's privileging of "density of detail and plausibility of action" (Meyer Spacks, *Novel Beginnings* 21) as well as to verisimilitude through sensual detail (as in Barthes's idea of the "reality effect" in nineteenth-century realist fiction, or Brooks's description of "the detailing of the material circumstances, the 'things' of man's existence, the *épaisseur de vie* [the thickness of life] surrounding him [...] [which are] at the center of the evolution of a certain kind of novel, from Richardson to Balzac to Joyce to Robbe-Grillet" (89–90).[48] But as many theorists have shown more recently, the novel is a pluralistic genre that evolved in various directions.

---

[48] Brooks's idea of worldliness examines a narrow body of texts inscribed not by realism, but by the notion of *mondanité* in seventeenth- and eighteenth-century French salon society. For Brooks, novels of worldliness "resolve themselves into scenes which represent and summarize aspects of human experience in society more than they advance the action" (91–2), as in the moral portrait, which "summarizes and fixes [a] whole life [...] in order to perform a critical census of society" (51). Although he critiques the limitations Watt places on the modern novel, Brooks reads Richardson only for his interest in the "particular," "patient detailings of private experience" (90 and 88), and then makes explicit that he does not see the novels of Richardson (because they do not take place in an aristocratic society) as comparable to French novels. In his study, Brooks invokes Roman Jakobson's distinction between "metaphoric" and "metonymic" language, where the metonymic is marked by passing time and an interest in atmosphere, history, and context, and works of metaphoric fiction "arrest action and fix life in order to permit final knowledge" (92). Analytical fiction, however, does not permit final knowledge—or in other words, there is no completion of the metaphor.

In many ways, the eighteenth-century novel—the principal subject of many critical studies of the genre—idealized the *homme sensible*,[49] the "sensible" man who either naturally felt extremely refined emotion or else learned to do so, who was quick to display compassion for the suffering of others (J. Todd 7). Thus, "sensibility" sometimes implies abundant (and even excessive) sympathy, sublimating feeling into descriptions of weeping or fainting. This implies a philosophical dimension as well. According to Janet Todd, Locke "taught the evanescence and primacy of impulse and suggested that sensibility—openness through sensation to the world—was the only route to knowledge" (Todd 24).[50] Adam Smith's *Theory of Moral Sentiments* analyzes the psychological role sympathy plays in the creation of moral theory. Smith's emphasis on aesthetics—that is, the faculty of seeing that informs our moral judgments—is also especially significant because it joins empiricism[51] to affect in what he describes as an open, sensible man, in whom "to see the emotions of [other men's] hearts, in every respect, beat time to his own, in the violent and disagreeable passions, constitutes his sole consolation" (Smith 27). Although Smith's treatise on morality, like Locke's comment, does not go as far as describing an "innate sensitiveness or susceptibility revealing itself in a variety of spontaneous activities such as crying, swooning and kneeling" (J. Todd 7), the economist's identification of understanding and moral judgment with sentiment and sensibility is representative of the eighteenth century's view of moral psychology. The *raison d'être* of the novel of sensibility was purportedly the desire to teach a reader how to feel, then to show the reader how to control those feelings and express them judiciously.

But analytical fiction stands in contrast to these representations of sensibility in eighteenth-century fiction. While many still depict excessive emotionality, the most analytical of these novels—just as in the previous centuries—also undercut the effusiveness of the passions with an ironic narrative that questions sensibility

---

[49] Sergio Moravia details the evolution of the idea that "an *exclusively* mechanical interpretation cannot explain either the specific nature of certain functions or the origin and the action of the forces clearly at work in every living being" (49, emphasis in original).

[50] This is the sort of sentimentality that Samuel Johnson mocks in his description of Miss Gentle, a fictional character whose portrait he paints in his journal *The Idler* (*The Complete Works of Samuel Johnson* 451).

[51] Enlightenment notions of empiricism, as Jessica Riskin has shown, were entirely bound up with the language of sensibility, and the idea that knowledge hinges on the capacity to feel. "By fusing sensation with sentiment, the inventors of the notion of sensibility transformed the meaning of scientific empiricism, for if knowledge arose from physical sensation, it must now originate equally in emotion" (Riskin 2).

(rendering it, rather, the more pejorative "sentimentality"). And as to the didactic element of the formulation above, it is doubtful whether these authors succeed in teaching readers how to manage their emotions. The eighteenth century did not create only habile empathizers across the literary board. Richardson's Clarissa Harlowe, Harriet Byron, and Charlotte Grandison, as well as Austen's Anne Elliot and Stendhal's Octave and Armance in the following century, are just as obsessively analytical, prone to error, and ambivalent about the possibility of true love, and their narratives are just as dominantly pessimistic and anti-romantic, as their early modern analytical ancestors.

But not every novel that has been described as eschewing the concerns of realism and sensibility is automatically a *roman d'analyse*. One tempting, though ultimately incongruous, correlation may be with what Alan Singer designates as the self-deceiver in literature:

> The literary characters who exhibit the sign of self-deception also give a defining contour to the history of the novel. Self-deceivers are so pervasive in the canonical texts of narrative fiction that, from a certain perspective, self-deception seems to be what the novel is about. Cervantes' Don Quixote, Sterne's Tristram Shandy, Flaubert's Emma Bovary, Joyce's Stephen Dedalus, Conrad's Marlow, Ford's John Dowell, and Nabokov's Humbert Humbert: in one way or another all of these protagonists act at odds with what they know. [...] Thus, we are bound to conclude that self-deception—from one perspective, an epitome of irrationality—rationalizes the longevity of the genre as a métier of human self-understanding. [...] The self-understanding typically waits upon a plot resolution that would prove them unrecognizable to themselves. (16)

Singer's plotting of self-deceiving characters within linear narratives in order to contrast what he calls the "present-ness" of personalities like Emma Bovary with the temporal changes inherent to the novels they inhabit is essential to a certain "aesthetic practice" exercised by the authors listed in the passage above. Such novels, however, hinge upon a particular kind of reading that Singer notes is "continuous with the un-self-deceived knowledge of self-deception that [Flaubert] makes available to any reader of *Madame Bovary* who scrupulously honors the novel's formal constraints" (29). Thus, the kind of novel that is examined in Singer's book produces knowledge in two directions, one sanctioned by the author and by linear time, and the other that functions against time, that is represented by the "present-ness" of the self-deceiving character. This account differs from the one in this present study in that characters in analytical fiction do not necessarily have access to any more or less knowledge than the narrators, authors, or readers. They are tragically aware of their self-deception, as lack of self-knowledge forms a central tenet of their philosophical belief.

The recognition that characters in analytical fiction are self-consciously self-deceived also helps to define the closed environment in which these types of novels take place, since they are universes constructed by the characters themselves. Analytical fiction's "closed" society functions by removing itself from the heroic, political, legal, financial, and, one might say, practical world and enclosing itself in a world made up of minds attempting to read other minds. In a text like *Clarissa*, which does not take place in an aristocratic milieu, the closed society is formed, as we will see in the chapter dedicated to Richardson's last two novels, by a feeling of being trapped long before Clarissa ever becomes Lovelace's physical prisoner. As Pingaud points out, a closed society remains impenetrable in the sense of *Huis Clos*: "The law of this society is appearance. [...] It is hell as imagined by Sartre, a closed world where everyone exists only in the minds of others."[52] In this book I examine what is simultaneously the opposite of and the complement to Brooks's concept of "worldliness": sociability's attendant interiority and analytical probing, which, I argue, rather than presenting completed, fixed knowledge, illustrate a closed world of obsessive analysis that inhibits the attainment of knowledge, as well as action. The mind is not a mirror to the world in analytical fiction; the divided psyche causes characters to turn every which way, toward multiple refracted untruths at once in the process of thinking, discovering, wondering, and speculating. Instead, as we will see in the following five chapters, the idea that the heart and mind—the soul—cannot be mapped by any system is what drives the pessimistic worldview of analytical fiction.

---

[52] "La loi de cette société est l'*apparence*. [...] C'est l'enfer tel que l'imagine Sartre, un monde clos où chacun n'existe que dans la conscience des autres" (82, emphasis added).

# 1

# The Unconsummated Life in Boccaccio's *Elegia di madonna Fiammetta*

> *Tomorrow, and tomorrow, and tomorrow,*
> *Creeps in this petty pace from day to day,*
> *To the last syllable of recorded time;*
> *[…] full of sound and fury,*
> *Signifying nothing.*
>
> (Macbeth 5.5.22–31)

In Apuleius's Latin novel *The Metamorphoses*, more commonly known as *The Golden Ass*, Psyche, a princess, must undergo a series of trials, first to redeem herself to the goddess Venus, whom she has offended with her beauty, and second to be reunited with her lover, Cupid, who had accidentally fallen in love with Psyche after being sent by his mother to destroy her. Urged on by her foolish curiosity, and with the unfortunate "help" of her jealous sisters, Psyche resolves to discover her lover's identity, since he had heretofore only appeared to her in the dark. Armed with an oil lamp and a razor to cut his throat if he is actually a monster, Psyche spies on her lover while he is sleeping. His magnificent good looks, his telltale wings, and his quiver and arrows on the floor reveal his true identity to her. Examining the god of love's weapons, she accidentally cuts herself with an arrow and immediately falls in love. Clumsy and overcome by passion, she spills some lamp oil on Cupid's shoulder, wounds him, and wakes him up. The beautiful palace which they had inhabited melts away, and Cupid attempts to flee, but Psyche holds on to him. Before he disappears, he drops her on the ground and warns her: "I shall punish you merely by leaving" (Apuleius 243).[1] Psyche

---

[1] "te vero tantum fuga mea punivero" (242).

wanders the earth in search of her lover, finally seeking out Venus herself for help. Venus tortures Psyche (with the aid of her maidens, Sadness and Sorrow) and then gives her a series of impossible tasks, culminating in a trip to the underworld to ask for some of Proserpina's beauty to give to Venus (she is helped by a tall tower from which she wishes to throw herself). Psyche, who is, above all, *pregnant* throughout her ordeals, having finally redeemed herself, and with the help of Jupiter, is made immortal. Psyche and Cupid are permitted to marry, and Venus even dances at their wedding. Psyche gives birth to a daughter, Voluptas, or Pleasure, and they live happily ever after.

The subject of this first substantive chapter in a book on proto-psychological fiction is, fittingly, a text whose lovelorn narrator has been described as "a new Psyche," and a "soul with a voice" (*The Elegy of Lady Fiammetta* xxi).[2,3] Boccaccio's *L'Elegia di madonna Fiammetta* (written between 1343–4) is a fictitious confessional novel about the suffering caused by jilted love, narrated by Fiammetta in the conventional language of lovesickness evidenced from Sappho to Petrarch.[4,5] Like the Psyche depicted in *The Golden Ass*, Fiammetta can be read as embodying spirit, curiosity,[6] and compassion (Ronchetti 210), while she suffers from abandoned love, although Psyche's misfortune ends "more quickly" (156) (literally, "with faster feet") than Fiammetta's.[7] Fiammetta also compares herself to Venus, though unlike in Apuleius's novel, where Psyche is naïve about her looks, Fiammetta is proud and often recounts the details of her self-adornment. And while Psyche disobeys her husband by bringing in light, a metaphor for knowledge (Doody 115), Fiammetta in vain searches for truth, anatomizing pain and the passions of the soul when, in fact, there was

---

[2] Mariangela Causa-Steindler points out that the connection between Apuleius's novel and the *Elegia* was first made by Walter Pabst, in his *Venus als Heilige und Furie in Boccaccios Fiammettadichtung* (*The Elegy of Lady Fimmetta* xxiii).

[3] By the soul (*anima*) here I mean, in a very general sense of Plato and Aristotle's terms, "a sort of principle common to all beings" (Küpper 96) or "the distinguishing mark of living things" (Lorenz).

[4] *Confessio* means both an admission of sin and providing a testimony of the self—although Fiammetta's story lacks an overt conversion narrative that acts as a counterpoint and resolution to the suffering. The *Elegia* is written in a form that defies generic classification. Following Hollander and Scordilis Brownlee, I read the *Elegia* as a novel rather than a romance, contrasting "the successful physical adventures of the outer world of the romance to the fragile novelistic inner world of the individual psyche" (Scordilis Brownlee 4), rendered in (often repetitive, if poetic) prose.

[5] One of the main features of the text is its referentiality; the *Elegia* is deeply indebted to Ovid's evocative letters by famous abandoned women, *Epistulae Heroidum*, or the *Heroides*, as well as to other amatory works by Ovid, Seneca's tragedies, and Dante's *Commedia* and other writings.

[6] "Psyche [...] suffers after trying to gaze upon what [she] should not" (Doody 115).

[7] "con piú sollecito piede" (*Elegia Di madonna Fiammetta* 238). All references to the *Elegia* are from Maria Pia Mussini Sacchi's edition from Mursia. English translations are by Mariangela Causa-Steindler and Thomas Mauch.

no clear reason for her lover's departure, not death, marriage, war, or destiny, but, in Fiammetta's mind, mere whim. Finally, and this is the most significant difference, instead of finding her lover after a series of physical trials, Fiammetta is restricted to gazing every day out her window, and there is no *deus ex machina*; her lover never returns.

The outer frame of the *Elegia* comprises a prologue and the final chapter, where Fiammetta describes writing a "piccolo libretto" ("little book"), composed as a substitute for herself to warn women of the dangers of overpowering, troubling love. Almost the entire action of the novel occurs in the first and second chapters: Fiammetta (whose fictitious name implies her ardor), a married woman, and Panfilo (the "all-loving" or "lover of all") fall in love at first sight[8] and engage in a relatively brief but passionate affair (although Fiammetta at some point offers a different version of their first sexual encounter, which I will discuss later in this chapter), before he leaves for Florence, never to return. Along the way, Fiammetta's nurse presents a number of arguments against love (which Gur Zak describes as "a parody of Stoic consolation" [5]), a vision of Venus appears to Fiammetta to convince her to surrender to her desires, and, after Panfilo's departure, Fiammetta recounts the stories of other abandoned and suffering women and debates with herself about how to manage her confused emotions. The story's "activity," as Margaret Anne Doody puts it, moves from the action of the love affair very quickly into "Fiammetta's solitary self-enclosed awareness" (Doody 202–03). During her extended period of anguish, Fiammetta over and over receives false reports of, in turn, Panfilo's marriage, his taking of another lover (this one is probably true), and finally his return to Naples (a kind of unfulfilled resurrection). With each new report, Fiammetta is launched into a new cycle of hope and despair, leading eventually to an attempted suicide, which also fails, and finally, before the novel abruptly ends, a return to the recursive pattern already described. Although the *Elegia* is not strictly an example of *unconsummated* passion, the story remains incomplete and the cure for love is perpetually deferred. The narrative describes the events of Fiammetta's abandonment, re-inscribing the past with present suffering, and depicts a lament for a kind of golden age of love, which, as we are likely to intuit

---

[8] Andreas Capellanus's definition of love in *De Amore* is "a certain inborn suffering derived from the sight of and *excessive meditation upon* the beauty of the opposite sex" (*The Art of Courtly Love* 28) ["passio quaedam innata procedens ex visione et *immoderata cogitatione* formae alterius sexus" (*Andreas Capellanus on Love* 32)]. Andreas's concept of love not only helps explain why Fiammetta's deep contemplation of Panfilo generates her passion, but also underlines the twinned experiences of pain and pleasure in the *Elegia* and *romans d'analyse* more generally.

from her story, had never existed at all. The reader presumes that long after the end of the narrative, Fiammetta continues to suffer from Panfilo's abandonment, from her unfulfilled passion, and from her inability to act.

The *Elegia* is a controversial work which has alternately been described as "the first psychological novel," as a failure, as a feminist work, and as an ironic satire.[9] In sorting through the scholarly reception of the *Elegia*, one is struck by the overall moralizing of the critics' voices, blaming Fiammetta for loving immoderately (which leads to her suffering from melancholy) and for being unwilling to pull herself out of it. In this chapter, I argue that the *Elegia* is a kind of inside-out psychomachia, in which the battle for the soul reaches, instead of a resolution, a kind of ἀπορία (aporia: an impasse or bewilderment) in cyclical representations of emotion and suppressed action. By presenting the *Elegia* as a work of analytical fiction, my interpretation focuses on two main elements: the text's cyclical narration that cuts off Fiammetta's access to making rational choices and making her doubt her own senses and beliefs, and the text's staging of a radical division between words and deeds, language and life, that reveals Boccaccio's nearly Platonic distrust of rhetoric in all guises.[10] The epistemological split between acts and words in the *Elegia* functions as a frame in this chapter for investigating the failure of mythological and historical exempla that are poor imitations of real anguish, as well as the instability of rhetorical argumentation and allowing the body to speak for distress. In this way, Fiammetta's self-deception is read as embodying a universal rule of the *roman d'analyse* rather than as Boccaccio's condemnation of a character's individual moral failing.

---

[9] One late nineteenth-century commentator on the *Elegia*, John Addington Symonds, describes the *Elegia* as "the first attempt in modern literature to portray subjective emotion exterior to the writer. Since Virgil's 'Dido,' since the 'Heroidum Epistolae' of Ovid, nothing has been essayed in this region of psychological analysis" (54). Warren Ginsberg writes that "so many consider [this text] the first psychological novel" (101), and Vittore Branca describes the *Elegia* as "primo romanzo psicologico e realistico moderno" (cited in Ronchetti 205) ("the first psychological and realistic modern novel"). Jacob Burckhardt is ambivalent: "in the 'Fiammetta' we have another great and minutely painted picture of the human soul, full of the keenest observation, though executed with anything but uniform power, and in parts marred by the passion for high-sounding language and by an unlucky mixture of mythological allusions and learned quotations" (204). Similarly, Michael A. Calabrese cites an "inflated sense of her own drama [...] [where] Fiammetta ruins her own case through her inflated rhetoric" (26), and, going even further, Katherine Heinrichs sees the book as "an exasperating work whose insistent and unrelieved psychopathology soon approaches burlesque, an effect clearly intended by Boccaccio" (156). Pamela Waley argues that this is true only "on a first and superficial reading [...] [while] subsequent study reveals a many-facetted and convincing portrait" (165) of Fiammetta's descriptions of her own suffering.

[10] Boccaccio was familiar with several of Plato's dialogues, including the *Phaedrus* (Andrei 172, endnote). In this famous dialogue, Socrates argues against writing, claiming "it continues to signify just that very same thing forever" (80–81).

## The Past Is Always Present: Cyclical Time

While the *Elegia* references seasons and holidays (Fiammetta first sees Panfilo at an Easter mass, he leaves her at the end of December, and he is absent for two winters), the narrative behaves as if outside of linear time, rendering time as a metaphor for Fiammetta's dilated but ultimately cyclical feelings of abandonment and despair. Fiammetta at first is ignorant of time's importance: "I spent more of my time utterly fulfilled and not considering that the pleasure I was then wholeheartedly enjoying would be the root and seed of future misery, as I, now fruitlessly, am painfully aware" (27),[11] but after Panfilo is gone, short January days seem to drag on longer than June ones. Despite substantively lamenting the unconscious ignoring of time, Fiammetta is simultaneously hyperaware of time; the chronology moves from the past to the future, almost eliding the present ("sí come io al presente […] conosco") ["as I, now […] am […] aware"]) in embedded adverbs. Furthermore, Fiammetta pairs love with loss; the term "senza frutto" ("fruitlessly") at the margin of this complex idea underscores the inconsequence of the realization come too late. Elsewhere, words like "unfortunately" and "ultimately" indicate this phenomenon as well ("whose advice unfortunately I had spurned" [16]; "Seeing what followed, [the vision of Venus offered] ultimately destructive advice, in which I unfortunately believed" [22][12]). Indeed, a single sentence can begin hopefully and end in devastation:

> while my Panfilo is alive […] seeing that human affairs are continually changing always leads me to believe that sometime he will again be mine […] but such hope, having no fulfillment, continually makes my life very onerous, and I consider myself burdened by a greater sorrow (145).[13]

Paradoxically, Fiammetta cannot give up hope, even as she has already given up hope. The past and future are always present in Fiammetta's writing, mingling the emotions of the time before she fell in love and the time after abandonment in a way that obscures and revises the very notion of a functional

---

[11] "e assai contenta, non pensando che il diletto il quale io allora con ampissimo cuore prendea, fosse radice e pianta nel futuro di miseria, sí come io al presente senza frutto miseramente conosco" (66).
[12] "li cui consigli male per me rifiutai" (50); "simigliante consiglio di distruzione ultima, qual fece ella, porgendomi" (59–60).
[13] "mentre che il mio Panfilo vive, […] veggendo le mondane cose in continuo moto, sempre mi si lascia credere che egli alcuna volta debba ritornare mio, […] ma questa speranza non venendo ad effetto, gravissima fa la mia vita continuamente, e però me di maggior doglia gravata tengo" (224).

present, all the while, paradoxically, depicting Fiammetta as arrested in a perpetual present of suffering.[14]

Instead of viewing time as linear and progressive, the narrative atmosphere and action bind themselves to cycles, like waves crashing on the shore, or like the cycles of the moon that Fiammetta counts and debates with. Fiammetta imagines the moon links her and Panfilo, and at first, she pictures Panfilo staring at the same moon, in a moment of imaginary, fantastical intimacy. But in the same thought, she dismisses this fantasy, correcting with "I now have no doubt that having already forgotten me, not only was he not looking at the moon, but neither had he a single thought about her and was probably in bed and fast asleep" (48).[15] This revision, like the other examples of time-confounding sentences above, inaugurates a linguistic pattern in the rest of the novel, and in analytical fiction more broadly, that a sentence can contain a cycle of time that loops back to just where it had started. This underlines the pessimistic worldview that all insights are ultimately discarded in favor of competing insights, ensuring that pleasure always comes mixed with pain.

The sense of dilated cyclical time is also amplified by the constant reopening of the possibility of restored love, which, when it vanishes, relaunches Fiammetta into even greater despair.[16] The story of what happens to Panfilo after he leaves Fiammetta is left ambiguous, and all the versions that Fiammetta hears are open to further scrutiny; they are false signals that impinge on Fiammetta's willingness to be more reasonable and make it impossible for her to "move on" (and in any case, where would she go?). These erroneous communications, conflating hearsay and eyewitness accounts, assaulting Fiammetta from outside (i.e., by the events of the narrative), resurrect her suffering such that just as she is "freed from one anguish […] [she is] plunged into another much greater [one]" (101),[17] and Fiammetta's misery is in fact not just written once, but over and over again, as her passion rekindles with each reminder of Panfilo.

---

[14] Although she does not analyze it in detail, Ronchetti also notes Fiammetta's entering "circular time" after Panfilo's departure: "past events, including past encounters with powerful cultural and literary models, are incessantly recalled, eliciting a virtually endless deconstruction of given meanings" (215). On the contrary, for Panfilo, since he has left Naples and his past behind, time continues to march on in a linear way (Ronchetti 216).

[15] "Il quale io ora non dubito che, essendogli io già uscita di mente, non che egli alla luna mirasse, ma solo un pensiero non avendone, forse nel suo letto si riposava" (94).

[16] Outside of the prologue and final chapter, which form their own circle, as Annalise Brody rightly points out (Brody 177).

[17] "io d'una angoscia uscita ed entrata in un'altra molto maggiore" (167).

In as much as readers have learned from the previous parts of the story that these types of renewed hopes only lead to fresh pains, we can only read skeptically, viewing the narrative as a cyclically repeating structure of hope and disappointment. For example, at the end of Chapter 6, Fiammetta obtains permission from her husband to sometime later go on a "pilgrimage," a journey whose true purpose is to seek out Panfilo.[18] It is, of course, unknown whether she will make this trip or not, since the book ends before she sets out (if so, it would alter the interpretation of the *Elegia* significantly). But the reader knows from experience that this new renovation of the possibility of contact, although powerful for Fiammetta ("the hope of a future journey held me back from [death] with no small force" [141][19]), will likely go nowhere. On a formal level, this renewed unknowing represents a redoubling of the narrative, a return to the middle of the text again, and to the painful reckoning of love's loss. And ultimately, the rekindled possibility of being reunited with her lover is more disquieting to Fiammetta than believing in a finished story, such as his marriage, or presumably his death (since, as Fiammetta observes flippantly, "dead things are usually forgotten" [146][20]); the persistence of hope, because it is always followed by disappointment, in fact causes suffering in analytical fiction.

## Fallible or Untrustworthy? Fictions in the *Elegia*

As Fiammetta remains fixed in the cycle of alternating hope and distress, we must keep in mind that "her shock and grief are harder to bear as she cannot confide in anyone" (Doody 202) except her nurse. Despite the passionate outpouring of emotion in her narrative written for compassionate ladies, Fiammetta is still "under cover"; her husband and friends do not know that she is living a double life. The entire narrative action of the *Elegia* unfolds on two paradoxical narrative levels at once: on the one hand, the "true story," that is, the secrets that Fiammetta divulges to her readers, and on the other hand, the occasionally reported outer life that Fiammetta (or whatever her real name is) performs for her husband

---

[18] Fiammetta is married to a handsome, rich, and good (if oblivious) man to whom she does not seem expressly attracted. Or perhaps he is merely too available: "la troppa copia del mio marito […] m'ingannò" (175) ("the excessive generosity of my husband […] misled me" [108]) into ignoring his many good qualities, writes Fiammetta. The beginning of this passage I quoted already in the introduction as the precedent for Montaigne's famous maxim about "soul error."
[19] "la speranza del futuro viaggio da ciò con forza non piccola mi ritiene" (219).
[20] "come mettere si sogliono le cose morte" (225).

and friends at all times. The "true" story (to which the reader is privileged to share) is not the "real" story that Fiammetta lives, and vice-versa. She denies the truth even as she proffers it.[21] This entire metaliterary conceit, along with the fashioning of time as inconsequential, as I just delineated, questions the validity of literary narration as an effective tool for communication more generally.

Before moving on to the discussion of storytelling, however, I wish to pause here to consider the question of what exactly constitutes an unreliable narrator, since Fiammetta is often designated as one. In addition, I wish to counter the particular ways in which Fiammetta has been treated as an "unreliable narrator" (I agree she is one, but for other reasons) because she does not conform to Christian ideals of chastity. Greta Olson plots "unreliable" narrators along a spectrum of intensity in two categories: "fallibility" and "untrustworthiness." In Wayne Booth's classic formulation of narrative irony, the conspiracy between implied readers (ideally ones who hold the same worldview as the author) and implied authors hinges on the author sending out textual signals that the reader, then, must use to read "against the grain [that is, the literal plane] of the text" (Olson 94). For example, Janet Levarie Smarr has Boccaccio's implied author in mind when she writes that "the classical allusions in the *Elegia* [...] [are] a useful means for working into the text moral warnings beyond those uttered openly to Fiammetta or her nurse" (134–35), which is what "Boccaccio would want readers to think" (Migiel 175) about the purpose of literature in Horatian terms, to instruct, as well as to delight. But, as Olson points out, one should be wary that "critics use the concept of the implied author to project their own values onto texts: first, they treat the narrator as a real person, whose lack of reliability they perceive as a personal, moral failure or, at least, a limitation" (Olson 97, citing Ansgar Nünning's view *contra* Booth). In other words, in designating a narrator "unreliable" we risk projecting too much of ourselves and our moralizing onto what is, in fact, an author's invention and a rhetorical tool. I will discuss this moralizing in more detail below.

In Olson's rubric, a "fallible" narrator is one whose "reports can seem insufficient because their sources of information are biased and incomplete [...] That is, external circumstances appear to cause the narrator's misperceptions rather than inherent characteristics" (Olson 101–02). Fiammetta may fit into this category because of all of the false accounts she receives about Panfilo's

---

[21] It is tempting to write that Fiammetta is a gift giver (in the Derridean sense, the gift being narrative) acting in bad faith.

actions and whereabouts, rendering her narration incomplete and misperceived. But on the other hand, as a homodiegetic narrator, Fiammetta is, as Olson puts it, "subject to the epistemological uncertainty of lived experience. [She is] not necessarily unreliable" (101) for having received false reports. Olson's second category, "untrustworthy," describes narrators whose speech "will be greeted by skepticism and rapidly amended when it is inconsistent" (Olson 102). In Olson's scheme, Fiammetta might be labeled as a "marginally unreliable" (103) untrustworthy narrator, in the vein of Moll Flanders, who "has been alternately identified as the eloquent speaker of London's poor or the object of Daniel Defoe's moral derision" (103). If we replace "London's poor" with "abandoned women" and "Daniel Defoe" with "Giovanni Boccaccio," no one would doubt we are speaking of Fiammetta. Just like Moll, Fiammetta "alternately styles herself as a victim, a fallen sinner, and an ambassador of morality" (Olson 104), or if not morality, exactly, then at least a critic of men's indifference and deception. This "marginally untrustworthy" category is also the most difficult to assess, according to Olsen, who concedes that "readers are required to do more 'detective' work to determine whether a narrator is trustworthy or not, and critics remain divided about how to characterize the storyteller" (104). I argue that as an example of analytical fiction, the *Elegia* already frames Fiammetta as a character who is aware of her own self-deception, but is powerless to change it.

Self-deception, as a story that we tell to help frame our view of ourselves, becomes necessary when there is no stable truth of the self upon which to rely. Avid readers of analytical fiction know that values such as "moral truth" (Levarie Smarr 146) and "correct choice" (Hollander 42) do not typically operate in these texts. At best, the Christian virtues of chastity and fidelity, or even social values like *bienséance* or reputation, are red herrings, an excuse that a character may use to cover up a much more deep-seated, personal, and existential fear about acting on their desires.[22] This is not to say that Fiammetta is amoral; she certainly has a moral compass that comes from her social milieu and Christianity (she is depicted as a Christian, if not a remarkably devout one). But moralizing about Fiammetta's fall from grace is not supported by the text, which depicts numerous young people extravagantly adorning themselves, speaking openly

---

[22] This is in no way to denigrate the danger that Fiammetta would have been in had she been a real woman. Stephen J. Milner reminds us that "the concern with honour, reputation, and social standing is indicative of a social world in which people observed, judged, commented, and gossiped about other people's business" (86). Having her identity and infidelity discovered would certainly cost Fiammetta her only asset, that is, her reputation as a virtuous woman (and potentially her life at her husband's hands).

(unlike Fiammetta) about their affairs, and cavorting at parties, resorts, and even in church. During jousts, for example, "the maidens gave joyful glances to their lovers, sometimes from high windows and sometimes from the doors below; and each one assured her lover of her amorous feelings, one with a new gift, another with a gesture, and still another with words" (131).[23] And Fiammetta, describing an encounter with a woman whom she guesses must be another of Panfilo's former lovers, writes, "I was jealous of the open signs of love she was showing" (60).[24] The nurse, moreover, tells Fiammetta that she has witnessed many young people enmeshed in the same kinds of adulterous affairs as her mistress, and of course the aim of Venus's discourse is to convince Fiammetta that "everybody's doing it." With the exception of the vision of Venus, perhaps, these examples indicate that Fiammetta herself constructs at least some of her concerns about virtue. Moreover, Fiammetta's allusions to reading about mythical romantic characters—from Paris and Helen to Tristan and Isolde—reflect an entire literary canon's investment in passionate romances of extramarital love, to which, even if ironically, the *Elegia* contributes. Not to mention, of course, that the tradition of courtly love literature, first theorized in Andreas Capellanus's *De Amore*, expressly condones love outside of marriage.[25] Fiammetta is far less of a morally corrupt fool than an ironic, anti-Romantic character (as all of the heroines depicted in this book on analytical fiction are), self-deceived because she is part of a literary tradition that questions the validity of introspection.

Above all, Fiammetta knows that she is self-deceived. She says in retrospect, "how falsely I was arguing and quibbling with the truth!" (45),[26] employing the Ovidian language of dissimulation to invoke her manipulative powers, and telling herself, "stop loving him, and show how you deceived him with the same art he used to deceive you" (57).[27] The parallelism of this phrase is quite striking. She also acknowledges that her suffering derives from being "self-deceived and deceived by you [Panfilo] and by your words" 61).[28] The word *"ingannare,"*

---

[23] "Le giovini donne [...] lieti sguardi porgevano a' loro amanti, ora dall'alte finestre e quando dalle basse porte, e quale con nuovo dono, e tale con sembiante, e tale con parole confortava il suo del suo amore" (206).

[24] "invidiosa che da lei sí aperti segnali d'amore [...] si mostrassero" (109).

[25] It must be noted that we should not conflate historical medieval views on adultery with literary ones. According to Henry Ansgar Kelly, "the opposition between love and marriage was very much a minority view, and hardly a serious one, contrary to what the theorists of courtly love have assumed" (38). For a more complex view of love and marriage in the medieval period, see Conor McCarthy's introduction to *Love, Sex, and Marriage in the Middle Ages: A Sourcebook* (1–23).

[26] "quanto falsamente argomentava, fatta sofistica contro al vero!" (91)

[27] "rimanti d'amarlo, e dimostra che con quell'arte che egli ha te ingannata tu abbi ingannato lui" (106).

[28] "dal tuo [Panfilo] parlare e da te e da me medesima ingannata" (111–12).

"to deceive," recurs frequently in the *Elegia*, and it is sometimes self-directed by the heroine. The recognition that she has been deceived both by Panfilo's words and by her own actions should give the reader pause to consider whether Fiammetta's narration is "unreliable," or whether her lack of self-knowledge is more critically a function of her tragedy.

## Imprisoned in Words, Excluded from Deeds

Despite her early act of adultery, the overall narration places Fiammetta squarely in what Teodolinda Barolini has identified in the *Decameron* as the feminine world of words (*parole*) as opposed to the world of deeds (*fatti*) (281).[29] After Panfilo leaves, Fiammetta becomes paralyzed, just like Boccaccio describes women suffering from melancholic lovesickness in the Proem of the *Decameron*: unlike men who have many active diversions to help them forget their pains, women remain "pent up within the narrow confines of their rooms"[30] isolated, burning with unrequited love, and suffering in silence. In order to help these women's recovery, Boccaccio proposes not exercise or any kind of action but, rather, reading: "Boccaccio offers [women] his *novelle*, his *parole*; men have deeds, women have words" (Barolini 282). Although the *Decameron* questions and often upends this gendered binary (as Barolini demonstrates), the *Elegia* is inextricably bound by it. Fiammetta finds herself, by the third of nine chapters of her story, suddenly excluded from the active world by Panfilo's departure. Confined to playing out her drama inside her house, under the control of her husband and society, Fiammetta remains imprisoned in her mental and physical suffering. When she does move her suffering outside, it is at her husband's suggestion; he takes her to the resort of Baia, where Fiammetta actually attempts all of the active pursuits advised to men (hunting, riding, swimming, dancing, etc.), and fails miserably at them. Except for this excursion to Baia, which I will discuss further below, the last three-quarters of the novel consist of Fiammetta explaining how she filled the time, perpetually hoping for Panfilo to return. Due to her sex, she is precluded from searching actively for him (the future "pilgrimage"

---

[29] Caroline Bynum warns, however, that too often the generalization "that vast binaries [...] marched through the medieval past from Plato to Descartes" is "not tenable" (16), and we should be careful to distinguish the competing theories of the mind/body problem (and its attendant rejection of the body as corrupt and feminized).

[30] "nel piccolo circuito delle loro camere racchiuse" (*Decameron* 6).

notwithstanding). Nor, because of the recursive narrative that continually refreshes her hope of his return, can she find a new occupation to distract her indefinitely. Psyche and Cupid apart, in much of the mythological fiction that Fiammetta reads, as Alessia Ronchetti puts it, "meaning is constructed through a plot based on the hero's journey from one place to another, one experience to another. [...] Women seem to have no choice but to function as markers of those territories that the hero crosses and eventually masters" (214).[31] Despite being a modern woman, Fiammetta is still subject to this paradigm (again, whether by choice or not is beside the point, suffice to say that the narrative is constructed in such a way as to make it so). Indeed, all of Fiammetta's attempts to bring Panfilo back turn out to be "more full of words than deeds" (129).[32] Furthermore, while Boccaccio in the *Decameron* proclaims that his text has therapeutic properties, Fiammetta explicitly pens *her* book as a plea for sympathy and a warning to women in love, not as an antidote. Fiammetta claims that recovery is not her goal; she tells her story "to make certain that the cause of my grief will *not* grow weaker through habit but stronger" (1, emphasis added),[33] suggesting that she does not expect (or perhaps even wish) to be cured.

Nevertheless, scholars debate whether the *Elegia* can be read, like the *Decameron*, as a curative text, or whether Fiammetta's experiences of hearing stories help her to alleviate her pain.[34] For example, in the passage in which Fiammetta gathers her maids around her to tell stories, *Decameron*-style *avant*

---

[31] "Panfilo is a mobile hero" (Ronchetti 214). However there is one scene in which Fiammetta paints Panfilo's new lover as endowed with the power to act, while Fiammetta cannot: "in che si stendono le mie parole?" ("how far do my words go?") Fiammetta roars in apostrophe at Panfilo's new lover (or to her imaginary picture of her, since we do not know if such a woman even exists). "Io ti minaccio, e tu mi nuoci" (181) ("I threaten you and you harm me by keeping my lover" [112]). Fiammetta endows this imaginary woman with the ability to hurt because she is empowered by Panfilo's love. Once he leaves her, she too will become a powerless Fiammetta.

[32] "più di parole che d'opere le trovai piene" (203–4). In this case, having tried all different kinds of remedies for her love, she attempts witchcraft, citing Medea as well as, implicitly, Lucian in *The Golden Ass*, but to no avail. Magic does not exist in this universe.

[33] "per lunga usanza *non* menomi la cagione, ma s'avanzi" (27, emphasis added).

[34] Zak posits that in the *Elegia*, Boccaccio maintains a general "mistrust of the use of tragic narratives as a source of consolation" (5). Brody concludes that "for readers who can see beyond Fiammetta's self-centered point of view [...] storytelling can break the cycle of sorrows and ideally heal from lovesickness" (182), but she earlier admits that "the *Elegia* can be read as a *failure* of a quest either to cure love sorrows or to attain a higher form of love" (176, emphasis added). As to whether the *Decameron*, as a comedy, effectively harnesses storytelling as a "better [form] of consolation [that] can be found in physical communion" (Milner 98) with friends is also up for debate. Zak provides a thorough review of the literature that investigates this question (footnotes pp. 1–2). To this list I would only add Irene Albers, who writes that in the *Decameron* "the 'therapy' is ambiguous, because the novella does constitute a distraction from the emotional fixation considered responsible for lovesickness, but also gives wings to the fantasies which should be quelled by it, so that readers might either be healed or infected" (35, footnote).

*la lettre*, Fiammetta does find distraction and even comfort. She reports that she had her maids tell her stories (although they are outlandish) and that they make her feel more cheerful (49). But this takes place within the promised initial four months of Panfilo's absence, and Fiammetta still trusts at this point that he will return. After she has more reason to believe that the departure is definitive, the evidence is more mixed. Of watching young people (of her own social class) happily in love, dancing and singing, Fiammetta reports that she was "quasi alcuna consolazione prendendo" (131) ("taking almost no consolation;" Causa-Steindler and Mauch's translation has it as "*as if* I were deriving some consolation" [75]), but on seeing people leaving early because their lovers are not present, she smiles to herself (though, she admits, only "faintly"), and feels a certain sympathy for the people whose lovers are absent. The smiling is ambiguous, however, and at best it is a mere inconsequential juxtaposition of her own pain with theirs. At worst, what she feels is akin to mere *schadenfreude*. In any case, the effect is altered from when Fiammetta asks her maids to tell her stories while she waits for Panfilo's return. Now that he is not returning, or it seems that way, Fiammetta interprets other people's love stories differently.

When Fiammetta hears young women singing songs about unrequited love, she writes that she wishes to learn them by heart "so that by *repeating* it to myself I would and could sometime lament in public in a more orderly and covert language" (75, emphasis added).[35] Here, Fiammetta hides her true motivation and mediates her suffering through an acceptable cover ("*coperto*") and thus is able to express openly feelings that were previously hidden. This device is a staple of analytical fiction, as we will see in future chapters. Singing the sad love songs also adds another layer to the *Elegia*'s cyclical structure: she repeats them and reexperiences the pain that Panfilo's departure had caused and continues to cause. Singing is not validated as therapeutic here, either, nor as a form of entertainment. The lament as a covert language acts as yet another delaying device, resurrecting and prolonging Fiammetta's suffering by allowing her to express it publicly.

At other times, Fiammetta remains unimpressed with conversations about love. She begins to see her pain and suffering as singular. At a wedding, for example, she reports, "I easily understood that no other love has been as passionate, as secretive, and as burdened with anxieties as mine, although there

---

[35] "acciò poi fra me *ridicendola*, con piú ordinate parlare e piú coperto mi sapessi e potessi in pubblico alcuna volta dolere" (130, emphasis added).

are a great many happier and less virtuous" (79).³⁶ Whereas before, Fiammetta did manage to find distraction and even consolation in hearing stories, as time goes on she finds less and less joy in any kind of entertainment. She begins to go out less frequently, she removes herself from society, and spends more time at home. She no longer finds comfort in entertainments or spectacles: "nothing pleased me, no festivity could give me any joy, and no thought or word could give me comfort" (131).³⁷ In fact, no other stories adequately compare to hers. This singularity, however, only brings Fiammetta suffering: she claims her uniqueness brings her no glory, only misery.

As the narrative progresses, Fiammetta begins to develop something akin to her own theory about the insufficiency of language to truthfully represent actions and emotions. While she collapses the limits between past, present, and future—since the recursive narrative makes time inconsequential—she builds a more concrete distinction between actual present *trauma* and narrative, which is yet another way of saying that the *Elegia* emphasizes the disparity between experience and words. For Fiammetta, the two kinds of suffering—literary and real—are in fact incomparable. Fiammetta indicates that storytelling is mimetically inadequate, claiming that there is no comparison between "the painted fire and one that truly burns" (155).³⁸ Thus, the *Elegia* introduces the Platonic principle that any kind of narrated passion is a weak and insubstantial copy of the real.

Some critics find Fiammetta's entire project suspect, but notably her representations of the exempla, unduly privileging the mythical fictions above her own narrative. For example, Fiammetta is "unable or unwilling to see the difference between life and literature. [...] [She], like Francesca, renounces reason to follow appetite, and in consequence is frozen in a hellish condition of permanent wretchedness" (Ronchetti 210 paraphrasing Levarie Smarr 129–30 and Hollander 48).³⁹ Zak interprets Fiammetta's statements as "sophistic and compassion-less readings" (18) and writes that she "remains utterly defiant in her dedication to her love despite all her torments" (11). Suzanne Hagedorn sees

---

³⁶ "agevolmente ho compreso niuno sì fervente né tanto occulto né con sì grevi affanni essere stato come il mio, avvegna che de' piú felici e de' meno onorevoli il numero ne sia grande" (136).
³⁷ "Niuna cosa mi piaceva, nulla festa mi poteva rallegrare, né conforto porgere pensiero né parola" (206).
³⁸ "dal fuoco dipinto a quello che veramente arde" (237).
³⁹ Inasmuch as Paolo and Francesca's souls wandered around the second circle of hell, they are nevertheless rendered as sympathetic characters by Dante the Pilgrim, and by Boccaccio particularly in his commentary on the *Commedia* ("it is Boccaccio, the great raconteur, who elaborates Francesca's story to novella-like proportions and whose imprint on it is most indelible" [Barolini 309]).

Fiammetta as a kind of female proto-Quixote, finding that "clearly, [Fiammetta's] intense psychological involvement in literature has arrested her own emotional development" (127).[40] For Calabrese, "in marshaling the entire host of women scorned by love or fate, then saying that none could possibly have suffered as she has, Fiammetta squanders any possible power that association with a famous heroine could bring" (26). Although these scholars take issue with Fiammetta's self-presentation and choices, it is significant that almost all of them identify Fiammetta as an inactive, static entity; Fiammetta is pronounced "frozen," "defiant," "arrested," and impotent.

Short of the reference to the Tristan myth (which I will briefly discuss below), so much has been written on the exempla that it would be futile to reiterate much more. I will only write that Fiammetta claims that the misfortunes of other abandoned women, including Hypsipyle, Medea, Oenone, and Ariadne, are less than hers, because "their tears ended with a fair vengeance, which mine do not have yet" (154)[41] and as far as we know will never have. In the case of the story of Tristan and Isolde, the only medieval romance explicitly cited in the *Elegia*—which in itself makes it significant—we see both similarities and contrasts between Fiammetta's story and that of the lovers. Like her and Panfilo, Tristan and Isolde fall in love accidentally and to a certain extent (though perhaps not for Panfilo) against their wills and better judgment. Both couples dissemble and engage in what E. Jane Burns calls "fictive discourse," whereby the couples "lie together as lovers, but [...] [also] lie together as tellers of a fictional tale" (80). This is where the similarities end, of course, and Fiammetta concludes that Tristan and Isolde were happy in their deaths because—once again folding together misery and joy—they "ended pleasures and pains at once" (146),[42] while Fiammetta's suffering continues. Similarly, she cites the metamorphoses and devices that delay, sublimate, or even celebrate death (as in the Tristan myth),

---

[40] Yet Hagedorn does not see Fiammetta as foolish.
[41] "ebbero termine con giusta vendetta le lagrime loro, la qual cosa ancora non hanno le mie" (235).
[42] "finirono [...] ad un'ora li diletti e le doglie" (225). It is not totally clear with which versions Boccaccio was familiar (Causa-Steindler writes that "it would be indeed surprising if the writings of Chrétien de Troyes and the poetry of the troubadours had not been part of Boccaccio's cultural background" [xxiv]), but the story that Fiammetta recounts (whereby a mortally wounded Tristan asphyxiates Isolde by hugging her very tightly so they can die together, "uno cuore et una anima" (Allaire 724) "one heart and one soul" [Allaire 725]) is only found, to my knowledge, in one manuscript, the *Tristano Panciatichiano* Italian prose version, housed at the Biblioteca Nazionale Centrale in Florence. However, there is so little passionate discourse in the *Tristano Panciatichiano* that it would be remarkable if this was Boccaccio's only source material. Instead, Fiammetta's introspective discourse and the thematic dilation of doubt of the *Elegia* most resembles that of Gottfried von Strassburg's epic *version courtoise* (published after his death in 1210), a *roman d'analyse* in its own right.

and again repeats that her own suffering is worse because it is ongoing. In other words, for mythological characters, there is some "out" that is inaccessible to Fiammetta. She is frozen in her present suffering in ways that the narrated stories are able to transcend.

In the fifth chapter Fiammetta despairs of the absence of the gods: "Where are you, Oh gods? Where have you turned your eyes now" (60),[43] she asks.[44] Fiammetta has no triumph of reason, no map, no gods, to help her out of the epistemological quagmire of obsessive love and pervasive self-doubt. But she does know (however ironically in a fictional work) that literary grief cannot compete with real trauma, and with this limited, skeptical, almost Cartesian knowledge (she suffers, therefore she exists) she makes her pain unique.

In this way, while Fiammetta's lament is protracted, expansive, and flowing, and it is emotionally open in many places, the narrative also withholds. Like many other authors in this study, Boccaccio, through Fiammetta, repeatedly claims that emotions or even deeds are beyond telling, even as Fiammetta has nothing but words to work with. For instance, we witness this trope of indescribability when she first hears from Panfilo that he is leaving Naples. She writes that only women who have been in love could understand: "I shall not try to explain it, since any other example besides the one I gave would be insufficient for us, as would any further talking" (31).[45] She claims Panfilo's cunning is "beyond my capacity to recount" (9)[46]; she declares she "shall not take the trouble to describe" (12) the changes in her behavior and appearance that lovesickness caused her "because it would take too long" (12).[47] In the figure of Venus, Fiammetta "experienced beauties impossible to express in words" (17)[48]; and when she is very angry she writes that she is incapable of illustrating "how vehement" (66) her anger is.[49] When Fiammetta spurns Shame

---

[43] "O iddii ove sete? Ove ora mirano gli occhi vostri?" (110).
[44] In the suicide attempt scene as well, we see a strong contrast between the classical literature that Fiammetta cites and the realities of fourteenth-century court life. Fiammetta hesitates about killing herself, in part, because the limitations of modern city living, the constant flow of servants around her, and the material necessity of poison, weapons, or fire to end her life are actually impractical. She cites not wanting to create a scandal in her family. Like the ineffectiveness of witchcraft to bring back Panfilo, committing suicide in medieval Naples is similarly and necessarily "more full of words than deeds" (129).
[45] "all'altre non curo di dimostrarlo, però che così come ogn'altro essemplo che il detto, così ogni parlare ci sarebbe scarso" (71).
[46] "oltre ad ogni potere raccontare" (40).
[47] "le quali tutte non curo di raccontare, sì perché troppo sarebbe lungo" (45).
[48] "io bellezze in lei da non potere con lingua ridire" (51).
[49] "quanta focosa ira" (117).

for not allowing her to be freer with her pen about her sexual encounters with Panfilo, she writes in irritation, "alas, how you offend me [...] believing perhaps that you are helping me!" (26)[50] and she concedes to writing in a kind of secret code, legible only to women who are sexually experienced and who can then help to translate the more intimate parts of the story for the uninitiated. In this rhetorical scheme, Fiammetta is prevented from writing (she asks personified Shame, "why do you hold back my pen [...]?" [26][51]). When the narrative itself forestalls action, signs (words) detached from their referents (actions), and their power and veracity diminish.[52]

Even the fact that she writes the book is not a clear indication of Fiammetta's ability to reconcile deeds and words, nor is it an indication of change or growth (Hagedorn 127). Nor does the act of writing prove either a consolation or a therapeutic act. Instead, writing *augments* Fiammetta's grief: "whenever I think that I must reveal [it] to others in writing, I am assailed by such self-pity that it drains nearly all my strength" (28).[53] At another time she claims that her book is delayed because "by writing of it I will feel as if I were reentering it" (100).[54] And similarly, Fiammetta and the nurse abandon their idea to write Panfilo letters that describe Fiammetta's anguish, questioning the effectiveness of letters and ultimately deciding that they would not do any good for her cause. She knows they would never be answered. The end result of Fiammetta's "little book" is a static catalog of suffering—her own and that of others from counter-exemplary literature and history—that does not bring the writer any pleasure or relief. Instead, the writing itself acts as yet another loop, another obstacle, in a painful *mise en abyme* of impossible love.

## "When We Practice to Deceive": Dissimulation and Deception

More often than not, like the many (usually false) reports of Panfilo's life, storytelling reopens the wounds of Fiammetta's suffering. Panfilo himself, Fiammetta explains, was a gifted storyteller (and liar: "alas, where are the gods

---

[50] "che tu mi offendi, credendomi forse giovare" (65).
[51] "Perché ritieni tu la mia penna [...]?" (65).
[52] Oddly, however, examples of this trope of indescribability disappear in the last two thirds of the text.
[53] "pur pensando di doverle altrui scrivendo, mostrare, tanta di me stessa compassione m'assalisce" (67).
[54] "perché, scrivendolo, in esso mi parrà rientrare" (165).

to whom you perjured yourself, O Panfilo? [...] Where are those false tears [...] full of deceit?" [103–4][55]). While they are still together, in public, Panfilo carefully hides his feelings for Fiammetta. He would delight her by recounting at dinner parties tales of the imaginary Greek couple Fiammetta and Panfilo or excitedly and wittily compare the jousting knights at tournaments to the heroes of antiquity. After his departure, dinner parties, celebrations, tournaments, and, indeed, church services seem hollow and painful compared to before, when with Panfilo there Fiammetta's joy was enlarged. Here again, the past overshadows the present and renders the present "fruitless," just as in the examples about time above. And to reiterate, while those events felt genuinely *active* before, Panfilo's leaving debases them into the world of mere appearances and empty language.

Panfilo, conflated with the god of love, is also the one who teaches Fiammetta to dissemble ("by speaking figuratively he managed to teach me to speak in the same way" [23][56]). And as Ronchetti points out, "'Fiammetta' *exists* as such because Panfilo has given her a name, or, to put it differently, 'Fiammetta' exists in her authorial function as a product of Panfilo's authorship" (211, emphasis added). On first glance, this inversion supports the interpretation of Boccaccio's "ventriloquism" (Calabrese 24)[57] of Fiammetta—i.e., her narration mediated through a male writer or creator, but, Ronchetti goes on, it has significant consequences for Fiammetta once Panfilo leaves. Ronchetti asks, what will happen to "Fiammetta" once Panfilo is gone? "What can she become?" (215) Can she gain a sense of authorship and authority? Yes and no. Fiammetta does not confess to her husband, à la *La Princesse de Clèves*; she dissimulates to him and to her friends the entire time. She endows love, as well as Panfilo, with the power to teach her to dissimulate, and seems proud of herself for learning to be able to speak on multiple levels at once. Whereas she says that previously she could only speak of simple matters, all of a sudden, "I picked up his manner of speaking with such enthusiasm that in a short time I could have outdone any poet in speech and fiction" (24).[58] In this quotation, which appears early in the narrative, Fiammetta manages to refashion herself as a new woman and as

---

[55] "dove sono ora, o Panfilo, gli spergiurati iddii? [...] Dove le infinte lagrime [...] piene del tuo inganno?" (170).
[56] "s'ingegnò, per figura parlando, e d'insegnarmi a tale modo parlare" (62).
[57] Calabrese is citing Elizabeth Harvey's book *Ventriloquized Voices: Feminist Theory and English Renaissance Texts*. Milner also uses this term in relation to all of the *brigata* of the *Decameron* (88).
[58] "con tanta affezione li modi del parlare di costui raccolsi, che in breve spazio io avrei di fingere e di parlare passato ogni poeta" (62).

a poet, capable of competing with the bards in lying. In this way, it is true, she seems to try to lessen the culpability of her infidelity. As Sarah J. Todd points out, "despite her extramarital dalliances, Fiammetta is keen to present herself in a pure and chaste light [...] raising questions regarding the reliability of her testimony" (81).

But the rewards of Fiammetta's education in dissimulation, inspired by and taught to her by Panfilo, are short-lived. True, her prevarications continue to the end of her narrative and her infidelity goes undetected. But the psychic toll is high. Fiammetta realizes the paradox of her situation: "Oh, deceptive world, if deeds are kept hidden, how much more powerful false faces are than righteous minds! I, who am more sinful than any other woman and afflicted by my dishonest feelings of love, am considered a saint because I conceal them under virtuous words" (96).[59] She may have taken joy in her double life while Panfilo was there living it with her, but her suffering is doubled by her need to present as a cheerful wife and friend after the abandonment. She now feels the imprisonment of her double life: "all the time keeping [the distress] in the heart and hiding [...] behind a cheerful face!" (114).[60] If Fiammetta succeeds in building herself up as a sort of lover-poet at the beginning of her story, it is only so that the implied author can render her fall all the more excruciating.

## Free Will versus Fate and the *Roman de la rose*

In Fiammetta's dream vision of Venus, the goddess defends infidelity on the grounds that Love "is the strongest, he annuls the laws of others by disregarding them and gives his own" (20).[61] Cataloguing love's conquests, Venus asks Fiammetta "What are your doubts? What are you running away from so madly?" (20).[62] Love's snares are literally everywhere ("heaven, earth, sea, and the underworld" [19][63]), and it is futile to resist. Strikingly, she exhorts Fiammetta to "love confidently" (20),[64] without reservation or thoughts of flight. While

---

[59] "O ingannevole mondo, quanto possono in te gl'infiniti visi piú che li giusti animi, se l'opere sono occulte! Io, piú peccatrice che altra, dolente per li miei disonesti amori, però che quelli velo sotto oneste parole" (159).
[60] "convenirle sotto lieto viso nascondere solo nel cuore" (184).
[61] "sì come piú forte, l'altrui leggi, non curando, anullisce, e dà le sue" (58).
[62] "Dunque che cerchi? Che dubiti?" (57).
[63] "il cielo, la terra, il mare, lo 'nferno" (56).
[64] "sicura ama" (58).

this mandate is in direct opposition to analytical fiction's main impetus of questioning and self-doubt, it corresponds to the construction of love presented in another, non-analytical, medieval text, Guillaume de Lorris and Jean de Meun's *Le Roman de la rose*. A foundational psychomachiac allegorical dream vision, the *Rose* inverts Prudentius's virtue-triumphing-over-vice structure with one in which passionate, consummative love overcomes modesty at the same time as action overcomes speech, and in its ending at least, epitomizes Venus's directive to Fiammetta to "love confidently."

Begun in 1230 by Guillaume and continued in 1275 by Jean (who composed more than seventeen thousand additional lines to add to Guillaume's four thousand), the *Rose* is narrated by a young lover who recounts a dream, "in which the whole art of love is contained" (*The Romance of the Rose* 3).[65] The text is punctuated by long speeches and debates by allegorical characters, including Love, Danger (or Dangier, meaning Rebuff or Resistance), Jealousy, and Venus (just like Fiammetta's nurse and Venus), acting as opposing agents who attempt to persuade the Lover to continue on his mission of seizing his love object, a rose locked up in a tower. Throughout both Guillaume and Jean's *Roman*, the authors juxtapose representations of idealized chivalric love with more realistic depictions of inhibited intimacy that lead, instead, to domination and jealousy. *Danger* is related to the concept of domination (etymologically "danger" derives from the Latin word *dominium* meaning "power" or "control" [Fleming 188]) and is connected to both active power and passive refusal (Braun 181–2). In the *Rose, both* Amour and Danger attempt to dominate the young Lover (one waiting to strike his heart with five good and five bad arrows, and the other constantly crouching and waiting to beat him with a club). The comparisons to Fiammetta are clear, although the genders are inverted—the Lover in the *Rose* is male, while the refracted and dissected love object is, admittedly, a flower, not a human (though we may say, she is more accessible than Panfilo). Fiammetta, too, interprets a number of various external forces that act on her like a kind of Danger, to thwart her potentially fulfilling relationship with Panfilo, and she is similarly dominated by fruitless Amour.

The figure of Danger is a complicated and ambiguous creature, an external, hypocritical force that acts on the characters and that in general destroys relationships and stifles the consummation of love. Danger (translated into

---

[65] "ou l'art d'amours est toute enclose" (*Le Roman de La Rose* 44).

English in a number of ways, including as Rebuff, Resistance, Reserve, and Shame) is a social and behavioral construct that keeps the lovers temporarily apart. He is a roguish, violent, and brutal peasant, and thus an outsider in the garden of Déduit (Pleasure). In Guillaume's text, Danger acts as a constant, debilitating, and hateful enemy for the Lover, and a force that simultaneously imprisons and protects the Rose (whereas Jean's treatment of Danger is as a defense that is easily overcome by Venus's flames at the end). Danger, who guards the rose bushes, stays very close to the Rose and to Bel Accueil (lest the latter make a mistake and let the Lover get too close). Danger's ubiquity also signifies that initial resistance is always there, like a sleeping dragon. As soon as the Lover approaches (with Bel Accueil ready to allow it), Danger wakes up, jumps out, and threatens an attack.

Amour (Cupid) also stalks and, just like his enemy Danger, tries to dominate the Lover throughout the text without managing to ever fully push him over the edge into attaining his goal. Amour claims that the Lover is caught in his net, despite his best defenses:

> Vassal, you are captured, there is no way to escape or defend yourself. Yield, and do not resist. The more willingly you surrender, the sooner you will find mercy. [...] You cannot struggle against me, and I wish you to learn that wickedness and pride will avail you nothing. Surrender. (29)[66]

But this is mere rhetoric and posturing. Within the context of this power struggle, the Lover becomes more and more inflamed, and he is continually thwarted in his desires; Cupid is just not strong enough to overcome the defenses of the Rose or to push the Lover into definitive action. The yearning for the Rose only increases after one of his teasing encounters with Danger. The Lover says:

> Now that I have tasted [love's] savour, the desire that inflames and excites my heart is all the keener. Now tears and sighs will return, and long, sleepless meditations, tremblings, lamentations, and complaints: I shall endure many such torments, for I have fallen into hell. (58)[67]

---

[66] 'Jeune homme, tu es pris, car ni les détours ni la résistance ne servent plus à rien. Ne fais pas d'histoires pour te rendre. Plus tu mettras de bonne volonté à te rendre, plus vite tu trouveras grâce. [...] Tu ne peux lutter contre moi et je veux d'ailleurs bien te montrer que tu n'as rien à gagner à la folie et à l'orgueil; rends-toi plutôt prisonnier' (145).

[67] "Puisque j'ai fait l'expérience de cette saveur [amour], le désire qui brûle et domine mon cœur en est d'autant plus intense. Maintenant reviendront les pleurs et les soupirs, les interminables pensées qui empêchent de dormir, les frissons, les douleurs et les plaintes. De ces souffrances j'en connaîtrai mainte, car je suis tombé en enfer" (249).

The language is very similar to Fiammetta's. The absence of the love object intensifies the Lover's ardor. We can compare the speech above to when Fiammetta laments:

> The more my ungrateful master acts in an extraordinary way against me and the more he sees hope fleeting from me, the more he blows onto his flames of desire and makes them greater; and as the flames grow, my tribulations increase, and since they are never soothed by a proper ointment, each becomes ever more violent, and the more violent they are, the more they torture my miserable mind. (142)[68]

It is significant that Fiammetta emphasizes how many "*more*" obstacles are put in her way by love, diminishing her free will. Indeed, the word "*più*" is repeated six times in this short passage, mirroring Fiammetta's own growing passion and frustration. But while the authors of the *Rose* experiment with a narrative *durée* that only threatens recursivity, in the *Elegia*, Fiammetta, who inhabits a *roman d'analyse*, will never find relief.

This is most evident in the second part of the romance, where Jean more explicitly contrasts the artificial ideals of "courtoisie" (or what Katherine Heinrichs calls "amor stultus" [foolish love] [162, and more generally 155–210]) with the harsh but ultimately preferable "réalités de l'existence" (*Rose* footnote 563). In the discourse of Ami (who gives marital advice to a misogynistic, jealous husband), we learn that Jealousy, just like Danger, creates a sense of domination—a lack of equality—between the sexes. A wife "no longer knows whom she can trust, when she sees her master [that is, her husband], with whom she had never been on her guard, now at her throat" (145).[69] Furthermore, the taint of jealousy or the desire to dominate kills love: "love cannot last or survive except in hearts that are free and at liberty" (144).[70] Without a definitive break in the cycle of domination, jealousy, and the Lover's resistance by Venus's flaming torch (which is what happens at the end of the romance), representing sexual love and procreation, these ideas could battle on indefinitely.

The differences between Cupid and Venus in the *Roman de la rose* are manifold. Cupid, within this universe, must also be regarded as a kind of villain

---

[68] "e tanto opera più verso me che l'usato il mio ingrate signore, che quanto più vede la speranza da me fuggire, tanto più con disideri soffiando nelle sue fiamme, le fa maggiori; le quali come crescono, così le mie tribolazioni s'aumentano; ed esse mai a unguento debito non essendo allenite, più ognora inaspriscono e, più aspre, più affliggono la trista mente" (220).

[69] "ne sait plus en qui se fier quand elle se voit dominée et pourvue d'un maître dont jamais elle ne s'est méfiée" (565).

[70] "l'amour ne peut durer et vivre que dans un cœur parfaitement libre" (563).

who inflames the Lover unnecessarily, while never accomplishing the task at hand, namely, to capture the Rose. For C. S. Lewis, "Venus is the sexual appetite—the mere natural fact, in contrast to the god of Love who is the refined sentiment. She is the generative force in nature" (121), as opposed to the romantic and chivalric impulse.[71] The Lover plays the fool throughout the Romance, while Venus, practically in one fell swoop, penetrates into the heart of the castle where the Rose is held prisoner, vanquishes Danger, and wins the Lover his beloved. In the face of passion, Danger does not use harsh words or empty threats, but simply moves to the side. The time for feigned modesty is over, and passion gives way to consummation, the Lover now having proven himself worthy to pluck the object of his desire and possess it.

*Fiammetta* can be read as a kind of adjunct or complement to the *Roman de la rose* in the sense that it shows how easily the castle is stormed when the Rose itself is, in fact, an active participant. But it also contrasts the *Rose* by demonstrating the *aftereffects* of the deflowering, that is, what can go wrong when the Lover eventually disappears, or when love fades, or when the characters are merely afraid. Even though the *Rose* is concerned with a complex psychology that leads to the consummation of love (and secondary characters like Ami warn against jealousy), the main story is disinterested in all the dangers that accompany a love affair after it has begun.

Due to this giving way to action, the *Rose*'s Venus may be said to represent a proponent of free will against the mindless domination of Amor and the prudish protectors of the Rose, including Danger. As an allegory, Venus's governing philosophy of uncomplicated, undoubted love makes sense. It is much less clear, though, for the *Elegia*, a novelistic (rather than allegorical) text. It is difficult to determine whether Fiammetta *chooses* to love Panfilo and then is responsible for her own suffering in her abandonment by him or whether she is ensnared by Love's trap, as she claims.[72] As Brody points out, Venus's speech at the beginning of the text equivocates gods, humans, and animals in their lack of mastery of themselves, in direct contrast to the Christian view of free will (181).[73] In a way

---

[71] Venus may or may not represent marriage in this case, as the authors of the *Rose* are ambiguous on the subject.

[72] The critical debate errs on the side of Fiammetta's having free will. For example, Hollander argues that "the 'moral drama' of Fiammetta concerns her *unwillingness* to make the correct choice" (42, emphasis added), and Levarie Smarr sees Fiammetta as merely justifying her desire: "reason may protest, but is impotent to redirect the will or to counteract the attractive power of lust" (129–30).

[73] Brody demonstrates that "Fiammetta remains trapped in a pagan world and the values of courtly love" (181). Although it must be stated that the references are all so jumbled up, and that Fiammetta, in turn, prays, ironically, to Fortune, Christ, and Juno (the goddess of marriage, of all things) to help her get Panfilo back.

that is evocative of the *Rose*, Fiammetta describes her ill preparation for the "battle" over her own soul, when she falls in love with Panfilo. She frames it in terms of divine intervention, that the gods failed to arm her properly for battle: "so that I would not go unarmed into that battle where I was to fall" (4).[74] But ironically, despite the fact that Fiammetta claims that the gods favored her, there is nothing they can do, despite being gods, to truly protect her. In the *Elegia*, fate seems arbitrary and its presence remains unfelt until there is no more time to change it. Fiammetta's insight always comes too late to do any good.

Fiammetta contends that her will was taken from her when she saw Panfilo ("my soul, free and until then mistress of itself, would that day renounce its sovereignty" [6][75]). One proof of this is her failed attempt at suicide. This scene involves a kind of "fortune," that is, coincidences and external phenomena that mislead the suffering heart. The nurse attempts to stop Fiammetta from running up to the roof of her house to throw herself off of it (another reminder of Psyche, who also fails in her jumping suicide attempt). Climbing the stairs, Fiammetta's dress gets caught on something and she falls. When the nurse tries to help her, Fiammetta laments: "my frantic hands, intending to untangle, were entangling myself" (124–5).[76] While this statement could be read as a metaphor for Fiammetta's own responsibility in her suffering, the action seems to transcend such debates: in the classic hunter/hunted dialectical paradigm, the harder Fiammetta works to free herself from love, the more ensnared she becomes in it.

It would be difficult to write about free will in the *Elegia* without discussing the scene in which Fiammetta accuses Panfilo of having raped her: "should I have screamed and brought endless shame on myself and death on you, whom I loved more than myself? As God knows, I resisted as much as I could, but as my strength was not equal to yours, you won and possessed what you were stealing" (63).[77] Calabrese reads this baffling passage as a commentary on medieval women's inability to consent (given that their "no's were taken to mean 'yes'" [32]), and Boccaccio's modeling, in part, of Fiammetta's story on Ovid's *Pamphilus de amore*, in which the (not coincidentally) namesake character

---

[74] "acciò che disarmata non venissi alla battaglia nella quale io dovea cadere" (33).
[75] "quello giorno la mia libera anima, e di sé donna, disposta la sua signoria, serva dovea divenire, come avvenne" (36).
[76] "le mani per la fretta, credendosi sviluppare, aviluppavano" (198).
[77] "Doveva io gridare, e col mio grido a me infamia perpetua, e a te, il quale io più che me medesima amava, morte cercare? Io opposi le forze mie, come Iddio sa, quant'io potei; le quali, alle tue non potendo resistere, vinte, possedesti la tua rapina" (114).

actually commits a rape. Calabrese, however, warns that too-presentist a reading of the alleged-rape denigrates the early modern text as well as our own contemporary accusations of violence against women.[78] Fiammetta's revised version of the story could also be a reference to Seneca's *Phaedra*, of course, a text from which Boccaccio borrows freely, with Fiammetta semi-consciously casting herself as the tragic character whose unrequited passion for her stepson cause her to falsely accuse him of violating her. As readers we have no way of knowing if she indeed consented, as she first claimed ("he obtained from me that which I wanted just as much as he did, *although I feigned the contrary*" [25, emphasis added][79]). Besides the fact that it was stated first, what reason is there to privilege the first account over the second? Neither this description nor the rape accusation is definitive. We do not know if the allegation represents proof of Fiammetta's real self-deception of amnesiac proportions or a spontaneous admission of a previously unacknowledged truth. This is an example of what Gerald Prince calls "disnarration," where "the disnarrated covers many instances when the writer wishes to make the reader aware of significant information that has been suppressed in the narrative" (Nichols 59). I would like to suggest that we can interpret this lacuna as a sign of unknowability. Throughout the *Elegia*, Fiammetta blames fate for her suffering and comments on the mutability of our mental states, personifying Fortune into a figure that manipulates the psyche. Boethius's idea of fortune, according to Lyons, is "the undependable, unstable, external world of matter [...] [contrasting] the inner citadel of the mind. [...] Fortune should be kept out of the mind and should not be allowed to take over with its illusions" ("From Fortune to Randomness" 160). Fiammetta ascribes to Fortune exactly that power, to vex her mind and breed mental disarray. Even though Fiammetta may be wrong about Fortune in a Boethian sense, she is not so far off in terms of her mind being affected: "Sappho wrote of love in terms of the symptoms of a disease, [...] Plato spoke of sexual love as a disease of the soul, and Aristotle assigned the origins of eros not to the soul but to a boiling of blood around the heart" (Beecher and Ciavolella, Ferrand 42).

---

[78] In contrast, Sif Rikhardsdottir points out that while certainly emotions are historically constructed to an extent, "the literary critic seeks not to identify the emotion of a medieval subject (which is inherently absent and obscure), but rather to understand why a particular author makes his or her protagonist exhibit a particular emotion and what it might have meant" (Rüdiger Schnell, quoted in Rikhardsdottir 76). Moreover, "an empathetic interpretation of emotive behavior is contingent on a certain degree of commonality in emotional responses across time that enables the modern reader to relate, for instance, to the internal turmoil of Hamlet" (76).

[79] "ebbe da me quel che io, sì come egli, *bene che del contrario infignessimi*, disiava" (64 emphasis added).

"And in the Senecan corpus, [...] love was characterized as an inexorable or irresistible force" (Kriesel 426). According to Lesel Dawson,

> whereas contemporary readers interpret such declarations of physical suffering as formulaic metaphors [...] the early modern subject understood the lover's melancholy to be a dangerous physical illness [...] which could inflame the body, take possession of the mind, and overthrow an individual's rational self-control. (12)

What Fiammetta calls "fortune," then, is actually a combination of bodily reactions and outside stimuli that constitute, as I have been arguing, the effect of the narrative thwarting Fiammetta's free choice at every turn. Read in this light, Fiammetta's rape accusation can be interpreted as no less reliable than any other statement she makes. Moreover, as Fiammetta says, "what can people in love do right? Our minds move according to impulses" (137).[80] Again, Venus's directive to "love confidently" proves impossible in this context since, as Fiammetta puts it, "love is something worrisome and full of fear" (137).[81]

Fiammetta's narrative represents a woman's suffering in the idiom of classical and medieval unrequited love poetry that also follows the conventions of other *romans d'analyse*: an obsessive dissection of emotions, a recursive structure that does not allow the female protagonist to change or grow, and the realization of a pessimistic, anti-romantic epistemology of love. To Fiammetta, this is a domestic tragedy no less profound than the Greek tragedies that she cites. Throughout the *Elegia*, Fiammetta weighs her own anguish against a variety of exempla and finds that the exempla come up short in comparison to her personal trauma. In this light, Fiammetta's rejection of fictional texts, as well as her denial that rhetoric can be curative, becomes legible as a further explanation of her powerlessness against a language that refuses her as much as she is compelled to refuse action. Fiammetta's narrative depicts a *life* that remains unconsummated, and there are no words or stories or even actions, so long as she is alone, that can redeem it for her.

In the *Elegia*, the fact that Panfilo is absent is in some ways incidental. In analytical fiction, the lover's love is always one-sided, as I explained in the introduction, and the discourse of the narrator exploits that loneliness to the

---

[80] "qual cosa possono gl'innamorati dirittamente fare? Come li impeti vengono, così si muovono le nostre menti" (214).
[81] "amore è cosa sollecita, piena di paura" (214).

extreme. It is a coincidence that the first chronological example in this study is also one in which the lover is abandoned early on in the narrative. But it corresponds to analytical fiction as an illustration of the narrative's focus on the suffering self, rather than on any kind of understanding of the Other. Subsequent examples in this book do not depict abandoned love in the same way, but the love object's physical presence in fact makes little difference in the mind of the lover experiencing the pain of passionate love and jealousy. In fact, the following two examples multiply the number of characters involved, yet, as we will see, love is still always impeded and knowledge is forestalled indefinitely.

2

# Link on Link: The "Chain of Dishonor" in Marguerite's *Novella 10* and Cervantes's "El curioso impertinente"

> *I am afraid our eyes are bigger than our bellies, and we have more curiosity than capacity. We embrace everything, but we all we catch is the wind.*[1]

The previous chapter established that the representation of love in analytical fiction is never confident or easy; there is always something either one-sided or warped in the way that the lovers are depicted, and there are always complications and obstacles that separate the lovers and inhibit action. In this chapter, we will see the same phenomena in narratives that are far more polyvocal. This chapter examines the motifs of deliberation and self-deception in Marguerite de Navarre's *Heptaméron* (1558) (the tenth *nouvelle*) and Cervantes's interpolated novel from *Don Quixote*, "El curioso impertinente" (1605). The male protagonist in each of these works, Amador in Marguerite's tale and Anselmo in Cervantes's, appears to go mad at some point during his respective story. For Amador, it is at the end of the novella, when deliberation, dissimulation, and honorable conduct have not yielded the results he seeks (the physical love of Florida), and Amador attacks his would-be lover in a seemingly insane rage. In contrast, Anselmo's suspension of the normative code of honor and his ostensible madness happen at the very beginning of his tale, in which, after having married the beautiful Camila, a woman whose moral trustworthiness he has no reason to doubt, Anselmo develops a plan to test his wife's fidelity by employing his best friend, Lotario, as a Lothario. Despite these plot descriptions, which may suggest a quick succession of action in the two works, the characters—male and female—find

---

[1] "J'ay peur que nous avons les yeux plus grands que le ventre, et plus de curiosité que nous n'avons de capacité. Nous embrassons tout, mais nous n'étreignons que du vent" (Montaigne I, 392–3).

themselves mired in ruminative analysis and paralyzing deliberation. This is sustained, no less, by the fact that in each story, almost every decision is formed counterintuitively; although reasonable, practical arguments are provided, characters seem to always choose contrary to their best interests, as we will see. Through a close reading of each work, I argue that deliberation always becomes inconsequential in these two tales, in which characters desire, but have, as in Montaigne's essay, "more curiosity than capacity." Ironically, in these two works, the greater the passion, the more the characters are driven apart, both by their very infatuation and by the narration itself.

## Marguerite's Tenth Nouvelle: The Tale of Amador and Florida

The outer frame of Marguerite's *Heptaméron*, a collection of purportedly "real" stories about people of all social classes and from around the European world, is not in itself a work of analytical fiction, even if, as Jacob Vance has demonstrated, the book "rules out the possibility of reciprocal love [and] 'aimer' and 'être aimée' [to love and to be loved] can never concord" (Vance S195). The *Heptaméron* tells the story of a group of ten *devisants*, all noble French women and men who find themselves lodged at an abbey in the Pyrenees, blocked from returning home from the spa town of Cauterets by a flood. They decide to pass the time by telling each other tales of love, seduction, deceit, and in general, the relations between the sexes. Each story is framed by a prologue and an epilogue in which the *devisants* engage in nuanced, spirited, and realistic intellectual debates, so that "no single interpretation is privileged and no consensus or conclusion is reached [...] [and] there is room for play in the space between the writing and the telling" (Gray 49).[2] Indeed, the storytellers rarely all agree as to the interpretation of a tale and, as P. A. Chilton observes in the introduction to the English Penguin edition, the *devisants* form "a three-cornered antagonism that runs throughout the *Heptaméron* [...] between female intelligence and love, masculine aggressiveness, and transcendent spirituality" (13). This gendered split (crossed over by only one of the *devisants*, Dagoucin, a man who believes in the existence of perfect love sublimated in spirituality) sets

---

[2] Theresa Brock proposes a strong feminist interpretation: "by training the storytellers to think critically and ethically about social injustice, the text encourages them to view women as subjects and to reject patriarchal abuse" (16).

up the frame tale as one that depicts love as "a kind of war necessitating a battle of the sexes" (Frelick 80), in which, unlike in the *Decameron*, "sex is rarely fun" (Chilton 14). On the contrary, as Nancy E. Virtue argues, "sex is almost always associated with violence, suffering, cruelty, deception, infidelity, incest, or rape" (67).[3] In this text, women describe men as dissimulating their "true motives, which consist of the desire for military glory, revenge, pride, and the subjecting of women through the manipulation of courtly modes of conduct" (Vance S193), while the men accuse women of using "public honor—which is defined by modesty, chastity, and patience—to conceal malicious intentions" (Vance S193). Neither the male nor the female *devisants* are entirely incorrect on this score, although the numerous rapes and attempted rapes by men in the stories—and the male *devisants'* condoning of these actions as adhering to the guidelines of "manliness"—would make many readers sympathize more with the women's arguments.

The tenth novella (day one, story ten) stands out among the rest of the seventy or so tales of the *Heptaméron*. Steven Rendall writes that "the story [...] appears much more 'literary' than the preceding ones" (74); it is by far the longest narrative, and, as we will see, one whose mode of narration itself is just as critically important as its content. Parlamente, the narrator of the tenth nouvelle and the *devisant* associated with Marguerite herself, positions her first story as a challenge to the men who believe that women's virtue is easily conquered. She prefaces her tale by asking—using the language of war, no less—whether her friends would believe a story describing a singular lady, "who had been truly in love, who had been desired, pursued and wooed, and yet had remained an honest woman, *victorious* over her heart, over her body, and over her would-be lover" (120, emphasis added and translation modified).[4] This description could frame the story as a proto-feminist tale, but I argue that the significance of the tenth novella lies more in its depiction of unconsummated, inhibited love and the mortal (rather than moral) struggle to abstain from passion. Indeed, in the tenth *nouvelle*, the female character's abstention from physical love has less to do

---

[3] Furthermore, Virtue notes that "the *Heptaméron* reflects a fundamental change in perception taking place in the late Middle Ages and Renaissance toward sexual violence and the emergence of what we might call a more 'modern' notion of rape" (67), whereas "medieval literature tended to 'conceptualize rape as a positive expression of love' (by glorifying, glossing over, or humorizing it)" (Virtue, quoting Kathryn Gravdal, 67).

[4] "bien aimante, bien requise, pressée et importunée et toutefois femme de bien, *victorieuse* de son cœur, de son corps, d'amour et de son ami" (93, emphasis added). References to the *Heptaméron* are from the Folio Classique, edited by Nicole Cauzaron. English translations are from P.A. Chilton's Penguin edition.

with the virtue of chastity than with fear and over-deliberation. The characters in the tale are constantly dissimulating, and, aware of their own feints, are simultaneously suspicious of each other's motivations. As is typical of the genre, love is deemed impossible in this *roman d'analyse*, and it is the narrative itself that keeps the lovers apart. As will become evident, the ebb and flow of intimacy is entirely linked, ironically, to the degree of characters' candor and reticence, respectively; their intimacy diminishes when they are too much in contact or too open about their mutual feelings for each other, and grows by way of careful hedging of emotion and incomplete avowals to themselves. Furthermore, this all happens as the plot cyclically separates them by war.[5] The tenth novella's narrative treats ungovernable passions by hiding them deeper and deeper, until they explode, creating misprision and self-delusion in the characters, underscoring Marguerite's fundamental pessimism regarding the attainability of knowledge.

The tale opens with a series of deliberations and ironic counter-moves that frame the novella from the beginning as one in which the lovers will constantly question, doubt, and revise what they believe to be true. During peacetime, the Countess of Aranda, accompanied by her twelve-year-old daughter, Florida, meet an eighteen-year-old soldier named Amador. Upon seeing Florida for the first time, Amador deliberates, gazes at her, considers, and finally decides to love her. Despite reason telling him that Florida is unapproachable, Amador consciously plans to act against the logical course of action. The words *contre* [against] and *délibérer* [to deliberate] appear frequently throughout the tenth *nouvelle*, as characters repeatedly analyze and reanalyze, and ultimately act against their intentions, against their hearts, and against better judgment.[6]

In this way, to overcome the impediments that keep him from remaining close to his beloved, Amador, "contrary to his previous intentions" (123),[7] marries Florida's best friend, Avanturada, so that he can at least live near Florida. Thus, a double *contre* is in play here: Amador acts against reason (this is, as any reader would immediately notice, an insane plan) *and* against his heart (he actively pursues and convinces to marry a woman he merely pretends to love). When Amador is called away to war, his letters to his wife are full of messages for Florida, who, ignorant of Amador's intentions, happily writes back with

---

[5] David LaGuardia also notices the fact that war multiple times "just happens to interrupt the development of their relationship at a critical point" (510), although he attributes it to the king's will, upholding "the law of legitimacy that is threatened by Amadour's actions" (510).
[6] As Floyd Gray points out, the word *déliberer* implies, rather than determination, that each character "weighs and ponders" (55) what to do or say.
[7] "contre la déliberation qu'il avait faite" (96).

notes enclosed in Avanturada's letters. What's more, in contrast to what may be expected, Avanturada is not bothered by his wishes to speak about Florida; not suspecting her husband's motives, she confides all of Florida's secrets to him. Avanturada even seems to love her husband more because he is also so fond of her friend. This is a conceit that we will see over and over in this novella, as well as in Cervantes's tale in the second part of this chapter.

Of course, Amador considers his marriage as only a cover ("*une couverture*," and later, "the death of his wife served merely as a cover for a much deeper grief" [145],[8] that is, when he has lost his proximity to Florida at the same time), because contradictions abound in the story from beginning to end. For example, even though Florida is the most beautiful lady at court and Amador is the most handsome man, as well as the best spoken, and the most valiant in war, their marriage is impossible for social and economic reasons. The story is doomed from its foundations. When he is first presented to Florida, Amador, the best speaker in Spain, becomes dumbstruck. Florida notices and graciously and articulately questions him, offering, "if there is anything I can do, I hope you will not be afraid to ask" (125),[9] but, since he is "transported with joy" (125),[10] he still cannot answer her. Both Amador and Florida's feelings are evidenced physiognomically, and each in turn is, at some point, rendered speechless by the other's presence. The first time he speaks to Florida, Amador barely keeps himself from fainting and, later, when he is near her, "the fire that burned in his breast would flare up so violently that, do what he might, the colour would mount to his cheeks and the flames of passion would gleam in his eyes" (129).[11] This description, which foreshadows another, much darker one at the end of the tale, emphasizes how the effects that violent passions, believed to emanate from the soul, are made visible on the body. As Nora Martin Peterson puts it about another *Heptaméron* character, they are always "aware of the dangers of having brought too much truth to the surface of [the] body" (*Involuntary Confessions* 33).

At first, Florida is quite open with Amador, since she remains ignorant of his desire to win her over (and clearly does not notice, or ignores, his change in color): with no passion in her heart she "went straight to Amador whenever she

---

[8] "le deuil de sa femme, duquel il couvrait celui qu'il avait au cœur" (116).
[9] "si en quelque endroit je vous en puis faire, vous m'y pouvez employer" (97).
[10] "était si très ravi" (97).
[11] "le feu caché en son cœur le brûlait si fort, qu'il ne pouvait empêcher que la couleur n'en demeurât au visage et que les étincelles ne saillissent par les yeux" (101).

saw him [...] [and] was quite unreserved in her behaviour toward him" (128).[12] David LaGuardia notes about this scene that "Floride proves herself to be quite adept at expressing the formulae of politeness, whose figures of speech contain a language of repressed sexuality that virtually explodes during the first encounter of the two main characters" (504–05), and that Marguerite here inverts the typical roles of male subject and female object (another contradiction). But Floride is still only able to eloquently speak to Amador because—even if LaGuardia is correct that, if read literally and not masked by formal speech, her "greeting would be a virtual invitation to a sensual relationship" (505)—Floride is still unaware of her love. This fact is significant for the progress of Floride and Amador's intimacy. So long as Floride does not suspect his being in love with her, and she herself is not yet cognizant of her own feelings, she is able to speak to Amador, regardless of the fact that it is against the custom of their land to do so. But the intimacy between them only grows so long as the characters remain ignorant of it.

After Amador and Avanturada's marriage, he is called away to war, and three or four years pass in which he visits Floride (and his wife) infrequently. Nevertheless, the Countess of Aranda adopts Amador as a son and, whenever he visits, grants him "opportunities denied him by birth" (Freccero 328), that is, free access to her house and to her daughter's company. As far as the countess is concerned, "there was always an open door. [...] He was trusted in everything" (128).[13] Amador is even permitted to go and speak to Floride unaccompanied. As long as she does not suspect Amador's true motivations, Floride speaks frankly with him, and Amador does not reveal jealousy, if he feels any. Speaking with *sagesse* and *froideur*, that is, wisdom and coolness, Amador constantly dissimulates in order to maintain political and social advantage. This may not even be conscious on Amador's part, and certainly not negative in terms of the worldview of sixteenth-century court life. As Floyd Gray points out, while it is possible that "*se delibera, couverture*, and *froidement* all suggest a devious seducer bent upon satisfying his illegitimate desires [...] Marguerite does not always use [these terms] negatively" (55). Similarly LaGuardia writes that "while we know clearly what Amadour wants—to possess Floride physically—this natural desire is forced to follow the circuitous path of courtly devotion, which is meant in the long run to provide a legitimating 'couverture' for the carnal

---

[12] "le cherchait en tous lieux où elle le voyait [...] [et] elle ne se gardait de nulle contenance" (100).
[13] "on lui ouvrait toujours la porte. [...] On se fiait en lui de toutes choses" (100).

act, and which all of the characters seem to understand as such" (509). And yet, Florida and Amador are incapable of acting on their love for each other despite all the covers they have created. Amador's pretended indifference to Florida also provides the perfect environment for her own love to grow undetected and even unbeknownst to herself. To protect this fertile simulated indifference, Amador speaks to Florida even more about the man she loves. Life imitates Amador's art here, and since he conceals outward signs of his love for Florida, he also feels no jealousy for her inclination toward the son of the Infante of Fortune. Instead, they both sublimate their love through speaking about him, just as Florida also mediates her love through Avanturada (Florida's feelings are expressed "*pour l'amour de sa* [Amador's] *femme*" ["for the sake of Amador's wife"] and later, "as if for Avanturada's sake, [she] expressed her joy"[14]). As Patricia Francis Cholakian puts it, "Floride is unaware of [...] her own attraction to him 'except that she felt a great contentment when she was near him'" (90). This state of "great contentment" comes as close as possible to direct admission of love in a *roman d'analyse*; but this blissful state cannot last long.

Just as Florida is beginning to feel love for Amador, and notwithstanding his dissimulation via Avanturada, Amador remains unsatisfied that he is doing enough to cover his affection. Concerned that Florida will detect some involuntary confession, as Peterson calls it—an uncontrollable blush or a certain gleam in his eye—he realizes he must even more profoundly conceal his love. To achieve this, Amador decides—counterintuitively—to court another woman, Paulina, so that he can create yet another layer of deception to cover his love for Florida. But Amador is already trusted by Florida's mother as an advisor and an almost-son. He is considered to be the "Achilles of Spain" and the greatest speaker, and he manages to deceive his wife. Why does he need to find yet another cover? There seems to be something else at play here, more than just fear of being exposed. It seems as though Amador needs to hide this love in order to keep it active. He irrationally complicates love—deliberating and then acting counter to what is reasonable—in order to prove to himself that it is real. Put in another way, the narrative drives Amador through his deliberations and counterintuitive actions, never allowing him to rest satisfied with what he already has. It is Montaigne all over again here, always pushing the limits of what is enough, all the while endangering the good that one already possesses.

---

[14] "[elle] s'en réjouit comme pour l'amour d'elle [Avanturade]" (110).

Of course, there are times when Amador attempts a slightly more direct approach, and these prove disastrous. Fearing that Paulina, since she is shrewd and experienced in love (and thus herself is growing jealous), might enlighten the true object of his affections, Amador, "to forestall any unfortunate consequences in the future" (129),[15] decides to confesses his passion to Florida. As Fontenelle writes in his *Science du cœur*, which defines the mental state of the lover, "the fineness, the delicacy, and the pleasure of the effects of passion exist in a space of contradiction."[16] A victim of Venus or Eros, the lover is left conquered, but uninstructed in the correct management of his love; "Amadour's declaration appears to be a strange mixture of candor and deceit" (LaGuardia 508). He tries to show his love and hide it simultaneously, and ends up lost in the kind of paradox that Fontenelle describes. Amador speaks with subtle and economic phrasing, revealing that he fears acting *"contre l'amour"* that Florida bears for the son of the Infante of Fortune. Thus, in order to reveal his love, he phrases it in negative terms, expressing merely what his love is *not* when he assures Florida: "I am not one of those men who would exploit this advantage. I desire no favour, nor pleasure, from you, except what is in accordance with the dictates of virtue" (130–1).[17] Furthermore, he fully admits that he married Avanturada and spoke so often of the son of the Infante of Fortune so as to be closer to Florida. And finally, Amador contrasts deceptive love ("une amour vicieuse") with the more virtuous kind of love that Florida displays and the kind that he himself believes he feels. The astonishing confessions about her best friend and lover strangely do not shock Florida, nor push her away. What she is worried about, by contrast, is whether Amador is lying, whether "there is some evil intent hidden away underneath all these fine words" (131–2).[18] In this way, Florida misses the more sinister clues yet again (before she did not notice Amador's blush and fiery eyes) in his speech; it is clear that she is already—i.e., she has always been—blinded by her own latent love for him.

Concerned that he speaks to her, as she puts it, "si affectionnément" ("with such affection"), Florida deliberates as well, using some of the same vocabulary Amador had used previously: "if I were to reject the noble love that you offer me,

---

[15] "pour éviter qu'il n'en vint inconvénient" (101).
[16] "la finesse, la délicatesse, enfin l'agrément de ces effets de passion, consistent assez ordinairement dans une espèce de contradiction" (85).
[17] "Je ne suis point de ceux qui prétendent par ce moyen avoir de vous ni bien ni plaisir autre que vertueux" (102).
[18] "il y ait quelque malice cachée pour décevoir" (103).

I would only be *contradicting* the way I've behaved towards you up till now."[19] Amador's and Florida's statements about love also mirror those of the frame character Dagoucin, whom I cited earlier as crossing the gender divide and aligning himself with the ladies of the group of storytellers (and whose name sounds a lot like, as Chilton points out in the prefatory matter of the collection, "*de goûts saints*" ["of saintly tastes"] [39]). In the preface to his first story (novella nine), Dagoucin idealizes men who would rather die than reveal their love (whereas Florida wisely—or perhaps fatally—tells Amador she would always "advise my friends to speak") (129).[20] Dagoucin's romantic notions of what he calls "perfect love," which is always kept hidden and unconsummated for fear of ruining his virtue, are mocked by some of the other *devisants* as unrealistic. But Dagoucin insists that "my love is a perfect love, and I fear lest showing it openly should betray it. [...] I scarcely dare think my own thoughts, lest something should be revealed in my eyes" (113).[21] This ascetic self-denial, even to the point of disavowing one's own thoughts for fear that they will be involuntarily divulged, describes an extreme version of the *"serviteur"* relationship, a vestige of courtly love that "can coexist with faithful marriage" (Chilton 19), one that aligns more with the model of the *parfait ami* (a Platonic ideal that Marguerite sometimes seems to endorse, in which love is sublimated into mystical devotion, but in practice in the *Heptaméron* can mean anything from intimate friend to passionate sexual partner). But, as Vance points out, "dissimulation and flattery constantly risk subverting" (S193) idealized forms of love, which, despite Dagoucin's claims, really are unattainable. Novella ten and the *roman d'analyse* more generally expose the impossibility, the unattainability of perfect love in these texts, as love is always depicted as tinged with jealousy and distrust, over-deliberation and self-doubt, or in this case, hidden violence. Amador, as we saw from the beginning, is no Dagoucin. He cannot fully control revealing his feelings for Florida, although he manages well enough for a time, mostly due to the fact that she either does not notice or chooses to ignore the signs he is giving off. Amador is a problematic character whom Parlamente defends as the noble friend of a friend, but who also seems to be modeled, not on Dagoucin, whose passive, perfect love conceals and sublimates all physical designs, but rather on

---

[19] "[c]ar de refuser l'honnête amitié que vous m'offrez, je ferais *le contraire* de ce que j'ai fait jusqu'ici" (103).
[20] "Je conseillerai toujours à mes amis de parler" (101).
[21] "j'ai si grand peur que la démonstration fasse tort à la perfection de mon amour, que je crains que celle de qui je devrais désirer amitié semblable. [...] Je n'ose penser ma pensée, de peur que mes yeux en révèlent quelque chose" (87).

her *devisant* husband, the proto-rake Hircan, who claims, in the outer frame of the *Heptaméron*, that women "are made solely for [men's] benefit" (119)[22] and that men should not hesitate "to demand from them what God himself has commanded that they should let us have" (119).[23] The other proto-rake, Saffredent, supports Hircan's point of view, implicitly citing the *Roman de la rose*, discussed briefly in the previous chapter, wherein "you've only got to attack your fortress in the right way, and you can't fail to take it in the end" (119).[24] Amador is a warrior "whose attempts to transgress social barriers and possess the young Florida lead not only to violence against the woman, but to the woman's violence against herself" (Chilton 15), and this creates, as Chilton indicates, "implicit structural parallels between military and sexual violence" (15). Love becomes weaponized in the tenth novella, and deployed when the façade of courtly love gives way to irrational passion.

But first, love is merely delayed. When Amador claims that he would rather die than reveal his feelings to anyone else, Florida is "filled with delight beyond bounds. Deep within her heart she began to feel stirrings she had never felt before" (133).[25] Yet, only a few sentences later, she becomes "craintive" (105), "nervous," and she begins to seek out Amador less than she had in the past. In contrast to the open pursuits of many other tales in the *Heptaméron* (when characters, even some female characters—in stories 3, 21, and 43, for example—recognize being in love, and they pursue their love object directly), the tenth *nouvelle* evades direct speech or action. As soon as Florida starts to take cognizance of her own feelings for Amador, she suddenly becomes jealous and begins to avoid him.

Although ultimately, Florida's jealousy is assuaged and she comes back around to Amador ("love, having been thwarted, was aroused now, and began to demonstrate its power" [134][26]). As the push and pull of now hidden, now revealed passions drives the narrative, Amador must leave for war again. On this expedition to Salces, he is captured by the King of Tunis. While he is imprisoned for two years, Florida marries the Duke of Cardona against her will, and the other man she had loved since she was a child, the son of the Infante of Fortune, dies. Again, the pattern repeats itself: as soon as the possibility of a growing

---

[22] "ne sont faites que pour [les hommes]" (92).
[23] "leur demander ce que Dieu leur commande de nous donner" (92).
[24] "onques place bien assaillie ne fut, qu'elle ne fût prise" (93).
[25] "commença en son cœur à sentir quelque chose plus qu'elle n'avait accoutumé" (104–5).
[26] "commença l'amour, poussée de son contraire, à montrer sa très grand force" (106).

intimacy between Florida and Amador presents itself, the war interrupts and pulls the two farther apart.

When Amador is taken prisoner, Florida, "who knew how to hide her true feelings [...] merely said that it was a great loss for all the family. [...] But seeing her mother weeping bitterly, she shed a few tears with her, lest her secret be discovered by being too well disguised" (136–7).[27] It is certainly interesting that the countess is so affected by Amador's capture (and, indeed, in the later part of the story she is far more of a confidante to Amador than to her daughter). However, as a mother figure to Amador, she is sanctioned to show her feelings openly. But for Florida, the process of crying together with the countess and Avanturada allows purportedly feigned tears to also secretly be real. Like in the several instances of playacting that I will discuss in the next part of the chapter about Cervantes's "El curioso impertinente," and like Fiammetta in the previous chapter, finding a cover to allow one to express emotions is a fairly typical narratological device in analytical fiction, although this instance takes it even a step farther, as Florida continues to dissimulate having feelings for Amador lest her indifference be discovered as feigned. Affecting indifference could reveal the truth, so she simulates even stronger feelings than she already has.

As Florida learns, dissimulation and deflection are the keys to success in her world, as is the sagacious interpreting of signs revealed by others, and the ability to hide the proofs of love in oneself, and from oneself. Indeed, characters in this work, as in all the analytical texts examined in this book, are obsessed with signs, insights, and their ability to read one another. As Lyons writes about *La Princesse de Clèves*, but which applies equally to Marguerite's tenth novella, characters "perceive the world as a set of *signs* and the people in it as producers and receivers of signs" (*Before Imagination* 166) rather than as actors in the world. The signifying mode in which characters constantly search for meaning in each other frames each work of analytical fiction as one in which action, or sensation, as Lyons puts it, always functions as secondary to signification and analysis.

We see this particularly after Amador has professed his love for her, and Florida is "*almost* won" (139, emphasis added). She is "*on the verge* of being ready not merely to accept Amador as a devoted servant, but to admit him as

---

[27] "qui savait bien dissimuler [...] dit que c'était grande perte pour toute leur maison. [...] Mais, voyant sa mère pleurer très fort, laissa aller quelques larmes pour lui tenir compagnie, afin que, par trop feindre, sa feinte ne fût découverte" (108). Although she does not focus on the epistemological implications, Cholakian points out that in this tale "mother and daughter are [...] engaged in a curious game of cat and mouse in which each hides from the other what both know to be true" (92).

a sure and perfect lover" (139, emphasis added and translation modified).[28] This quasi-self-avowal, of course, is neither here nor there. While later, Florida will have to face the fact that she is truly in love with Amador (although it is completely contrary to what she knows she *should* feel), for a long time, she hides this knowledge from herself and experiences only the edge of love, caused by the false signs of non-threatening, silent, and ultimately unconsummated "perfect love." Florida does not, however, prefer this kind of love because she is *pudique*; she must work very hard to suppress her passions, even suffering from nosebleeds because she represses her feelings so much. After the imprisoned Amador is permitted to return to Spain in order to find ransom money to free himself, their mutual love, though still unconsummated, grows: "she made up her mind to take consolation in her love for Amador and the sense of security it afforded her, though she never once dared declare to him her intent" (139).[29]

Florida now knows that she loves Amador. So when he returns from Tunis, she again conceals her love for him in happiness for Avanturada. Now that Florida is conscious of being in love with Amador, her behavior changes, she deliberately hides herself from the crowd. She goes down a back staircase which was "dark enough to prevent anybody seeing whether her cheeks changed color" (138).[30] Here again, Florida's double disguise makes the truth itself function as a cover, although her blush risks revealing her true feelings. Nevertheless, she embraces Amador and resumes her openness with him, revealing to him her suffering at "having had to marry against her inclinations, and at having lost the man whom she loved so dearly" (139),[31] that is, the son of the Infante of Fortune. Yet again, the narrator implies that she manages to express her love for Amador while only ever speaking of her love for another. Thus, just at a moment when the would-be lovers might reveal their passion for each other, were this another kind of narrative, Amador and Florida bury their true feelings, and manage to express intimacy only in ways that, ironically, keep each other at arm's length.

But again, as soon as their quasi-intimacy flourishes, the King calls Amador away. Dejected at this news, Avanturada faints, falls down a flight of stairs,

---

[28] "presque toute gagnée" (111); "[s]ur le point [...] de le recevoir non à serviteur, mais à sûr et parfait ami" (111).
[29] elle "se délibéra de prendre la consolation en l'amour et sûreté qu'elle portait à Amadour, ce que toutefois elle ne lui osait déclarer" (110).
[30] "tant obscur que nul ne pouvait connaître si elle changeait de couleur" (110).
[31] "d'être mariée contre son cœur que d'avoir perdu celui qu'elle aimait tant" (110).

and dies. During his short period of mourning, Amador, in whose "heart was such despair that he thought he would lose his reason" (139–40),[32] not because of the death of his wife, but because it would separate him from Florida (whom he was only able to see because Avanturada lived with her), seems to go insane. Something changes in the novella after Florida's marriage and after Avanturada's death. When Amador again tries his hand at a confession, his feelings are revealed to be less virtuous than he had previously claimed, and he argues, to cover up his bad act, that "passion leaves no room for reason. And [...] the passion of love [...] blinds all the senses" (142).[33] He rationalizes that since Florida is now married, she has "a cover and your honor is safe. So what wrong can I possibly be doing you in asking for what is truly mine?" (141).[34] He attempts to rape Florida. Now Amador is willing to risk everything ("he made up his mind to make one last desperate gamble—to risk losing all, or to gain everything" [140][35])—his reputation, his rank, potentially even his life, as well as his relationship with Florida—in order to possess something that earlier, in his first confession, he claimed to have never wanted.

When Florida upbraids him for his actions, Amador claims the he was merely testing her virtue.[36] Now a more adept reader of love's complicated twists and turns and the deceptions men use when they are dominated by irrational love, Florida is not fooled by Amador's claim that his actions were inconsequential. But nevertheless, the narrator also reveals that she cannot stop loving him. While Hircan and Saffredent in the outer frame tale will later claim that Amador did not pursue his case far enough, and these two *devisants* categorize the attempted rapes (another comes at the end, as we will see) as early modern "seduction" plots, it does not seem to be the intent of Marguerite to either support Amador's choices or blame Florida for the attack. Nevertheless, Amador's "fall," as Lucien Febvre calls it (212), while it leads Florida to see that she was deceived about him, also, again counterintuitively, acts as a force that amplifies Florida's cognizance

---

[32] "eut tel désespoir en son cœur qu'il cuida perdre l'entendement" (111).
[33] "la passion ne donne lieu à la raison. Et [...] la passion d'amour [...] aveugle tous les sens" (113). The Princess of Clèves claims at the end of Lafayette's novel, by contrast, that "les passions peuvent me conduire; mais elle ne sauraient m'aveugler" (306) ["passions may drive me, but they will never blind me"].
[34] "maintenant que vous l'êtes [mariée], et que votre honneur peut être couvert, quel tort vous tiens-je de demander ce qui est mien?" (113).
[35] "il se délibéra de jouer à quitté ou à double, pour du tout la perdre ou du tout la gagner" (111–12).
[36] We see similar tests in Boccaccio's *Decameron*, Ariosto's *Orlando Furioso*, in several novels of Lafayette, in Shakespeare's *Merchant of Venice*, in Richardson's *Clarissa*, and of course in "El curioso impertinente," as we will see in the next section. See also David Kaplan's article on this subject.

of her own love: "while in accordance with reason, she was determined to love him no more, the heart, over which none of us has control, would never yield" (144).[37] This deliberation recreates a distorted mirror of the much earlier one in which Amador decides to love Florida. She attempts to "deliberate" not to love him, but the force of love is too strong. She must merely go on hiding her passion, although the reader of analytical fiction knows that this very act of hiding her love will probably end in making it grow.

The greater irony, moreover, is that Amador was much closer to attaining his goal when he pursued it only in a clandestine manner (moments before, Florida had resolved to console him by "joining her tears to his" [140][38]). But Amador becomes "bereft of all reason through the violence of love" [141][39]), awakening Florida to the danger of her situation, despite her enduring passion for him. Not surprisingly, after this event, Amador leaves for the war again. Three or four more years pass, during which Florida resolves to never see Amador, although, counter to what we might expect, she writes him letters in which "she made sure that he would realize that they were written out of obedience, and not from any inclination of her own" (145).[40] Even though she knows that he is unstable and violent, Florida risks reopening their relationship by being unable to stop writing to him, just as she cannot stop loving him.

Freccero and Cholakian in particular interpret most of Amador's behavior as conforming to a malicious strategy wherein "from the beginning, Amadour is depicted as a maker of devious plots" (Cholakian 89). He also certainly dares to think his thoughts (Dagoucin had said previously that he is afraid to think, lest he commits some kind of moral thought crime), and many of them are violent. Within this interpretation, when Amador asks Florida whether it

---

[37] "combien que, selon la raison, elle était délibérée de jamais plus l'aimer, si est-ce que le cœur, qui n'est point sujet à nous, ne s'y voulut onques accorder" (115–16).
[38] "pleurer avec lui" (112).
[39] "avait perdu toute raison par la force d'amour" (113).
[40] "c'étaient lettres qu'il pouvait bien connaître venir plus d'obéissance que de bonne volonté" (117). In the interpolated letter from Madame de Thémines to the Vidame de Chartres in *La Princesse de Clèves*, Madame de Thémines wishes to make the Vidame think her love has cooled by the act of pretending to hide less passionate feelings. She proceeds to write him "des lettres tièdes et languissantes" (211) ["lukewarm and languishing letters"] so that he can show them to his lover "pour jeter dans l'esprit de celle à qui vous les donniez que l'on cessait de vous aimer" (211) ["to show them to your other lover and have her believe that I've stopped loving you"]. [...] Clearly borrowing from Lafayette, Marcel will renounce his love for Gilberte in almost identical terms in Proust's *À l'ombre des jeunes filles en fleurs*, composing letters to her wherein he responds to her invitations "en protestant que j'en étais désolé comme j'aurais fait avec quelqu'un que je n'aurais pas désiré voir" (159) ["as if I was sorry but in a way that one would write to show that he did not really wish to see them"]. (See Kudish, "[La] plus Jolie" 59 and endnote on 66–7.)

is better "to speak or to die" (29), the answer is a foregone conclusion; he has already decided to love her, and in a way that highlights that "dissimulation is a condition of, but also a direct threat to the augmentation of virtue through courtly friendship" (Vance S193). Amador's ultimatum also shows how "Parlamente's story repeatedly dwells on the relation between language and force and suggests that Marguerite is well aware that speaking is [...] a form of coercion" (Rendall 79). And similarly, Nancy Frelick reads Amador's speech as breaking down the meanings of words such that the use of "*amour* and *amytié* [love and friendship] also underscores the semantic slippage in these terms that can be used to signify both [...] selfless compassion [...] or its opposite—the kind of brutal concupiscence that is so often used by characters and *devisants* to justify taking what they want by force" (82). As soon as Florida consents to Amador's speaking freely, he backs her into a corner in what Rendall describes as a "gangland 'offer that you can't refuse'" (75) that indicates what kind of lover Amador will prove to be. Eventually, Amador's perfect façade begins to chip away and he is revealed to be far more like Hircan (whose "voice is that of the flesh [...] [which] is always moving, scheming, and desiring—regardless of sex [...], [adding] a carnal power to the text that [...] the *Heptaméron* does indeed wish to emphasize" [Peterson, *Involuntary Confessions* 32]), though even less self-controlled, since Hircan merely boasts about sex (and imagined rape, as in the discussion of the fourth story and at the end of the tenth as well) while Amador actually attempts to violate Florida twice. Following this line of argumentation, it would be easy to "praise Floride and condemn Amadour, depicting her as innocent and virtuous and him as calculating and violent" (Gray 55).

But are they? It is unclear that this is truly what Marguerite wishes to depict in her story. While the tense sexual politics are quite evident in the realistic frame of the *Heptaméron*, to paint Amador as a calculating rapist who has been scheming from the beginning (as is truly the case in novella two, for example) and Florida as the saintly object of Amador's violence is not truly supported by the narrative. As LaGuardia puts it, "the relation of Amadour and Floride is [...] not exclusively one of a manipulative male character who attempts to rape a female character bewildered by her own desires" (509). And Gray argues that Amador's "love is not calculated nor calculating; rather he is deceived by love. [...] From the beginning, therefore, all of the connections [Marguerite] initiates between the characters are impossible, questionable, contested, denounced" (56); "both Floride and Amadour are victims, less of unreciprocated desire than of its impossible fulfillment" (Gray 59). This interpretation falls very much in line with my own of the tenth novella functioning as a work of analytical fiction. Between the plot that constantly pulls Florida and Amador apart by war, and their own inability to speak to each other directly, it is evident that individual action is less consequential in this tale than systemic and narratological forces that preclude the possibility of a happy ending.

Just as strong as the patriarchal system of the king, who, as LaGuardia writes, is the supreme power attempting to thwart Florida and Amador's possibly transgressive love, is the control that the narrative itself exerts over the characters. The discoveries that the lovers have made about their feelings throughout the novella are upset by false impressions and by their own self-deception about what they think they desire (e.g., Florida's unnecessary jealousy of Paulina and Amador's subsequent distrust of Florida's reaction to it; or when Amador suddenly tries to take Florida by force, and then when Florida looks for excuses to absolve him: "[she] thought he must be out of his mind. Rather that, than have to admit he had desired to stain her honour" [141][41]). And the subtle, somewhat passive and certainly hidden process of analyzing the passions—the rumination, deliberation, and dissection of looks and feelings—actually heightens them, bringing Amador and Florida closer together, until another plot twist—confession, jealousy, violence, or war—draws them farther apart again.

Moreover, Parlamente, whose name, as Marc-André Wiesmann points out, carries "ambiguous onomastic resonances [...] [and] can suggest both a respect for the truth (Parler/'mens,' to speak one's mind) and a propensity to lie ('Parler/mentir')" (438), indulges in the same trope of indescribability that I discussed in the previous chapter. This device is used even more frequently here than in Boccaccio's text and it is little evidenced in other tales of the *Heptaméron*. To cite a few examples, Parlamente says, when Amador and Florida have prevailed over their initial conflicts following his confession, "I could not begin to tell you" (134)[42] what was the manner or the content of their conversation that dissuaded them from feeling mutual jealousy. After Amador is freed after two years in the Tunisian prison and is reunited with Florida, Parlamente states, "I shall leave you to imagine the words that passed between him and Florida" (139).[43] While Florida, already feeling so much regret for what had happened

---

[41] "[elle] soupçonna plutôt qu'il fût hors de son sens que de croire qu'il prétendît à son déshonneur" (112).
[42] "Je ne saurais entreprendre de vous conter" (106).
[43] "Je vous laisserai à penser les propos que Floride et lui purent avoir ensemble" (110).

between them, continues to secretly and irrationally love him, the narrator tells us that she "shall not try to describe Amador's feelings. […] It would be impossible to set such anguish down in writing. It is difficult even for anyone to imagine such anguish" (143).[44] These remarks suggest that Marguerite does not seem willing to either comment on, condemn, or fully praise any of the characters. Gray reads these narrative inclusions as "rhetorical devices which the narrator uses […] to suggest, through […] several abridgements, the achievement and complexity of the whole in relation to the essentials retained here" (52). But in some cases, such as the last one quoted, there is nothing truly "essential" or whole to glean from the narrator's statement. It is fully ambiguous whether Amador's "*douleur*" ("pain") constitutes anger, regret, frustration, sadness, or all of these mixed together. The narrator refuses to disclose, and leaves it to the reader to deliberate and analyze. The tenth *nouvelle* is not an exemplum; it does not exist to fulfill the Horatian precept to instruct and to entertain. Instead, the reader becomes complicit in a text—in a society—where moral ambiguity and dissimulation are the norm. We experience the mingled pleasure and pain of love as we read this story, but it ultimately leaves us just as baffled as the characters. Parlamente's narrative withholding illustrates that if characters do not know how to think and feel, then one should not imagine that the narrator or the reader does either.

The cyclical story could go on indefinitely. Three more years go by, with Florida sending Amador letters that merely underscore her indifference to him (and yet, why does she write, if not to reopen the relationship?). Amador is preternaturally successful in war, but he begins to feel hatred for Florida and calls her an enemy ("son ennemie" [117]). But rather than forget her and never see her again, he arranges to get himself called back to Aranda so that he can visit her. The Countess, who never learned about the attempted rape, encourages her daughter to meet with him. Florida, terrified that Amador will attack her again (and blaming herself for the first attack), purposefully disfigures her face with a large rock since she "could not bear the thought that this beauty of hers should kindle so base a fire in the heart of a man who was so worthy and so good" (146).[45] Florida's misprision of Amador is painful to read. She blames her own appearance for sparking malice in Amador and even as she injures herself,

---

[44] "Je n'entreprends point vous dire la douleur que sentait Amadour écoutant ces paroles, car elle n'est seulement impossible à écrire mais à penser" (115).

[45] "aimant mieux faire tort à sa beauté en la diminuant que de souffrir par elle le cœur d'un si honnête homme brûler d'un si méchant feu" (117–18).

she cannot stop loving him. She seems to feel as though disfiguring herself is, in fact, an act of love. As Freccero puts it, "her (self)-defacement is rhetorically motivated; […] she dissimulates her own desire […] in order to represent herself as undesirable" (237). While I agree that Florida brutally disfigures herself in order to gain some fleeting control over her own life, her course of action is anything but successful. Like all other acts in the *roman d'analyse*, Florida's self-harm is rendered inconsequential. It is just another violent wave in the ocean as far as the plot is concerned.

Nevertheless, Florida's self-disfigurement represents the breakdown of language in the *roman d'analyse*. Incapable of keeping Amador away with words, Florida attempts to stop him with actions—although she fails again because the only person she ends up harming is herself. Florida is in bed recovering from the wounds of her self-injury when, despite the bandages on her face, Amador attacks her again. This time, Amador's façade matches the deliberations within; just as his intentions have become warped, so has his countenance become distorted and unnatural:

> The fair complexion was flushed with fiery red. The kind, gentle face was contorted with a terrifying violence, as if there was some raging inferno belching fire in his heart and behind his eyes (147).[46]

This description mirrors the earlier one in which Amador blushes in Florida's presence. In fact, the same verb, "étinceler," is used both times. The "gleam" or "sparkle" is much more violent, much more dangerous here. Amador has allowed his madness and his obsession with Florida to consume him, and furthermore, Florida is now aware of it and is on the lookout. Thus, he is no longer able to dissimulate, and there is no more strategy to "read" into his behavior. The courtier who cannot master his passions and whose appearance corresponds accurately to what he is feeling within is in a great deal of danger. So then why does Amador take this major risk; why does he assault Florida? Whether it is because his pride has been wounded or because he truly goes mad in the last part of the tale, or because his passion has reached its limit and now belongs to the realm of cruelty and savagery, Amador's behavior cannot be analyzed as part of a broader strategy. He refers, toward the end of the novella, to his relationship with Florida as a war. He devises a scheme "to score a victory over her as his

---

[46] "le plus beau teint du monde était rouge comme feu, et le plus doux et plaisant regard si horrible et furieux qu'il semblait qu'un feu très ardent étincelât dans son cœur et son visage" (118).

mortal enemy, for that was how she now appeared" (145).⁴⁷ It is significant that Parlamente uses the same word, "victory," to describe Amador's desire here, since it is the same word that she used to portray Florida's mastery over her own feelings in the preface to the tale, and over Amador's determination to take her by force. Commenting on this passage, Freccero suggests that "'love' […] is not all that different from war. […] The two are juxtaposed […] producing an appearance of difference while operating according to the same logic" (232). In analytical fiction, to quote Shakespeare, "nothing is but what is not" (*Macbeth* 1.4.155); paradoxically, love is war—violent, irrational, and destructive—in any *roman d'analyse*, whether the war is an internal one within a character, or, as here, being waged against a former love object.

Late in the story, in order to distance herself from him and to convince her mother to stop favoring Amador over herself (Florida's mother "was convinced that Florida was just being perverse, and had taken it into her head to dislike anyone that her mother was fond of" [150]⁴⁸), Florida herself devises a plan to make her mother see Amador's true nature.⁴⁹ Again, it is a labyrinthine, counterintuitive thought process: "dropping for a day or two her hostile air" (150)⁵⁰ so as to trick him and allow her to speak to him again, Florida counsels Amador that a woman named Loretta is in love with him, and she encourages him to pursue this love affair. Thus, rather than just avoiding him, Florida chooses to bring him into her confidence. She deliberately sends out false messages to Amador (all the while saying it will be her last communication with him), which has the effect of, at least in Amador's mind, reopening the possibility of love. For his part, rather than re-declaring his love for Florida, he believes her and starts to make advances to Loretta. His complacency in courting Loretta at first pleases Florida (because it makes her mother take notice, and she stops idealizing Amador), but it also works counter to her intention. In reestablishing contact with Amador for any reason, she really does rekindle for him the possibility of her love.

When Florida hears that Loretta's jealous husband has sworn to kill Amador, she again breaks her promise to abstain from speaking to him and warns him of the husband's plan. Amador seizes the opportunity and promises to never again see Loretta if Florida will grant him three hours of her conversation each day.

---

⁴⁷ "pour avoir la victoire de son ennemie, puisque telle se faisait contre lui" (117).
⁴⁸ "pensa pour certaine qu'elle fût si déraisonnable qu'elle haït toutes choses qu'elle aimait" (121).
⁴⁹ She forges a plan "de tromper Amadour" (121) ["to deceive Amador"].
⁵⁰ "laissant pour un jour ou deux son visage étrange" (121).

She refuses, but Amador's hopes are still renewed. Having reached this impasse, Amador is called away to war again. He performs a kind of insane *aristeia*. Florida's husband dies, and Amador, rather than be captured by the Moors, commits suicide. Florida, without telling her mother or mother-in-law, enters the Convent of Jesus and sublimates the love she still holds for Amador into the perfect love of God ("thus she took Him as lover and as spouse who had delivered her from the violent love of Amador" [152][51]). She lives for many years as a nun, and upon her death "commended her soul to God with the joy of the bride who goes to meet her bridegroom" (152).[52] It is important to note that even though Amador kills himself, it is not explicitly because of his love for Florida and her unwillingness to reciprocate it physically. Amador transfers his passion into another sign—war—in order to end this tale.

Although Parlamente frames Florida as virtuous and victorious, Florida only "triumphs" over her would-be lover because the two can only express themselves in, at first, half-truths and coded language (and they are often reduced to silence), and later in irrational outbursts of violence that can yield no happy resolution. That is to say, contrary to what Parlamente claims, no one wins anything in the tale. The tenth novella bears multiple marks of analytical fiction, including the love triangle structure (i.e., Florida's indifference to her marriage and the presence of Amador as a possible lover—although it becomes quite a larger polygon when we consider all of the secondary characters whom Amador and Florida pretend to love, and all of the people these secondary characters actually love, thus creating a sense of dilation and delay), the detached stance of the self-proclaimed unreliable narrator, who periodically reports that she "cannot begin to tell" what characters are feeling, and the overall lack of confidence in the possibility of faithful and uncomplicated love. In fact, the only trusting character, Florida's mother, is so deceived by Amador that she is in part responsible when Florida is nearly raped by him. Moreover, the narrative's clear distrust of not just love, but also the possibility of reason, justice, or fair speech renders the tenth *nouvelle* a *roman d'analyse*. Unlike in the *Elegia*, the narrative presents multiple points of view, but still traps the characters in inaction and false impression. Here again, no kind of communication can succeed. Language always doubles back on itself in dissimulation and doubt, and is rendered unstable and inconsequential.

---

[51] "prenant pour mari et ami Celui qui l'avait délivrée d'une amour si véhémente que celle d'Amadour" (123). The yoking of "mari" and "ami" here is quite interesting, in that the two, as I discussed in the introduction, normally do not go together. It is only in the spiritual realm that such a marriage—because it is a metaphor—is possible.

[52] "lui rendit son âme en telle joie que l'épouse a d'aller voir son époux" (123).

## Cervantes's "El curioso impertinente"

While Amador's madness only manifests itself at the end of Marguerite's tenth *nouvelle*, the next story examined in this chapter suggests that the male protagonist, Anselmo, has lost his reason almost at the very beginning. Within the larger narrative of the madness of Don Quixote, it is unclear whether Cervantes intends the reader to view this disease as a temporary condition from which a character can suddenly be undeceived (such as in Cervantes's later exemplary novel, "El licenciado Vidriera" ["The Glass Graduate"], published with the other *Novelas ejemplares* in 1613), or whether Cervantes is challenging that notion, both in the interpolated novel, "El curioso impertinente," and in its larger frame. In either case, it is clear that the two—*Don Quixote* and the embedded novella—function reciprocally, and each informs the interpretation of the other. But the deeper philosophical concern that casts doubt on whether one's actions, and, moreover, one's motivations, can have more profound historical repercussions is prevalent in both texts. If in literature it is proven that they cannot, Cervantes seems to ask, what are the ramifications for larger questions of truth and knowledge outside the literary realm?

In the middle of *Don Quixote de la Mancha*, Part I, the innkeeper, Juan Palomoque, pulls what can be called Cervantes's first exemplary novel out of an old trunk. It is an odd tale, an interlude, and an interruption. The reader at first does not know whether this will be a comedy or a tragedy. But very quickly, it becomes apparent that this story illustrates something not evidenced in the rest of the *Quixote*, that which we might call a proto-psychological universe of intellects reading and misreading each other, exploring the labyrinthine trajectories of the Baroque psyche. *Don Quixote* and "El curioso impertinente" simultaneously present a series of distorted mirrors of each other. Or, as Alvaro Molina has put it, "Cervantes's literature [...] does not double the world—as a mirror would, in the classical understanding—but it re-constructs fragments or perceptions of it into a new construction. The 'classical mirror' thus turns into a 'shattered glass' mirror" (8). Reality is fictionalized and distorted, but to better reflect reality, to satirize so as to allow readers to see themselves more clearly. But ultimately, the questions of reality and knowledge remain open. For McKeon, the interpolated stories play a role in Cervantes's "real commitment to empiricist epistemology" (*The Origins of the English Novel* 278), whereby "romance completeness is founded on the strictly authorial manipulation of main story and digressive dilation" (279). McKeon later ascribes this literary phenomenon to a more political cause: that "the promise of an objective history and of a transparent narration was a real one in [the] early modern Spanish culture" (293) of the "historiographical crisis" (293) of the Inquisition (although the preference for "true history" ["*la historia verdadera*"] in fiction is evidenced since Aristotle). If we follow McKeon's argument that *Don Quixote* is a text that responds in a multifaceted way to the Inquisition's desire to control and reshape the historical narrative of Spain, "El curioso impertinente," which McKeon does not include among his analysis of the digressions of Part I of the novel, can be viewed as another provocation against this Counter-Reformationist ideology of historical unity. This is further evidenced through Molina's analysis of glass metaphors, though providing a more literary and less political interpretation for the novella, which posits that

> "El curioso impertinente" deals with one fracture after another. The first to give way is Lotario's better judgment under Anselmo's pressure; then Camila's better judgment in Anselmo's absence; then Lotario's own friendship with and fidelity to Anselmo; and finally Camila's marital fidelity under Lotario's pressure. But all along, as a figure fashioned out of glass, as a child born of these infidelities, what develops is a new very fragile creature, which is the fiction of fidelity itself. (15)

This is to say, as well, the fragility of *fiction* itself. Cervantes seems to ask throughout the *Quixote*, "what is *real* in storytelling?" Is a story more real if it is framed by (an albeit fictional) paratext and "discovered manuscript" trope?

The *Quixote*'s canon tells the curate that he would prefer to see a story "with a whole body for a plot, with all its members complete, so that the middle corresponds to the beginning and the end to the beginning and the middle" (478).[53] On first reading, "El curioso impertinente" seems to provide just that, a whole story, told from practically the birth of the characters to their untimely ends, where each part corresponds to the other. On the other hand, the "Curioso" functions as an interruption within a much longer narrative, and it itself is interrupted by the episode of the wine skins (borrowed from Apuleius), facts

---

[53] "un cuerpo de da fábula entero con todos sus miembros, de manera que el medio corresponda al principio, y el fin al principio y al medio" (491).

which then make it seem as though, in Sancho's words, the narrator "has made a pretty kettle of fish of everything" (549).[54]

By interrupting the narrative multiple times, both with the text of the novella itself, as well as with meta-discussions about its appropriateness by various characters in the novel, Cervantes further questions the possibility of epistemological certainty in both historical and narrative terms. "El curioso impertinente" is also fragmented in its representation of incomplete perceptions, in its depiction of radical uncertainty, and in its focus on the unknowability of and unaccountability of desire, as we will see. Furthermore, this interpolated story creates a tragic, anti-romantic counter-narrative to the other successful mini-marriage plots embedded in *Don Quixote*, including the stories of Dorothea and Don Fernando, Lucinda and Cardenio, and the captive and Zoreida. The elements might all point to Cervantes's questioning of the possibility of attaining what are, as we have already seen, the "big three" targets of analytical fiction's skepticism: love, knowledge, and truth.

One of the ways in which Cervantes indicates this questioning, pertaining to "El curioso impertinente," is how other characters in the novel react to it. The bachelor, Sansón Carrasco—having now metaliterarily read Part I—suggests in Part II that "El curioso impertinente" "is out of place and has nothing to do with the history of his worship, Don Quixote (549)."[55] Although the bachelor, who, in the second half of the *Quixote*, takes everything literally, including Don Quixote's knight errantry, is about as good a literary critic as Sancho, his analysis of the interpolated story's place in the novel prefigures much of the real literary criticism regarding "El curioso impertinente," that it is an unnecessary interruption.[56] Cide Hamete Benengeli, the fictitious narrator, himself defends the "elegance and fine craftsmanship" (833)[57] of the inserted stories, but writes, via

---

[54] "*mezclado* [...] *berzas con capachos*" (571), literally "mixing up cabbages with baskets." J. M. Cohen translates this phrase as "a fine mix-up of everything" (489).

[55] "no ser de aquel lugar, ni tiene que ver con la historia de su merced del señor don Quijote" (571).

[56] J. M. Cohen, in his 1950 translation of *Don Quixote*, advises his readers "to skip" the interpolated story, since "neither its morality nor its psychology bears a moment's examination. [...] It is difficult to see what amusement the average reader can find in it" (15). Furthermore, as Diane de Armas Wilson notes, "Vladimir Nabokov's scornful dismissal of its plot as 'incredible nonsense, deceit and eavesdropping being the usual bedsprings of the thing' [...] [and] Madariaga's authoritarian criticism [...] [as] *a frank intruder*, smuggled into the work by a simple contrivance" (11) goes to show how some critics in the first half of the twentieth century viewed "El curioso impertinente." Although other mid-century scholars like Raymond Immerwahr ("the reading of the 'Curioso' is central in respect to the main action" [126] of *Don Quixote*) and Bruce Wardropper, who writes that "the short story is a pointer, a clear indication of at least some of the things that *Don Quixote* is about" (595), defy their contemporaries.

[57] "la gala y artificio" (877).

a long digression, that he will further refrain from any additional interpolations. This delaying and dilating device is something we have seen before. Ironically, "Cide Hamete," in resigning himself to never again interrupt the narrative, interrupts it further with this long explanation of how he will craft the story from now on. The false authorship device here allows Cervantes to comment on and defend his own story, which had already, since the publication of Part I, met with criticism. At the same time, however, Cervantes ends in persevering in his style, delaying and interrupting the narrative in order to comment and extend, and to put off the finality of an ending and of knowledge.

"El curioso impertinente" revolves around three main characters, Anselmo, his best friend Lotario, and Anselmo's new wife, Camila. Anselmo is a man consumed with the idea of testing his wife's fidelity—a theme that is evidenced in the bible, in Boccaccio, and in Ariosto, among others—by soliciting Lotario to seduce her. While Lotario holds out for some time, even dissembling courting Camila but not really going through with it, eventually the inevitable happens and Lotario and Camila become lovers, working together to deceive the all-too-willing husband. However, Lotario eventually becomes jealous as well, imagining that he sees another of Camila's lovers leaving their house. Here he turns the tables on Camila and indicates his own desire to test her fidelity. The "Curioso"—like the larger narrative of Don Quixote that frames it—illustrates the ways in which the imagination can create an uncontrollable and obsessive passion that clouds judgment and forestalls self-knowledge.

As the title implies, the interpolated tale hinges on an obsessive and destructive curiosity, which, I will argue, stems as much from self-doubt and doubt about others as Anselmo's madness. Anselmo appears as an empiricist, but in reality, he is interested only in what he perceives to be ontological truth (i.e., *a priori* knowledge, separate from evidence). As Alison E. Krueger points out, "according to Anselmo's logic, if Camila resists, she is virtuous; if she fails, her previously virtuous behavior must have been caused by a factor other than her virtue" (145). Later, Lotario falls into this philosophical trap as well, confessing to Anselmo that Camila has fallen in love with him (though omitting his own participation in the affair), and claiming that "if she was what she should be and what we both thought her to be, she would already have informed you of my wooing" (352).[58] In this way, both Anselmo and Lotario's *a*

---

[58] "ella, si fuera la que debía y la que entrambos pensábamos, ya te hubiera dado cuenta de mi solicitud" (355). The Spanish text is the Real Academia Española edition, edited by Francisco Rico, and the English translation is Walter Starkie's.

*priori* judgment of women's lack of fidelity belies their claims to empiricism.[59] But besides misogyny, and besides folly, or even madness, Anselmo's fatal curiosity stems from an impulsive and contradictory need to experiment and test, and from an even more desperate fundamental skepticism about the idea of virtue in general. Like the *Elegia di madonna Fiammetta*, as Frederick A. De Armas makes clear, Cervantes's interpolated tale has roots in Apuleius's Cupid and Psyche story—itself an interruption of the main narrative of the *Golden Ass*—wherein "curiosity to see what must remain invisible brings about Psyche's downfall, much in the same manner as Anselmo's desire to render visible his wife's invisible qualities (her fidelity) brings about his destruction. [...] Seeing what should remain invisible (a god or an intangible virtue) brings about great suffering" (De Armas 191–93) in both works. Anselmo's curiosity, folly, and skepticism combine in a perfect storm of irrational behavior in this tale that both reflects and distorts, on a far more domestic scale, Don Quixote's impossible quests to fulfill the adventures and ideals of knight errantry and for the love of Dulcinea.

Similar to Marguerite's tenth *nouvelle*, the story of "El curioso impertinente" is also the story of two people who *believe* that they are best friends, but whose very tests of friendship (since Anselmo is, unconsciously, not just testing his wife, but his friend as well) serve to drive them farther apart. In fact, some readers may too-quickly skip over the beginning of Cervantes's interpolated novel, and believe that "El curioso impertinente" begins with Anselmo's desire to test Camila, when in fact, the first few paragraphs of the story center on the friendship between Anselmo and Lotario, and the fact that, after his marriage, "Anselmo noted the falling off in Lotario's visits and raised many complaints" (327).[60] This is well before Anselmo develops the "madness" that drives him to test his wife (Jorge Garcia López notices that "Anselmo seems to suffer from the distance that his marriage has put between himself and Lotario"[61] and Ashley Hope Pérez notes that "it is abundantly clear which relationship is the focal point of the narrative" [85]) indicating that Anselmo's trial is intended as much for his supposed best friend—once that best friend has stopped coming around as often—as it is for Camila. But if the story begins with Anselmo and

---

[59] McKeon discusses the relationship between "naive empiricism and extreme skepticism" (*Origins of the English Novel* 118) in *Don Quixote* as well, and writes that "the text of *Don Quixote* encloses a development from the self-criticism of romance, to the naive empiricism of 'true history,' to a final orientation of extreme skepticism" (273).

[60] "notó Anselmo la remisión de Lotario y formó dél quejas grandes" (328).

[61] "Anselmo parece estar dolido por la distancia que su matrimonio impone entre él y Lotario" (142).

Lotario's friendship, this bond is not without its problems. As René Girard's now classic interpretation of "triangular desire" makes evident, Lotario and Anselmo's "ardent friendship is accompanied by a sharp feeling of rivalry. But this rivalry remains in the shadows. [...] [Anselmo] pushes the loved woman into the mediator's arms in order to arouse his desire and then triumph over the rival desire. He does not desire *in* his mediator but rather *against* him" (50–51, Girard's emphasis). And Molina writes, "from the beginning Anselmo's obsession threatens and then obliterates that category of 'dos amigos'" (7), while Pérez points out that the story "brings Camila into an affective economy wholly based on the rivalrous dynamic between the two men" (84). Perhaps like Amador, who must continue to speak about Florida's love for the son of the Infante of Fortune to persist in his love for her, Anselmo could desire Camila only when she "is already desired by another man, desiring her, in fact, because of the other man's desire for her" (Quint 25).

Like the tale of Amador and Florida, the characters in "El curioso impertinente" arrive at decisions and see the world in general counterintuitively. But whereas Amador only eventually accepts his obsession, justifies his irrational passions, and ultimately acts as though all is fair in love and war (he has no problem to, as Fiammetta puts it, "trespass the limit"[62]), Anselmo at the very start is prepared to act on his violent impulses, although he dissimulates being ashamed of his curiosity. He dances around the topic and puts off revealing his consuming desire to test his wife for as long as he can, using what Lotario calls "circuitous" means of revealing his irrational passions:

> I am the most dissatisfied and peevish mortal in all the world, because of late I have been troubled by a whim that is so peculiar and so unaccountable that I marvel at myself. I revile myself when I am alone and I try to stifle it and banish it from my thoughts, but in vain. In fact it seems as if I intended all along to proclaim it to the world. (328)[63,64]

---

[62] "trapassare il segno" (Boccaccio, *Elegia Di Madonna Fiammetta* 60).

[63] "vivo yo el más despechado y el más desabrido hombre de todo el universo mundo; porque no sé qué días a esta parte me fatiga y aprieta un deseo tan estraño, y tan fuera del uso común de otros, que yo me maravillo de mí mismo, y me culpo y me riño a solas, y procuro callarlo y encubrirlo de mis proprios pensamientos; y así me ha sido posible salir con este secreto como si de industria procurara decillo a todo el mundo" (330).

[64] Krueger points out that "Anselmo's tone is reflective of the predicament described by the skeptic Francisco Sánchez (1550-1623) in the aptly titled *Qvod Nihil Scitvr* (*That Nothing Is Known*), in which Sánchez writes: 'as it is, I am tortured incessantly by grief, in despair of being able to know anything completely'" (quoted in Krueger 148).

Cervantes purposely delays both Lotario's and the reader's knowledge about Anselmo's intention not so much to create suspense as to protract Anselmo's deliberation. When Anselmo finally confesses what his obsession actually is to Lotario, he reveals that even he finds his feelings "unaccountable," and yet, he cannot be dissuaded from continuing to nurture his obsession to have Lotario test his wife.

Looking at the method of argumentation in the novella, Krueger finds instead that Anselmo and Lotario each argue on the side of either experience or authority, respectively: "Anselmo and Lotario talk past each other; their respective approaches to knowledge and to assessing the situation at hand are so different in that neither character adequately responds to the points presented in the other's arguments" (Krueger 138 footnote). Anselmo begins with a completely illogical premise: he asks "what reason [...] has one to thank a woman for being good if no one has tempted her to be bad?" (329).[65] The only thing that Anselmo is tempting here, of course, is fate. Lotario, a more sensible man, at least at first, attempts to dissuade Anselmo from testing Camila (Garcia López argues that "in his discourse, Lotario credibly foretells—in literary, social, and even psychological and pathological terms—what will be the course of Anselmo's story and destiny"[66]), but his arguments cannot win against Anselmo's irrationality.[67]

The counterintuitive misreadings continue when Lotario has finally conceded to help Anselmo in his mad plan: "Anselmo embraced Lotario affectionately and thanked him for his offer *as if his friend had done him a great favor*" (337–8 emphasis added).[68] This last clause represents the voice of the narrator, commenting on Anselmo's self-destructive foolishness. But from the beginning, Anselmo approaches his marriage to Camila through Lotario; he has his friend woo her for him and negotiate with her parents and he cannot love her until he believes that Lotario has attempted to seduce her. The code of

---

[65] "¿qué hay que agradecer [...] que una mujer sea buena si nadie le dice que sea mala?" (331). Anselmo's question, as we will see, is repeated by Lovelace—via a reference to Ariosto—in *Clarissa*, pointing out Richardson's rake's skepticism and foolish and cruel curiosity.

[66] "Lotario describe en su discurso con perfecta antelación y lujo de rasgos creíbles—en términos literarios, sociales e incluso psicológicos o patológicos—cuál será el derrotero de la historia y el destino de Anselmo" (144).

[67] In any case, it is disputed whether Lotario's arguments are in fact sound. They are rather misogynistic, comparing Camila to, among other things, a crystal mirror and an ermine. As Krueger, who investigates the tale from the point of view of rhetoric and philosophical argumentation, points out, "the appropriate method for discerning truth and as to how we may understand the relations between truth, knowledge, and life" (121–2) reaches no conclusions in "El curioso impertinente".

[68] "Abrazóle Anselmo tierna y amorosamente, y agradecióle su ofrecimiento *como si alguna grande merced le hubiera hecho*" (341, emphasis added).

honor here (and "honor" is important since Anselmo writes at the end that he was the "architect of his own dishonor") is clearly inverted, as the husband tries to make his friend into a husband-substitute so that he himself can become the lover.

At first, Lotario purposely avoids Camila when they are left alone together, although he persuades Anselmo that he is pursuing his wife with the zeal of a devil. Rather than placating Anselmo, however, Lotario's lies only strengthen his obsession. Again, counterintuitively, Anselmo is not satisfied with mere words; he wishes to see action, offering Lotario money to buy presents for Camila to attempt to win her over. Again Lotario refuses, and Anselmo becomes suspicious. He decides to hide and listen in on Lotario and Camila's conversation, in the famous keyhole spying scene. Discovering only silence between his wife and his friend (and not realizing that all of this time spent together, even in silence, is just laying the groundwork for a future affair, as looking can be more productive than speaking) Anselmo becomes angry and even accuses Lotario of acting dishonorably against their agreement.

Narrative distancing is created here also, as the narrator purposely suspends the tale in order to point out the flaws in Anselmo's thinking. For example, when Lotario's reasoning with Anselmo fails, the narrator directly addresses the foolish husband: "hapless and ill-advised Anselmo, what are you doing?" (341)[69] the narrator asks (though of course, Anselmo cannot hear him, thus negating the force of the interruption and rendering it merely stylistic on the author's part). Anselmo's project is haunted by the fact that he publicizes private matters, dragging up from underground and setting into motion that which is unstable, unknowable, and dangerous. He shares his most intimate obsessions and fears with Lotario and creates problems where none previously existed. After Lotario and Camila have fallen in love, the narrator interrupts again to remind the reader that Lotario would have done better to continue to deceive Anselmo by purposely distancing himself from Camila. In elevated prose, the narrator offers the following maxim, which is very much in line with the mode of analytical fiction: "only superhuman powers can overcome those too human ones of love" (346).[70]

Despite the fact that eventually, Lotario becomes dishonest, his dishonesty consists of just what Anselmo has asked him to do. Lotario falls in love with

---

[69] "¡Desdichado y mal advertido de ti, Anselmo! ¿Qué es lo que haces?" (344).
[70] "menester fuerzas divinas para vencer las suyas humanas" (348).

Camila in a way that is typical in analytical fiction. He does not speak to her for three days, but those three days give Lotario plenty of time to contemplate Camila's beauty: "Lotario gazed at her all the time he should have been talking to her, thinking how worthy of being loved she was" (342).[71] Whereas before his lies were intended to keep Anselmo happy and everyone involved morally irreproachable, Lotario now begins to seduce Camila and justifies his courtship as ultimately less dishonorable than Anselmo's schemes. Long before Camila submits, represented by the chiasmus "Rindiose Camila, Camila se rindió" ("Camila surrendered; surrendered Camila"), Lotario has entirely surrendered to Camila's charms (as well as to Anselmo's insisting), merely by looking at her.

Camila, for her part, also reacts counterintuitively. For example, she is so happy to have married Anselmo that "she continually thanked Heaven and *Lotario*, the joint artificers of her present happiness" (326, emphasis added).[72] Understandably, she does not praise her husband in winning her over, since he did nothing to make the marriage come about, to the point that Ruth El Saffar even speculates that Camila is secretly in love with Lotario when the marriage is celebrated (*Beyond Fiction* 72). When Lotario visits, Camila always welcomes him, justifying his visits because they are mediated through her husband's fondness for his friend. That is, until Anselmo tells her that he wants to leave her alone for several days with Lotario. Camila protests and considers running away to her parents' house. Ultimately, however, she decides to stay and to allow Lotario to visit her alone, "lest she give her servants cause for gossip" (345).[73] Lotario, by now, has fallen in love with Camila, and has started to press his case more overtly than she anticipated, even despite her growing affection for him: he "wept, beseeched, promised, feigned, flattered, and swore with such passion and with such signs of genuine feeling that he overwhelmed Camila" (345–6)[74] despite her modesty. And eventually, the long silences and longer looks have an effect on Camila as well, whether it is because Lotario is truly an attractive match for her or because of the attention he pays her (which she does not receive from her husband). She decides, against reason, to stay silent about

---

[71] "Mirábala Lotario en el lugar y espacio que había de hablarla, y consideraba cuán digna era de ser amada" (346).
[72] "que no cesaba de dar gracias al cielo, y a *Lotario*, por cuyo medio tanto bien le había venido" (328, emphasis added).
[73] "por no dar que decir a sus criados" (347).
[74] "Lloró, rogó, ofreció, aduló, porfió y fingió Lotario con tantos sentimientos, con muestras de tantas veras, que dio al través con el recato de Camila" (348).

Lotario's pursuit. Deceiving herself, she believes that she can fend off Lotario and whatever language he attempts to use to seduce her, without even needing to get Anselmo involved. But, of course, the lack of communication becomes a conduit for her own growing feelings toward Lotario. Being forced—or so she says, since fearing what the servants might think is merely a cover—to stay in the house with Lotario, slowly, Camila begins to reciprocate his love. Whereas before she had written to Anselmo complaining of Lotario's too-overt attentions (and Anselmo, when he receives the letter, couldn't be happier), Camila now, merely days later, thinks of ways of excusing Lotario's behavior if her husband were to ask (though he does not). In this way, the very woman whom Lotario had warned was made of glass[75] and thus should not be tested, lest she break, is subjected to the most rigorous of trials. She fails, and in fact, would have succumbed in a most un-analytical fashion, where it not for one phrase, which is the narrator's interjection that Lotario "won the triumph he most of all desired *when he least expected it*" (346, emphasis added).[76]

Camila and Lotario become lovers, but eventually Camila becomes afraid that her love was given too easily, too quickly. She and her maid, Leonela, debate the value of love (whether the proverb—which inverts Montaigne—"there is no reason why a thing should lose its value because it's easily given" or "what costs little is little prized" [349][77] is more apt for the situation). Like Venus in the *Elegia*, Leonela questions Camila's need for complication in love: "what is it that frightens you and has you in such a dither?" (350)[78] She proceeds to list Lotario's qualities, and, ironically, attributes Camila's passion to "a glimpse of Lotario's entire soul in his eyes" (350)[79] as if he were the most honest man that had ever lived, underscoring another element that we often notice in analytical fiction, that is, the deceptiveness of the gaze; Lotario dared not speak to Camila, so he watched her instead, and thus he fell in love, causing more damage, perhaps,

---

[75] Later, in one of Lotario's poems, he compares the unrequiting lover's heart to granite (349), and in the seduction scene, Lotario's prowess is said to be able to overcome Camila's modesty, even if she were made of bronze.

[76] "vino a triunfar de *lo que menos se pensaba* y mas deseaba" (348, emphasis added). These words are echoed later, when Lotario tells Anselmo that he believes that Camila really is unfaithful: "absorto, suspenso y admirado quedó Anselmo con las razones de Lotario, porque le cogieron en tiempo donde menos las esperaba oír" (356) ["Anselmo was dumbfounded, amazed, and stunned by Lotario's statements, for they caught him at a moment when he least expected to hear them" (353)].

[77] "no está la monta ni es causa para mengua de la estimación dares lo que se da presto" or "lo que cuesta poco se estima en menos" (352-3).

[78] "de qué tu espantas, o de qué temes […]?" (353).

[79] "en los ojos […] toda su alma [de Lotario]" (353).

than speaking would have. As we have already seen, and as we will see in other works of analytical fiction, silence often breeds a kind of pseudo-intimacy.

After they begin their affair Lotario continues to lie to Anselmo, but in the completely opposite fashion than he did previously. Finally, there is a real love to conceal, rather than a disingenuous one to fake. Speaking both truth and lie simultaneously, Lotario tells Anselmo that there is no more need to test Camila (as the reader knows, she has failed the test). Lotario also goes on to assure Anselmo that he need not try Camila with an "another pilot,"[80] that is, another lover. It is just at this moment, when Lotario and Camila have settled into a comfortable pattern, of course, that the narrative takes a much more complex turn. Perhaps Lotario is worried that if Camila acquiesced to him then she would to another man as well (and, as we will see, Lotario also catalyzes the destruction of all of these characters by jumping to conclusions and growing jealous). And yet, Anselmo, either because he still does not feel confident, or because he is truly enjoying himself at watching the spectacle, or perhaps because he still needs to prolong the trial to continue to either augment his love for or separate himself from Camila (or embroil Lotario even deeper), "begged [Lotario] nevertheless not to abandon the enterprise even if it was merely for the sake of curiosity and entertainment" (347).[81] Anselmo, cast by Cervantes as a fool who, the narrative tells us, is the cause of his own demise ("el fabricador de su deshonra"), does not ever suspect anything duplicitous in Lotario and Camila's speeches. Anselmo becomes more of a spectator by the middle of the story, having largely been replaced by Lotario as husband.

This is most obvious in the "ghost lover" scene, when Lotario (who was at their house at daybreak, though it is unstated why he is there) becomes irrationally and uncontrollably jealous, believing that Leonela's lover is actually another lover of Camila's. While the expectation may be that it would be Anselmo to notice the presence of an unauthorized man in the house, it is actually Lotario. And although the narrator attributes all of this trouble and confusion to Camila's "wicked" actions, it is clear that it is, on one level, Lotario's fault for being jealous and jumping to conclusions, and on another level, not due to any one character, but rather the fault of the narrative patterns of the *roman d'analyse*, where no insight is stable or correct, and misreadings are the default setting for interpretation.

---

[80] "otro piloto" (349).
[81] "le rogó que no dejase la empresa, aunque no fuse más de por curiosidad y entretenimiento" (349).

## "The Play's the Thing": Acting in "El curioso impertinente"

One figure through which the analytical features of "El curioso impertinente" are easily evidenced is the metaphor of playacting that is deployed throughout the narrative. As I wrote in the introduction, many works of analytical fiction share the features of a stage drama, but without the Aristotelian recognitions necessary for a successful tragedy. Instead, the misreadings and misinterpretations pile on one after another until some outside force (in this case, Leonela's lack of discretion in carrying out her own love affair) sets the ending scenes (I will not say climax, as there is none in a work of analytical fiction whose narration is cyclical, rather than pyramidal) into motion. According to Garcia López, "what Anselmo does, in essence, is attempt to transform Lotario and Camila into puppets to act out his idea, in a 'playhouse' driven by his obsessions."[82] But it turns out that Anselmo is the least capable puppet master in this whole production, as first Lotario (who deceives Anselmo so well throughout) and then Camila (as she sets up an elaborate stage scene for deceiving Anselmo later on, as many critics, including Garcia Lopez have noted) emerge as more effective directors. As El Saffar observes, for example, all three characters are "launched into a series of 'plays' in which each character in turn believes himself to be the 'author,' successfully manipulating the actions of the other two" (*Distance and Control* 72, quoted in Pérez 98).

The episode in which Lotario writes love poetry to Camila under Anselmo's watchful but misunderstanding eye also represents a kind of playacting, just as it creates a warped *mise en abyme* of perceptions, insights, and misreadings. Anselmo induces Lotario to recite love poems to Camila, addressed to another woman, so that she will believe that Lotario is no longer in love with her, and to then test Camila's potential for jealousy (it is fortunate that Lotario warns Camila about this part of the plot, because otherwise "she would no doubt have fallen into the hopeless tangle of jealousy, but as she was forewarned, she survived this trouble unharmed" [347])[83]. Lotario recites the poems, which of course are indeed written for Camila, who is already his lover. Camila knows the poems are really meant for her, but in order to hide this information from her husband, she receives Lotario coolly. Because of her behavior toward Lotario,

---

[82] "lo que hace Anselmo, en esencia, es intentar convertir a Lotario y Camila en actores de una idea, en marionetas de un espacio dramático dominado por sus obsesiones" (141).

[83] "ella sin duda cayera en la desesperada red de los celos; mas, por estar ya advertida, pasó aquel sobresalto sin pesadumbre" (350).

Anselmo continues to believe that his wife is faithful and incapable of jealousy. The sonnets are recited and the duped husband praises the words that his friend sincerely wrote for his wife. The narrator again interjects to comment on Anselmo's culpability in this own deception:

> And so, in this manner he continued to add link on link to the chain that he was forging for his own dishonor, for the more Lotario dishonored him, the more he convinced himself of his spotless honor. And likewise, the deeper Camila sank in her gradual descent into infamy, the higher she rose in her husband's estimation toward the topmost pinnacles of virtue and renown. (349)[84]

The love poems that Lotario writes and can recite openly because they are addressed to "Chloris" communicate different and contradictory messages to each member of the love triangle. While Anselmo believes that he knows the truth, trusting that the love sonnets are disingenuous, they also capably transmit Lotario and Camila's faked-but-real love. And just as Fiammetta can acknowledge her love for Panfilo through love songs at Baia, and Florida can credibly hide her love for Amador by praising his wife, so Lotario can speak of his love for his friend's wife openly in front of him without being detected.

In the real playacting scene, Lotario and Camila plan to deceive Anselmo by making him hide behind a tapestry while they perform a play that will assuage his fears about being deceived. As a spectator, unable or unwilling to act, Anselmo vacillates between intervening in what he believes is a real scene in which Camila swears revenge against Lotario, and staying where he is, greatly enjoying the spectacle. He "restrained this impulse [to jump out], so great was his desire to see how his wife's high-spirited and honorable resolution would end" (356).[85] During her performance, Camila dissimulates rage and even madness, waving around Anselmo's dagger and threatening Lotario for attempting to dishonor her. As Anselmo watches them, Camila and Lotario (and Leonela) perform impeccably and "both of them made their imposture ring truer than truth itself" (358)[86] with their speeches and actions. In the end, Camila pretends to stab herself (although she inflicts only a minor wound), which we can juxtapose

---

[84] "y de esta manera iba añadiendo eslabón a eslabón a la cadena con que se enlazaba y trababa su deshonra, pues cuando más Lotario le deshonraba, entonces le decía que estaba más honrado; y con esto todos los escalones que Camila bajaba hacia el centro de su menosprecio, los subía, en la opinión de su marido, hacia la cumbre de la virtud y de su buena fama" (352).

[85] "tal cose no se hiciese, pero detúvole el deseo de ver en qué paraba tanta gallardía y honesta resolución" (359).

[86] "los dos la mentira y la verdad más disimulada que jamás pudiera imaginarse" (434).

with Florida's self-harm in the *Heptaméron*. The differences between these two episodes are obvious: the reader knows that Camila's self-injury is deliberately minor because she is performing, whereas Florida's injuries are more serious and more gruesome. But both women injure themselves deliberately because words will no longer serve to repel dangerously curious men, each of whose sense of boundaries is warped by madness. At the same time, though, neither act of self-harm leads to any significant results; Amador is still inclined to rape Florida—in fact he seems to become even more angry with her when he exposes Florida's self-mutilation as having been deliberate, and Camila's self-imposed wounds ironically (inasmuch as he does not seem particularly frightened for his wife's health) assuage Anselmo temporarily, but not indefinitely. Soon another suspicion creeps in, and he begins to doubt her fidelity and his own sense of control over his household.

Even here, where it seems at first that Camila is the one pulling the strings, the reader is only privileged to her reactions, which are mediated through the two men in her life. As Pérez has written in response to interpretations that claim Camila's proto-feminist agency in her later role in the novella, "whatever her self-assertion, eloquence, and genius in acting, Camila is still brutally subjected to the punishments that so often await wayward women of early modern Spanish literature: the convent and the coffin" (84), and "Camila is drawn into an ever-darkening triangle of dependence, deception, and desire that ultimately leads to her destruction" (Pérez 85). Certainly, Camila is only a "conduit" of the other two men, as Pérez writes (97), and her own agency is limited to playacting in a theatre circumscribed by the men in the tale and the patriarchy more generally.[87]

But the roles that are scripted for Anselmo and Lotario are almost as limiting. As Aciman writes, "the novel tortures the jealous lover. […] It presents him with evidence that is either misleading, hence dismissible; or it provides him with evidence that compels him to revise all previous assumptions—only so as to

---

[87] In a brilliantly attractive deliberate misreading of the failure of Camila's dagger scene which also contrasts fictive reality with historical truth, Pérez asks, "could Camila-as-herself, appearing in a fragmentary flash from outside the bounds of this two-man society, perhaps act for a vengeful justice that is larger than what Camila-as-actor knows? With the dagger, she could destroy the triangle. Lotario's death by Anselmo's dagger in Camila's hand: it would be a kind of perfect comeuppance. […] But we cannot know. As witnesses to this scene, we also remain in radical uncertainty as to whether Camila really intends the dagger for the breast of Lotario. […] The absolute opacity of Camila's performance suggests that *all along* she has been more than they (or we) can know. And yet the content of the self that seems to exist beyond this triangle of desire cannot be expressed within it" (101).

have his newer assumptions prove to be equally misleading" ("The Recursive Matrix" 95). Whether it be skepticism, empiricism, fear, or madness, Anselmo is still enslaved by his own obsessive, misdirected passion (as is Alonso Quijano); Lotario is placed into a psychological bind by his possible latent passion for Camila or for Anselmo (or both; or, possibly, neither, since we learn at the beginning that Lotario is less interested in romance than in hunting). Anselmo and Camila seem to be living in an unconsummated relationship that binds them in mutual failure, while Camila's relationship with Lotario is based just as much on deceit and manipulation. None of these characters, any more than any of the characters in any work of analytical fiction, have agency over their actions. Their beliefs are manipulated by the force of the narration itself that undercuts any possibility of truth or uncomplicated love.

For most of the tale, Anselmo remains the most happily deluded man in the world, with every insight that he may have into being deceived immediately replaced with another, counterintuitive one that keeps him complacently unsuspecting. The deception continues for some time, until "fortune turns her wheel," and "their artfully concealed wickedness became public, and Anselmo's curiosity cost him his life" (362).[88] One day, Camila disappears. Anselmo is left on his own to realize physically what has already happened emotionally. After a cursory search for Camila, Anselmo is told by a stranger that she has run away with Lotario. It is interesting to note that Anselmo, who had hitherto been so obsessed with proof and knowledge, does not investigate the rumor he hears. He takes Camila's absence, as well as that of Lotario, at face value, and, ironically, finally interprets the situation correctly. At the end of the text, he abandons his empiricism, intuitively putting together the pieces of the puzzle himself. Before he dies of grief, Anselmo writes a deathbed confession:

> A foolish and ill-advised desire has cost me my life. If news of my death should reach Camila's ears, let it be known that I forgive her, for she was not obliged to perform miracles, nor did I need to ask her to do so. [...] I was the one who fashioned my own dishonor. (370)[89]

---

[88] "volvió Fortuna su rueda y salió a plaza la maldad con tanto artificio hasta allí cubierta, y a Anselmo le costó la vida su impertinente curiosidad" (365).

[89] "Un necio e impertinente deseo me quitó la vida. Si las nuevas de mi muerte llegaren a los oídos de Camila, sepa que yo la perdono, porque no estaba ella obligada a hacer milagros, ni yo tenía necesidad de querer que ella los hiciese; y, pues yo fui el fabricador de mi deshonra" (373).

Similarly, one could argue that in the end, only right before he dies, Don Quixote admits to his own former foolishness and, although it is too late, he embraces rationalism and the quiet and pious lifestyle that better suits his age and station in life:

> My judgment is now clear and unfettered, and that dark cloud of ignorance has disappeared, which the continual reading of those detestable books of knight errantry had cast over my understanding. Now I see their folly and fraud, and my sole regret is that the discovery comes too late to allow me to amend my ways by reading others that would enlighten my soul. (1045)[90]

Don Quixote, or Alonso Quijano, as he now wishes to be called again, renounces knight errantry, and, more importantly, chivalric romances (and Sancho touchingly in desperation and sadness tries to convince him to take them up again), and moreover, he emerges from his madness more or less unharmed by it. The narrator tells us that Quijano dies peacefully of a natural death so that no other author (besides Cide Hamete Benengeli) could resuscitate him. Even though the household grieves for a time, in the end, everything and every person returns to normal. Therefore, while Don Quixote does see the error of his ways, it is in no way stated that either his previous behavior or his death-bed renunciation have any serious impact on himself or anyone else. Moreover, as much as the reader would perhaps like to believe that Don Quixote has been cured of his madness, in death he *still* blames books for his condition (and wishes that he could have read different ones before his death to "enlighten" himself, illustrating his continued dependence on fiction to guide his behavior, rather than truly relying on either empirical evidence or reason).

The ending of *Don Quixote* sheds light on the consequences (or really, inconsequence) for Anselmo. In spite of his own belief that he has been the architect of his own demise, Anselmo is only correct to a point. Just as Quixote's niece, squire, and housekeeper continue to eat and drink and spend money, the Florentine people, we learn at the end from the *ciudadano* who shares the news about Camila and Lotario, have also been following this story as a juicy piece of gossip, but, of course, are not affected by what is merely, to them, an interesting story. The fantasy of the closed society is instantly shattered and the

---

[90] "Yo tengo juicio ya libre y claro, sin las sombras caliginosas de la ignorancia que sobre él me pusieron mi amarga y continua leyenda de los detestables libros de las caballerías. Ya conozco sus disparates y sus embelecos, y no me pesa sino que este desengaño ha llegado tan tarde, que no me deja tiempo para hacer alguna recompensa leyendo otros que sean luz del alma" (1100).

real world of sixteenth-century Florence is revealed to comment on the ultimate inconsequence of the *curioso impertinente*. It is true that Camila and Lotario's lives have been destroyed by the catalyst of Anselmo's foolishness, but they are also victims of analytical fiction, whose uneasy revision of love, ubiquitous jealousies, and distrust of both actions and words render self-knowledge and happiness impossible. Their lives become fodder for gossip in the outside world, and are thus simultaneously narratized and fragmented. The three deaths at the end of "El curioso impertinente" are just as counterintuitive as the novella's beginnings. Anselmo dies ostensibly of a heart broken not only by Camila but by Lotario as well ("when he found [Lotario] gone and when his servants told him that their master had departed that night and had taken all the money he had with him, he thought he would go out of his mind" [368][91]). And although Camila bravely runs away from Anselmo's house, as Pérez points out, "Lotario's reaction belies his professions of love—or at least nullifies their currency beyond the triangle that also includes Anselmo. [...] Faced with the very outcome he once desired—to get away from Anselmo—Lotario is now paralyzed" (104). Camila, thinking that she and Lotario will start a new life together, is abandoned in a convent, where she soon hears about her husband's death, and Lotario, without any kind of explanation, runs away and is killed in battle (nowhere previously had Lotario's military service—let alone a war—been mentioned).[92] Camila is left hovering ambiguously between Lotario's presence and absence, refusing to take the veil in the convent until she hears of his death. Finally when Lotario dies, Camila does become a nun and dies shortly after.

Whereas initially it may seem that this story—contrary to the *Quixote* at large—is meant to illustrate that actions have consequences, on closer inspection, the ultimate outcomes are rather arbitrary as well. The repetition, mirroring, and theatricality of the tale of foolish curiosity stem from all three characters' irrational fears and jealousies, and a lack of self-control on the part of Anselmo when he clearly recognizes that what he wants to do is morally and socially wrong. And yet, it is as if he cannot help himself; his propensity to error

---

[91] "cuando no le halló y sus criados le dijeron que aquella noche había faltado de casa y había llevado consigo todos los dineros que tenía, pensó perder el juicio" (372).

[92] As Louis Lo points out, the reference is to the historical battle of Cerignola that took place when France invaded Naples in 1503. Moreover, the story of the battle is recounted in "a book called *la Historia del Gran Capitan Gonzalo Hernández de Córdoba* [...] which is found in a cloak-bag together with two other large books and the manuscript of [of course!] *El curioso impertinente*" (72) at Palomoque's inn. Thus, historical reality and fiction reshuffle once again in Cervantes's fictive world.

and self-deception are stronger than reason, love, or friendship. The same can be said of Lotario and even Camila, who become embroiled in the same foolish curiosity as Anselmo.

In the *Heptaméron*, Amador marries a woman he does not love in order to be closer to the woman he does love; in *Don Quixote*, Anselmo marries a woman he does not love in order to be closer to the *man* that he does. They all play their roles, at first quietly and at a distance, hedging their bets, and with long, deliberating looks and subtle gestures. It is through these subtle communications that Amador and Florida and Camila and Lotario fall in love. However, once that love is out in the open, it becomes vulnerable to the pressures of the analytical mode: jealousy, deception, fear, and tragedy. While Anselmo describes himself as the author of his own dishonor, it is actually the analytical mode of narration, mirroring an epistemology of impossible love, that has written it, just as it has written Amador's.

The model of honorable conduct for men and women is debated openly by the *devisants* of Marguerite's tale, and although no one model is identified as the most virtuous, the debate itself is significant in its questioning of and playing with early modern modes of self-governance and reputation management. Cervantes's far more novelistic project does largely the same thing, and indeed both texts include substantial interlacing (a term that Quint uses in *Cervantes's Novel of Modern Times* to indicate "thematic connections between […] episodes" [85]). *Don Quixote*'s premise is the inversion of a minor aristocrat's sense of self-governance and honorable conduct, and each episode of the *Quixote* serves as an inversion of right behavior for the early modern man. Less immediately obvious, perhaps, is the Spanish novel's preoccupation with the range of heterosexual relationships (from friendship to sexual consummation) entangled in the chivalric mythos, as illustrated by Don Quixote's misdirected passion and inability to form what today we would call "healthy" sexual relationships. "El curioso impertinente," diffusing meaning outwards, presents those relationships explicitly. But similar to the *Heptaméron*, no one stable meaning or code of conduct is privileged and both texts, I argue, ultimately question the possibility of truth and honor.

3

# Sign Seeing and Failures of Mind Reading in Lafayette's *La Princesse de Clèves*

*"If you judge from appearances here, [...] you will often be deceived; truth and appearances seldom go together"*[1]

In this chapter, I wish to take a closer look—and the word "look" is loaded—into the particular style that we typically think of as "Baroque"[2] but which is also a key to identifying and analyzing the formal workings of analytical fiction. Ocular metaphors and verbs of seeing and seeming, "to look into," "to appear," "to resemble," and "to watch," appear with increased frequency in literature of the sixteenth and seventeenth centuries. Such empirical accounts of experience and knowledge through visual intelligence are no doubt related to sixteenth-

---

[1] "Si vous jugez sur les apparences en ce lieu-ci, [...] vous serez souvent trompée: ce qui paraît n'est presque jamais la vérité" (Lafayette, *La Princesse de Clèves et Autres Romans* 157). The original text is quoted from the Pingaud edition, while the translations are by John D. Lyons in cases where the pages are cited; other translations are mine.

[2] The term Baroque originally referred to architecture and painting. In *Renaissance and Baroque* (1888), Heinrich Wölfflin defines this movement as a "painterly" style that conveys to the observer a sense of spirit, movement, and psychology. Wölfflin compares the distinction between Renaissance and Baroque as follows: "where the linear style employs the pen or the silver-point, the painterly uses charcoal, red chalk or the broad water-colour brush" (30–31) to make a sketch. The charcoal sketch "works with broad, vague masses, the contours barely indicated [...] [in which] the entire composition [is] made up of areas of light and dark" (31), as opposed to a linear outline. Moreover, "light and shade contain by nature a very strong element of movement [...] a mass of light tends to a movement of dispersal, leading the eye to and fro" (31). This type of work emphasizes at the same time the asymmetry of the individual parts, the grandeur and exaggeration of the whole work, as well as a model of dialectical dual focus that, because the eye is constantly redirected from the parts to the whole, creates a sense of movement and of emotion. In the same way, the element of chiaroscuro "gives an illusion of physical relief, and the different objects seem to project or recede in space" (31), which in *trompe l'oeil*, for example, creates an artificial sense of movement on a flat surface. It is important to note that Wölfflin's preference for sketch over outline directly opposes Aristotle's sense of aesthetics in the *Poetics*: "if an artist were to daub his canvas with the most beautiful colors laid on at random, he would not give the same pleasure as he would by drawing a recognizable portrait in black and white" (40).

and seventeenth-century advances in the study of optics, but are also part of a larger system of knowledge, or *episteme*, developing at this moment in time. McKeon places the interest in the "metaphor of visual sense perception" in a philosophical "revolution [...] that [...] entails a transformation of metaphysics and theology [to] epistemology. [...] Thus, the psychology of the knower, and of his sources, will become paramount" (*Origins* 83) in the rapidly secularizing early seventeenth century. Although, of course, we have witnessed in this study already a great interest in epistemological questions in relation to what characters see and glean from each other from much earlier.

Like Cervantes's challenge to the limits between fiction and reality, we begin to see such investigations in every art form. For example, Foucault begins *The Order of Things* with a long description of Velásquez's painting *Las Meninas*. This work of art can function as a legend for understanding Baroque tropes of illusion not only as contrasting with reality, but as becoming reality itself. *Las Meninas* contains a painting within a painting, a *mise en abyme,* and multiple subjects and scenes acting at once. We see the artist himself on one side in the foreground, forming one end of a central scene with the Infanta Margerita and her entourage. The scene depicts the King and Queen of Spain having their portraits painted. But these subjects are omitted from the foreground, and instead they are reflected in a mirror in the far background and just off-center of the scene; they are two small figures gazing at the spectator as if from a painting within a painting. They are, though central, oddly distant. And then again, they are oddly central, too. Foucault conjectures that what Velasquez manages to show us is the world of "pure representation" (228) or the non-linear ways in which the Baroque mind structures the world in figures of seeing and being seen. Encapsulated within the represented painter's gaze out toward the spectator is "this slender line of reciprocal visibility [that] embraces a whole complex network of uncertainties, exchanges, and feints [...] the observer and the observed take part in a ceaseless exchange" (Foucault 5) between illusion and reality. Indeed, the figure of the painter in the painting is looking at the people he is painting, but in fact, he is looking at the viewer, implicating us in the creation of representation and meaning. In this way, writes Foucault, "no gaze is stable. [...] Subject and object, the spectator and the model, reverse their roles to infinity" (5). The significance of the gaze between subjects both present and absent, or somewhere in between, is reciprocity to the infinite power. The artist insists that the viewer take part in the painting.

A homolog to this study of the meaning of looks and the vocabulary of seeing and seeming can be found in prose. In literature and philosophy, the seventeenth century was an age of anatomizing, of analyzing, and of searching for what may be hidden in plain sight.³ The use of mirrors, verbs of seeing and seeming, and scenes of hiding and spying are far more than tropes in seventeenth-century art and literature; visual metaphors shaped society's way of thinking, "framing" the way a person defined herself as reflected and refracted in the eyes of others. As Julia V. Douthwaite points out, the verb *"voir"* ("to see") appears 419 times in *La Princesse de Clèves* (1678), making it the fourth most frequently used verb in the novel, after *être* ("to be"), *avoir* ("to have"), and *faire* ("to do" or "to make") (in *Approaches to Teaching Lafayette's* La Princesse de Clèves 112). "Seeing" is central to *La Princesse de Clèves*, and: "as a baroque painter might use a mirror to introduce otherwise extraneous objects into a picture, and to give their reflected, stylized presence a certain necessity, which a direct representation would not have, Mme de Lafayette often shows us extraneous material refracted through the intellect of another character" (Kaps 72). In Lafayette's work, "violent passions struggle to find an adequate medium of expression [while] [...] an alternative language of vision subtly competes with words" (Koppisch 757). According to Helen Karen Kaps, *"voir* is often used by Lafayette to represent an intellectual process (understanding, learning), as well as a sensory one" (72). Lyons writes that these verbs "provide the signposts of a novelistic structure based on the characters' constant interpretation of the voluntary and (more often) involuntary physical details that come to their attention [...] for these perceptions are the basis of the inferences that the characters are constantly making" (*Before Imagination* 177). John Campbell also sees verbs like *se représenter, rêver, songer,* and *voir* as verbs "denoting the act of thinking. [...] These terms coexist with expressions pointing to the need to see clearly (e.g., *s'avouer, se reconnaître*), and with others suggesting defeat for any such attempt (e.g., *s'abandonner, se flatter, se tromper*)" (*Questions of Interpretation* 151).

As we will see throughout this chapter, reflections, doubling, spying, and deliberating create in the novel the same kind of vacillation and interior movement as are rendered in Baroque painting. This is not a movement forward, however. Like in other works of analytical fiction, the characters become mired

---

³ According to Dorothy Dallas, the discursive, pastoral, *précieux* novels of writers like Mademoiselle de Scudéry had all but disappeared by 1670, and were replaced by novels wherein "le jeu des passions et l'analyse des sentiments prendront une si grande importance que les auteurs les plus lus seront ceux qui partage toutes les inquiétudes et les joies des personnages" (21) ["the game of passions and the analysis of sentiments take on such a huge importance that the most-read authors were those who made use of characters' anxieties and joys as much as possible"].

in ruminative analysis that stagnates linear time and progress. The movement in the novel takes the form of a *mise en abyme* (as Richard Hodgson points out), that reflects back onto itself. Each sentence in *La Princesse de Clèves* seems to be built out of revisions: truth and counter-truth, insight and counter-insight.

In analytical fiction, being seen means to be caught without one's mask on, but it also means having to examine oneself honestly. It is in this dialectical, doubled, infinitely regressing milieu that Mademoiselle de Chartres, later known as the Princess of Clèves, is exposed for the first time to intrigues and political maneuverings. Beautiful and rich, but having been kept away from society until the age of sixteen, the future princess is naïve about the manner in which courtiers behave. After Mademoiselle de Chartres arrives at court and is married off to the Prince of Clèves, she falls almost immediately in love, in spite of herself and her mother's counsel, with a man who is not her husband. More problematically, she cannot dissimulate indifference, revealing her love for the Duke of Nemours through blushes and bouts of speechlessness (and in fact, several of the characters are rendered speechless on various occasions of being surprised). She falls victim to certain cataleptic impressions—"blind, unbidden surge[s] of painful affect [...] rather course and blunt instrument[s], lacking in responsiveness and discrimination" (Nussbaum 269)—that paralyze the princess in flustered inaction. While the Stoic definition of a cataleptic impression, according to Nussbaum, is "that which is imprinted and impressed by what is real" (270), reality is, of course, subjective in this world governed by skepticism.

Throughout Lafayette's novel, the princess experiences unarticulated, corporeal representations of sensation that Nemours himself, in the novel, identifies as the "the bizarre effects of passion."[4] For example, characters are unable to master their reactions (the princess blushes while Nemours blanches); their *trouble*, trembling, embarrassment, and their experience of bitterness (*aigreur*) are referred to frequently. The princess, her husband, and her would-be lover all lose affective control at some point in the novel, and it destroys their sense of self and place in the world. As I noted in the previous chapter, "involuntary confessions of the flesh," as Nora Martin Peterson delineates them, are "distilled signs of truth, unmarred by the competing codes of courtliness and confession" ("Competing Codes" 251). And for Leah Chang, the blush functions as "a textual figure for reception, for the publication and circulation of the text, and for a privileged relationship between the text and its readers, the intimate relationship

---

[4] "[les] effets bizarres de [la] passion" (245).

of decoding, knowing, and understanding" (20). But self-knowledge can never be complete in *La Princesse de Clèves*, because truth is slippery and unstable. When a character thinks that she knows and understands another, she is usually mistaken, and even bodily signs of truth can be mistaken and misread. We learn at the beginning of Lafayette's novel that the sixteenth-century court of Henri II inhabited by the characters of *La Princesse de Clèves* is unknowable. The advice Madame de Chartres gives her daughter upon her introduction to court life in *La Princesse de Clèves*, which provides the epigraph for this chapter—if one were to judge based on appearances, one would often be mistaken—is representative of Lafayette's worldview as well as of the more general worldview of analytical fiction. This maxim appears early on in *La Princesse de Clèves* and is a focal point to which the novel always returns.

This chapter provides new insight on some of the scenes in *La Princesse de Clèves*—a novel that has been written about extensively—specifically from the point of view of analytical fiction. In highlighting certain episodes that centralize spying, agitation, and conflated emotions, I delineate Lafayette's ironic juxtaposition of the search for truth and the impossibility of knowing, a contrast evidenced throughout the novel. By reexamining scenes of unilateral spying, contradictory or counterintuitive action, as well as the almost-pervasive trope of indescribability—which are ultimately all examples of failed reading—I hope to shed light on the ways that *La Princesse de Clèves* refuses the possibility of real insight. In Lafayette's work, neither marriage, nor love affairs, nor any of the other myriad words for love present in the novel that Campbell cites—*inclination, galanterie, affection, aventure, charme, commerce, passion, intérêt, sentiment, tendresse* (*Questions of Interpretation* 16)—manage to fulfill the mandate of what we today would call love.

Instead, *La Princesse de Clèves* operates on what I have called elsewhere "affective contradictions," or a mingling of emotions, usually pleasure and pain. Spinoza writes that a *"state of mind that arises from two contrary emotions is called wavering of spirit*. Accordingly it is related to emotion as doubt is related to imagination" (108).[5] For example, when Nemours goes to speak to the princess after her mother has died, "Monsieur de Nemours' speech gave her pleasure and offense equally."[6] Later, when the princess half-painfully and

---

[5] Proposition 17 states: "If we imagine that a thing which habitually affects us with an emotion of sadness has some similarity to another thing which habitually affects us with an equally great emotion of joy, we will hate it at the same time as we love it" (108).

[6] "le discours de Monsieur de Nemours lui plaisait et l'offensait quasi également" (193).

half-joyously realizes that she has inadvertently revealed her love to Nemours, "this last impression was not entirely painful, and it was mixed with some sort of tenderness."[7] And only three paragraphs later, when she is led to believe by the dauphine that Nemours loves someone else, her thoughts become so confused that she cannot keep them straight. When Nemours weeps from his hideout near Madame de Clèves' country home, the narrator explains that he is feeling both pleasure and pain, just as earlier he had felt "a hundred times happy and unhappy all together."[8] Similarly, the rumor-tormented Monsieur de Clèves feels a violent chagrin, and yet his pain is also mingled with a sudden feeling of comfort, he *almost* believes his wife's sincerity. This leads to "such painful and opposite feelings that he could not contain himself."[9] When her husband dies, "all these pains mingled,"[10] as the princess feels intermittently distraught at the thought that she was the cause of his death as well as because she had too hastily promised not to marry Nemours afterwards. These affective contradictions steer the narrative back and forth, as it unfolds cyclically and episodically, always doubling back on itself, just as pain follows pleasure.

## A "Douleur Sensible": The Mind in Pain

After the death of the princess's mother (and after the princess has fallen in love with Nemours), the responsibility of educating Madame de Clèves as to the duplicitous nature of courtiers falls to her husband. In a key intercalated scene, Clèves brings the princess an astounding revelation about their friend, Madame de Tournon, a seemingly virtuous young widow who had unexpectedly died the day before. Clèves reports that Madame de Tournon had been involved in two liaisons simultaneously, with Sancerre and with Estouteville, and that she had given each man hope that she would marry him. While Sancerre had gone to Clèves with the devastating news of Estouteville himself (I will analyze Sancerre's shattered emotional state in a moment), Clèves explains that he had discovered Sancerre and Madame de Tournon's affair on his own. He reveals his sagacity and sensitivity to subtle clues and fleeting impressions, performing

---

[7] "cette dernière douleur n'était pas si entière, et elle était mêlée de quelque sorte de douceur" (209).
[8] "cent fois heureux et malheureux tout ensemble" (245).
[9] "des sentiments si opposés et si douloureux qu'il ne les put renfermer en lui-même" (290).
[10] "toutes ces douleurs se confondaient" (295).

a kind of mind-reading on his friends.¹¹ The prince discovers the truth about Sancerre's relationship with Madame de Tournon through a meticulous process of deduction that rests on the assumption that everyone is always hiding their true motivations, and, simultaneously, that everyone also loves to spread gossip. Clèves had heard some time before, through a "network of confidences" (Shoemaker 50), an exciting rumor about the King and Madame de Valentinois from Monsieur d'Anville, which he repeats to his friend Sancerre, swearing him to secrecy. Later, at the house of his sister-in-law, the prince meets Madame de Tournon, whom he overhears spreading the very same gossip that Clèves had told Sancerre. Clèves' sister-in-law then repeats it back to Clèves, not realizing that it was he who had put the gossip item into circulation in the first place. He immediately begins to piece together the truth by watching and listening to the characters. Madame de Tournon looks embarrassed, and he remembers that Sancerre had previously praised her; "all these things opened my eyes, and I soon decided that there was a love-affair between them, and that he had seen her after he left me" (31).¹² In this way, the prince disentangles the mystery of Madame de Tournon's and Sancerre's liaison, with the frequently occurring metaphor of eyes being "opened."

All of this mind-reading and eye-opening may lead the reader to believe that such perceptiveness represents the key to penetrating the truth in Lafayette's novel when characters are unwilling to confess on their own. However, just as we are reading about Madame de Tournon's duplicity, the narrator's attention suddenly turns to Madame de Clèves, who is listening to her husband's tale. The prince's story stirs in the princess a kind of overwhelming anxiety, caused by the fact that she is, herself, secretly in love with another man, although she has not and does not intend to act on her passion. While her husband is reporting to her about Sancerre's anguish at discovering that his mistress was deceiving him, Madame de Clèves blushes, finding that there is "a certain likeness to her own condition which surprised her and distressed her for some time" (32).¹³ But Clèves is so busy recalling how he had ferreted out Madame de Tournon's treachery that he misses his wife's tacit confession of her own adulterous feelings. Unable to recognize his wife's suffering, the story of Madame de Tournon leads Clèves to

---

[11] With the term "mind-reading" I mean to reference Lisa Zunshine's *Why We Read Fiction: Theory of Mind and the Novel* (especially 123–53 on the "concealing mind" in the detective novel).

[12] "Toutes ces choses m'ouvrirent les yeux, et je n'eus pas de peine à démêler qu'il avait une galanterie avec elle, et qu'il l'avait vue depuis qu'il m'avait quitté" (179).

[13] "un certain rapport avec l'état où elle était, qui la surprit, et qui lui donna un trouble dont elle fut longtemps à se remettre" (181).

ironically pronounce that he is pleased to have a spouse as faultless as his own, since as a group, "women are incomprehensible" (29).¹⁴ This misreading, or really lack of reading, as it is an ellipsis on the prince's part—no less at a moment when he is demonstrating his remarkable ability to extract knowledge at court— highlights Lafayette's use of an ironic structure that centralizes, simultaneously, a kind of plumbing of the psyche and an almost systematic drive toward self-deception.

Throughout the novel Lafayette contrasts Madame de Clèves' not-yet-fully-realized pain as she struggles to understand her own misplaced passion with Clèves' arrogant self-deception. Clèves considers himself an excellent mind-reader, and in fact, he often is.¹⁵ But his occasional inability to understand his wife's emotions reveals his interpretative shortcomings. This interpolated scene about Sancerre and Madame de Tournon also contrasts Clèves' (unwarranted) self-confidence and composure with Sancerre's delirious outpouring of emotion: on the day that Madame de Tournon has died, Sancerre (his name confirms both the ease with which she deceives him and the transparency of his passions) hyperbolizes that no one has ever felt such pains at once: "I suffer at the same time grief for her death and for her faithlessness—two misfortunes which have often been compared, but have never been felt at the same time by one person" (34).¹⁶ Annihilated by ambivalence and antagonistic passions, Sancerre declares that "all my feelings are wrong" (35)¹⁷ because he is caught in an in-between state, receiving neither consolation from her death nor is he able to hate her. Affective contradictions abound and he is overtaken by chaos and negation, he feels love and loathing at once, and sees himself as incomparably suffering. Later in the novel, Clèves will also undergo a violent affective upheaval and will utter the same sorts of ravings as Sancerre—a loss of control that ultimately leads to his death—ironically forgetting both his own falsely prophetic advice, that if his wife were to confess that she was in love with someone else that he would be "distressed without being angered, and should lay aside the character of [...]

---

¹⁴ "les femmes sont incompréhensibles" (174).

¹⁵ For example, he famously interprets his wife's blushes as coming from modesty, rather than love, early in the novel. Because the princess has not yet felt passionately about anyone, she cannot even dissimulate loving her husband. She protests, claiming that propriety keeps her from expressing her emotions, but again, the prince is not fooled; he intuits that the princess is only using propriety as a cover for her lack of passion. He correctly perceives that she is merely putting on a kind of performance, without even knowing it. Yet, in this scene, Clèves does not notice his wife turn red.

¹⁶ "j'éprouve à la fois la douleur de la mort et celle de l'infidélité; ce sont deux maux que l'on a souvent comparés, mais qui n'ont jamais été sentis en même temps par la même personne" (185).

¹⁷ "tous mes sentiments sont injustes" (185).

husband to advise and sympathize with her" (32)[18] and his pronouncement that luckily, his own wife, Madame de Clèves, is uncomplicated and virtuous.

Lafayette also counteracts almost every instance of sagacity and penetration with a contrasting impression evidenced through blushing, paling, trembling, speechlessness, and vaguely articulated sensations of *trouble* (agitation or turmoil), *inquietude* (anxiety), and a state of being *accablé* (overwhelmed or overtaken). Physio-mental states are rendered through feeling, as in the phrase "*une douleur sensible*," a felt or visible pain suggesting sorrow and anguish, which is used numerous times throughout the novel to explain, in turns, the recognition of unrequited love, coping with the death of a child, and the realization of one's requited love. In English, the word "feeling," of course, has the double meaning of "sensible" and something akin to "emotion." In French, the word "douleur" can mean both physical and mental pain. This elusive, somatic language creates an affective environment of anxiety, shame, and distrust in *La Princesse de Clèves*. Pain in the body and mental pain conflate in this novel. In fact, one of the most powerful non-verbal signs in Lafayette's text is the tendency for characters to fall ill when they are unhappy. Monsieur de Clèves becomes sick from a strong mental agitation, and even dies of a broken heart.

Instead of physical descriptions (we learn very little about what the characters look like), Lafayette reveals psychical ones, delving into characters' motivations in order to reveal something akin to the corporeal. It is only rarely that the narrator describes actual physical movement in this novel; even the word "movement" is more often than not used metaphorically, referring to the heart. During the *aveu*, Clèves stands immobilized, "outside of himself [...] he thought he would die of anguish."[19] Then, in a scene that is parallel to the one that recounts Sancerre's suffering, after Clèves is mistakenly led to believe that his wife has had an affair with Nemours, "on all sides he saw nothing but precipices and steep abysses" (78).[20] Clèves becomes increasingly jealous, not a little bit because Nemours openly boasts about being in love and being loved back and the story circulates. Clèves confronts his wife, and seems to have gone mad: "I am torn by wild and uncertain feelings that I cannot control; I

---

[18] "j'en serais affligé sans en être aigri. Je quitterais le personnage [...] de mari, pour la conseiller et pour la plaindre" (181).
[19] "hors de lui même [...] il pensa mourir de douleur" (241). The same language is used when Nemours spies on the princess alone in her *cabinet* as she gazes at a painting of the siege of Metz, which features a portrait of himself. He is transfixed, and is "tellement hors de lui-même" (282) ["so much outside of himself"], indicating the similarities between the two men.
[20] "il ne trouvait de tous côtés que des précipices et des abîmes" (261).

find myself no longer worthy of you—you seem no more worthy of me. I adore you and I hate you. [...] I have lost all my calmness, all my reason" (87–8).[21] On his deathbed, Cleves threatens his wife that no one else will love her the way he did, and that someday someone will hurt her the way she is injuring him. As Campbell points out, "*agitation, incertitude, douleur, tristesse* are henceforth the paradoxical expressions of something called 'love' which brings [the Prince] to an early grave" (*Questions of Interpretation* 29). Clèves's suffering is exacerbated by his ambivalence as an unusual man who had loved his wife as a lover; in a statement that echoes Sancerre's pronouncement of singularity, he feels "at the same time a mistress's infidelity and the mortification of being deceived by a wife" (94).[22] Clèves' astonishment at being faced with what he believes is the truth—that his wife has deceived him with Nemours—overturns the entire worldview that he had blindly constructed for himself, and it ultimately kills him. When Clèves loses control of his emotions—when he not only becomes violently jealous but admits the jealousy to his wife—he also loses the strict, calm, calculating persona that had been so easy to maintain when his friend suffered. His heart having been broken, Cleves, like Sancerre, feels annihilated. His speech when he confronts the princess becomes fragmented and composed of contradictions, and his comprehension of himself, his wife, and the world disintegrates into ambivalence. To lose control over one's power to dissimulate in this novel is to lose oneself. His death is the death of the strategically constructed image of the self under which, ultimately, is left only ambivalence, fear, and pain.

According to the dictionary of the Académie français, 1694, the word "agitation" signals a sense of movement, or vacillation, but also meant, in the seventeenth century, "distress and passions."[23] A century later, the word had come to mean, figuratively, "the kind of distress that the passions create in the soul."[24] These agitations signal a profound sense of instability that influences

---

[21] "Je n'ai que des sentiments violents et incertains dont je ne suis pas le maître: je ne me trouve plus digne de vous; vous ne me paraissez plus digne de moi; je vous adore, je vous hais [...] il n'y a plus en moi ni de calme ni de raison" (276–7).

[22] "en même temps la douleur que cause l'infidélité d'une maîtresse et la honte d'être trompé par une femme" (289). This not only renders his experience parallel to Sancerre's, but also recalls and inverts another story that Madame de Chartres's tells her daughter: the example of a woman who mourns the coincidentally simultaneous deaths of both her husband—a man for whom, like the princess, she felt no particular inclination—and her lover, so that the tears she sheds are genuine, thanks to the death of the more beloved man: "elle eut ce prétexte pour cacher sa véritable affliction, sans avoir la peine de se contraindre" (160) ("she was able to conceal her real grief without an effort" [21]).

[23] "des troubles et des passions."

[24] "[le] trouble que les passions causent dans l'âme" (ARTFL Project).

characters in visceral ways. As Peter H. Nurse notes in his introduction to the 1970 Harrap edition of *La Princesse de Clèves*, "in spite of the calmness of the surface of things, [...] *La Princesse de Clèves* can generate an unsurpassed intensity of emotion" (xxix). Nurse uses the word "intensity" again when he characterizes Lafayette's style as an example of free indirect discourse, in which "the broken rhythms of the prose contribute to accentuate the exceptional intensity of the inner conflict" (xxxi). Similarly, Gilles Deleuze and Félix Guattari discuss free indirect discourse (though not specifically in the context of Lafayette's work) as having "exemplary value: there are no clear, distinctive contours; what comes first is not an insertion of variously individuated statements, or an interlocking of different subjects of enunciation, but a collective assemblage resulting in the determination of relative subjectification proceedings, or assignations of individuality and their shifting distributions within discourse" (80). The double meaning of "*agitation*" in the court of Henri II (when it is described as being full of "agitation sans désordre" [143]) highlights the importance of constant movement—on the one hand, a kind of "collective assemblage" of voices and passions that make it exciting, both for the courtiers within the novel and for readers, and on the other hand, an unending stirring of passions (which is also linked with words like *trouble* and *saisissement* [seizing]) that renders it so dangerous for a young person like Madame de Clèves.

Before the princess even recognizes that she is in love with Nemours, "her interest in the prince caused an agitation which she could not control. [...] Hence she sat without saying a word" (39).[25] Further on, when the princess believes that Nemours loves another woman, she is left "so astonished and agitated that she could scarcely move" (49).[26] We witness the same phenomenon in Nemours when he feels "such a great confusion of strange thoughts [...] [that] made it impossible for him to control his face. [...] [It] so seized him that he could not answer."[27] The narrator hovers over Nemours' ambiguity and inaction almost to absurdity—in a novel with so many ellipses (as Joan DeJean points out) and that is characterized by such economy of language—in the dedication of several paragraphs to Nemours' passionate deliberations in the

---

[25] "l'inclination qu'elle avait pour ce prince lui donnait un trouble dont elle n'était pas maîtresse. [...] Elle demeurait donc sans répondre" (193).
[26] "si étonnée et dans un si grand saisissement qu'elle fut quelque temps sans pouvoir sortir de sa place" (210).
[27] "une si grand confusion de pensées bizarres qu'il lui fut impossible d'être maître de son visage. [...] [Ça] lui causa un saisissement qui ne lui permit pas de répondre" (255).

*cabinet* scene, to the extent that it renders the passage rather ironic. Spying on the princess while she is alone in her room, resolving now to make himself seen and to speak to her, and again recoiling in fear of alarming her or making her angry, the duke waivers in front of the princess's window. Then, because this moment may have lasted forever if it were not interrupted, a hasty movement forward makes Nemours' scarf catch on something, making an unexpected noise that startles the princess, and sends her fleeing from the room. She believes that she has *almost* seen him, and then rationalizes that perhaps it was an effect of her imagination.[28]

## Ellipsis and Narrative Refusal

The description of emotion in *La Princesse de Clèves* varies widely. On the one hand, we witness extreme outpourings of emotion like Sancerre's and Clèves's, which are gendered masculine, whereas, by contrast, the women in the novel, save for the princess, are models of affective opacity (and it is the minor female characters' ability to live double lives that contrast the princess's—and many of the men's—lack of emotional self-control[29]). But just as frequently as the characters feel overwhelmed or agitated by their emotions, the language of feeling is omitted, and Lafayette employs the trope of indescribability that indicates it is the reader's responsibility to understand them. Lafayette often employs the pronoun "on" to suggest, rather than describe, the mental or physical states of the characters. The princess's pain (*douleur*) is unprecedented and often described as unspeakable. When Nemours is spying on Madame de Clèves in the cabinet scene, the narrator reports that it would be impossible to express what he is feeling. When an emotion is extremely strong, it cannot be articulated; when the princess is stirred by jealousy, it cannot be represented.

---

[28] "un effet de son imagination" (283). Soon, however, the princess resolves to remain unsure: "elle trouva qu'il valait mieux demeurer dans le doute où elle était que de prendre le hasard de s'en éclaircir" (283) ["she found that it would be better to remain doubtful than to take the risk of discovering the truth"]. Madame de Clèves is so intoxicated by her internal vision of Nemours, and she has so entirely lost herself in her daydreaming, she no longer maintains control over herself. This idea of remaining "dans le doute" even further illustrates Lafayette's tendency to forestall the movement forward of the plot.

[29] Besides Madame de Tournon, about whom I wrote above, another example is that of the queen. At the beginning of *La Princesse de Clèves*, we learn that the queen's calm and her tolerance of the king's mistress stems from an almost unprecedented self-control ("une si profonde dissimulation" [130] ["such a profound ability to dissimulate"]) and an "humeur ambitieuse" (130) ["ambitious nature"]).

When she is truly mortified, her agitation and embarrassment are rendered "outside of what can be imagined,"[30] or after the death of the princess's husband, the narrator reports that "the horror that she felt for herself and for Monsieur de Nemours cannot be expressed. [...] This princess's pain transcended the boundaries of reason."[31]

Through the ironic combination of hyperbole and narrative silence—one term that might be used is *adynaton*, a comparison to the impossible or "a confession that words fail us" (Lanham 3), or simply, a refusal to tell—*La Princesse de Clèves'* narrator elides emotions. Both DeJean and François comment on Lafayette's taciturn style more generally as one that readers "must read between the lines: they must interpret (verbalize) the unsaid and even the unsayable, for the language of Lafayette's heroine is a language of lack, of silence, of repression, of gaps" (DeJean 899), and as "a mode of presenting in such a way as to withhold, of giving in such a way as to neutralize the value of the gift" (François 70). DeJean's groundbreaking essay focuses on Lafayette's use of ellipsis, ("simultaneously absence and presence, ellipsis gives a plenitude to silence" [DeJean 890]), pointing out the central omissions of Lafayette's narrative. On the other hand, I am interested in something a bit different. As Arielle Saiber points out, ellipsis differs from adynaton in that ellipsis "is an incomplete expression. [...] [It] leaves something out—something to be understood by the reader" (128) (an example would be when the narrator implies that she casts doubt on her own understanding of Madame de Clèves' motivation just before the cabinet scene. The narrator tells us that Nemours' portrait was among those that hung in her house "and that was *perhaps* why Madame de Clèves cared for the pictures" [87, emphasis added][32]). Whereas adynaton is "a device in which the speaker says that he or she must stop speaking because words cannot convey what he or she wishes to say" (Saiber 128).

Even while the narrator purports not to know herself, we comprehend the princess's turmoil. There is a certain transfer of knowledge that happens through the very suspension of descriptive emotional language throughout the novel.

---

[30] "au-delà de tout ce que l'on peut s'imaginer" (255). In French, it is worth noting, "on" creates an insular subjective environment, folding the narrator and reader into the text because of its double meaning of "one" and, colloquially, "we," whereas the English "one" does not entirely capture that inclusion, especially when it is translated by the passive voice. I am grateful to Jason Schneiderman for pointing this out to me.

[31] "l'horreur qu'elle eut pour elle-même et pour Monsieur de Nemours ne se peut représenter [...] La douleur de cette princesse passait les bornes de la raison" (294).

[32] "et c'était *peut-être* ce qui avait donné envie à Madame de Clèves d'avoir ces tableaux" (278, emphasis added).

This transfer is perhaps expressed best by a word that Lafayette uses often, an "impression" that is transmitted based on the anxious affective atmosphere that is established early on by the princess's mother and by the exemplary (or, rather, counter-exemplary) stories that are told to emphasize for the princess the nature of dissimulation in the court. The "impression" also recalls the idea of cataleptic or grasped knowledge discussed earlier. As Chang puts it, the princess arrives at court a *tabula rasa* (15), with white skin presenting itself to be written upon. The idea of the impression is figurative, of course, but nevertheless evocative of some kind of physical mark, some kind of depression or imprint on the character's being—on that blank slate—that stays. The cataleptic impressions of *La Princesse de Clèves* are inconsequential—they will not change the princess's course of action—and thus they cannot function in the Stoic sense of the term as knowledge (Nussbaum 267). Instead, they are traumatic experiences that might have produced self-knowledge were self-knowledge possible. However, since it is not—since a doubt or a false impression is just as powerful as a truthful one, or because truth is always subjective in Lafayette's world—the princess's experiences of love and jealousy, pain and pleasure, remain confused and opaque, but no less real. They are still imprinted on her psyche. Even when change is impossible, the felt—even if ineffable—pain of experience remains. Just as in the *Elegia*, where Fiammetta claims that language is an inadequate medium to describe her trauma, Lafayette, by transferring emotional and other knowledge to the realm of imagination, simultaneously negates knowledge. Thus, knowledge is sublimated into mere being.

At the end of the novel, just before she moves to a convent, the princess famously says to Nemours, who has come to confess his love, that "passions can drive me, but they will never blind me."[33] The princess knows that her passions will always steer her. But at the same time, she will not allow herself to fall off that precipice, however artificial she realizes it is. Throughout the novel, the repetition of the verb *voir* has, as Campbell puts it, "a near hallucinatory effect" for the princess looking at Nemours. "Perhaps because of the '*tabou* of physical contact,' the mere fact of being in his presence, of looking at him and allowing him to gaze at her, is a kind of surrender" (Campbell, *Questions of Interpretation* 29). At some point, the princess simply stops looking; Campbell calls it her "last line of defense" to avoid Nemours' presence. By refusing to see him, the princess thinks that she is avoiding succumbing to blindness. It is the same refusal to see,

---

[33] "les passions peuvent me conduire; mais elles ne sauraient m'aveugler" (306).

to tell, to articulate, that the narrator has espoused all along. Even the princess rejects epistemology at the end in favor of first, just being, and then not being, as equivalent states. She wishes to make herself "impossible to tell" and impossible to see.

## Sign Seeing

It seems, on first reading, that *La Princesse de Clèves* begins where most novels end: with a marriage. However, on closer inspection, we see that Lafayette's text actually starts with the subject of infidelity ("the magnificence and the gallantry [...] in the last years of the reign of Henri II,"[34] wherein "galanterie" means "love affair") and a digression on the power of Diane de Poitiers, the king's mistress (a full two paragraphs before the queen, his wife, is mentioned). As Hodgson puts it, the princess lives "in a society in which the King's infidelity has become institutionalized and in which politics is such a dangerous game, [that] *agitation* is an integral part of every facet of social life" (59). For example, the queen, as I mentioned already, is ambitious and loves to rule, so she tolerates the fact that her husband keeps the Duchesse de Valentinois as a mistress. She is so capable of dissimulating her true feelings that they are completely inscrutable to many members of the court, although this also functions as an open secret. Thus, the significance of infidelity is not a moral problem; everyone has affairs. Instead, its implications lie in psychology and social mores, and the darker, hidden effects on the psyche that cause *trouble* and *agitation*, a stirring of the passions, especially if anyone else were to discover the infidelity. The courtiers in Lafayette's novel must constantly decode each other's dissimulations, and must persistently be on the lookout for deceptive behavior. To understand this complex social matrix, characters must interpret the signs correctly; but very often, they merely see them. This focus on not just decoding—but failed decoding—throughout *La Princesse de Clèves* frames Lafayette's work not only as a history or a romance, nor as a text that merely wishes to expose corruption at the court, but rather as a fully developed *roman d'analyse* that aims to reveal the limitations of introspection. From a narrative point of view, the infidelities and cover-ups that make up the plot, or, rather, plots, of *La Princesse de Clèves* demonstrate that the text is written in point and counter-point; false

---

[34] "la magnificence et la galanterie [...] dans les dernières années du règne de Henri second" (129).

belief is soon followed up by a harsh reality, followed by a new layer of self-deception. Despite the potentially dangerous motif—and moreover in a novel that has been long considered a *roman à clef* for seventeenth-century politics—Lafayette exploits infidelity as a metaphor for dissimulation and the way in which appearances are invariably deceiving. The uncertainty and sense of fear evidenced throughout the novel casts a darker shadow over the purported "magnificence" of the court.[35]

How do characters in *La Princesse de Clèves* fall in love? The Prince of Clèves sees Mademoiselle de Chartres and loves her not only in spite of her very indifference, but even because of it. In other words, he loves her because of the signs she *does not* give him. As the princess points out much later, the prince's passion is fueled by searching for something that she cannot give him. The fact that his wife is calm and untroubled in and of itself troubles the prince, and that augments his passion even more. And though she gives him no reason to feel jealous, he seems to be almost searching for that feeling, loving her all the more not only in spite of her absence of love, but because of it (at the end of the novel, she says, "perhaps, too, his love only survived because he found none in me" [103][36]). This is again a repetition of Montaigne's maxim that we overmuch desire the things that we do not have.

During the first part of the novel, we see into the mind of the princess only when her thoughts and feelings are guessed at by other characters, such as her mother and the prince de Clèves. Against her mother's wishes, she becomes a set of signs or an open book to be read and interpreted. From Clèves, who is as desperate to win Mademoiselle de Chartres's affections as he is to marry her, we learn that while she is kind to him, it is his own passion and his own desire that drives his feelings for her. In fact, Mademoiselle de Chartres is indifferent to him, leading him to feel dissatisfied after they are married. He enumerates the signs that she reveals and the ones that she lacks, namely passion, impatience, and agitation, signs that he would interpret as proofs of love. Thus, a dark cloud hovers over the Clèves' marriage, evidenced by a pessimistic tinge and a certain irony that permeates the description of the prince's state of mind.

---

[35] In fact, there are many tragedies in the novel, indicating that there is occasional disorder: the Vidame de Chartres is exiled because he is caught deceiving the queen, the king dies as a result of a horrible accident, the Prince de Clèves dies of a broken heart, and outside of the story, the dauphine, Mary Stuart, is executed by Elizabeth I.

[36] "peut-être aussi que sa passion n'avait subsisté que parce qu'il n'en aurait pas trouvé en moi." (306).

The Princess and Nemours fall in love indirectly, by way of surprises, subtle clues, and the things they hear said about each other. These are not the overt declarations of the prince, which only serve to push the princess away from him. Lafayette's narrative is built on these kinds of clues and signs, these *marques de l'admiration*. Gestures, looks, and occasionally speech are interpreted not only for their surface meaning, but also for the motivations, beliefs, and feelings behind them, and for clues as to how a character has interpreted and reinterpreted what another character has said or done. A poorly read sign can also catapult a character into a state of extreme bliss or terrible suffering, and yet they cannot stop themselves from engaging in looking for signs. Although the trajectory of the princess and Nemours' relationship is quite different than that of Camila and Lotario's in the Cervantes story discussed in the previous chapter, there are tangible correspondences between Clèves and Anselmo. Neither can be satisfied with the love he is given, and they both torture themselves to death with their jealousy. However, the princess does not understand, cannot even conceive of love, until she meets and falls in love at first sight with Nemours.

When Nemours and the princess first meet, Lafayette uses the vocabulary of *surpris* and *étonnement*; these "belles personnes" ("beautiful people") who are, like Florida and Amador, the most beautiful people at court, are surprised and astonished to meet each other. Given her lack of experience in love affairs, the princess does not yet recognize the signs that her passions reveal to her, and her reason and knowledge lag far behind. The narrator reveals the princess's thoughts (beyond her earlier embarrassment and confusion) for the first time only after she becomes cognizant of her love. Meanwhile the thoughts and deliberations of Nemours take center stage.

A few paragraphs after they meet, Nemours' passion for the princess has grown so strong that he needs to send out false messages that confuse everyone into thinking he is in love with the princess's friend the reine dauphine. He begins to frequent the dauphine's salon more often than usual, because Madame de Clèves spends a good deal of time there, and also because he wishes people to intuit what they will. This is, again, reminiscent of the *Heptaméron* in its levels of strategy. Even passionately in love, Nemours very carefully plans out how to go about pursuing the princess without revealing too many signs at once, and without allowing anyone to guess the truth about his intentions.

The scene of the princess and Nemours' mutual absence at the ball given by the Maréchal de Saint-André functions similarly, although the outcome, as we will see, is ultimately inconsequential. The Princess overhears a courtier say that Nemours believes that a woman who is in love with a man should attend a ball that he gives, but should abstain from going to someone else's ball if he will not be present. Being immediately affected by this theory, the princess decides that she will not attend the Maréchal's ball while Nemours is away in England (supposedly wooing the future queen Elizabeth), and uses both the pretexts of illness and that the Maréchal had been in love with her (and it would seem inappropriate for her to attend the party of a man who may still harbor feelings for her). Thus, as Peggy Kamuf puts it, she "had contrived to send an encouraging message to Nemours through […] absence" (217). She also wishes to send the duke a sign of her affection by merely listening to and following his advice. In this way, the two lovers send each other furtive signs, sometimes unintentionally, sometimes intentionally. The princess's absence speaks in such a way as to send him a positive sign of her love, although she cannot be sure that he will ever discern her meaning.

One would think that the princess's decision not to attend the ball, and the duke's learning that information, is significant to illustrate a growing intimacy between them, all communicated by mutual absence. However, that is not the way in which the story is resolved. In fact, there is no definite knowledge gained at all. When the princess appears at the dauphine's a few days later, looking quite healthy, the dauphine repeats the rule that Nemours had developed, teasing Madame de Clèves about being in love. Nemours, of course, happens to be there as well. The princess is embarrassed and her mother—realizing, by her daughter's blush, that the dauphine had guessed correctly that it had to do with feelings of love—assures the party that her daughter had indeed been very ill. The duke, too, sees the princess's blush, and he suddenly feels the pleasure of suspecting that he has discovered the truth about the princess, that she is in love with him and that that accounts for her absence at the ball. The princess does not know what to think. The narrator tells us that at first Madame de Clèves is perturbed because she realizes that she had let slip signs of her true feelings for Nemours and that he had suspected it, but then, simultaneously, she feels a twinge of regret at her mother's completely dispelling that notion. Madame de Chartres, for her part, is not entirely sure whether she has succeeded in intercepting the message, and she ends on shaky ground. Nemours, in turn, has his attention pulled away from the princess as he becomes wary of the Maréchal, whom he intuits as a rival who constantly observes Madame de Clèves and himself (since he is also in love with the princess). The focus of the scene then passes on from insight to this idea of spying and observation. In this way, Madame de Chartres's message is lost because Nemours becomes distracted by jealousy.

Nevertheless, signs are occasionally interpreted correctly, although they remain inconsequential. During the horoscope scene that takes place in the Queen's rooms, Nemours and the princess, forced to be together by circumstance and coincidence, are engaged in a conversation about whether or not to believe in horoscopes and predictions. Nemours teases Madame de Clèves by whispering in her ear that he does not believe in horoscopes because it was once predicted to him that his ardent passion would be returned by the woman he loves. Meanwhile, the princess is trying to avoid Nemours, but does not manage to completely steel herself when he begins to whisper to her. She attempts to ignore and avoid him, but in spite of herself, "certain things inadvertently escaped her which convinced this prince that she was not indifferent to him" (42).[37] While a man with less penetration than the duke would perhaps not have noticed, Nemours is able to pick up on the princess's small and unintentional signs very quickly. As we saw in the analysis of earlier texts, in analytical fiction, love between characters is often expressed in understatement; "I do not dislike you" becomes code for "I feel a violent passion for you." The litotes in the passage above ("qu'il ne lui était pas indifférent") is striking and highlights the subtlety of the messages the princess is inadvertently sending the duke. In fact, he notices that she was working hard *not* to send him any signs, which then functions to *alert* Nemours of her growing affection.

## Scenes of Unilateral Spying

It is often through spying that the characters are able to catch glimpses of the truth—the truth about their own feelings, that is. This interest in watching is evidenced, for example, in the episode in which Nemours steals the princess's portrait, and she is paralyzed by fear and embarrassment in a moment of tension between not two, but three characters. The passage follows the gaze of the princess, Nemours, and the reine dauphine:

> Madame de Clèves was able to see Monsieur de Nemours […] pick up something from [the] table. She at once guessed that it was her portrait. […]

---

[37] "certaines choses qui partaient d'un premier mouvement, qui faisaient juger à ce prince qu'il ne lui était pas indifférent" (198).

The crown princess noticed and asked her what she was looking at. At these words Monsieur de Nemours turned round and met Madame de Clèves's eyes fastened on him. (45)[38]

Here, Madame de Clèves is caught, *in ambiguo*, between two very sagacious characters, the dauphine who is reclining on the bed, and Nemours who is standing at the table, hidden from the dauphine by a curtain. The act of stealing the portrait reveals, in this tumultuous moment of the princess's *anagnorisis*, the fact that Nemours is indeed in love with her, something which up to this point had been unclear. Locking eyes with Nemours, he seems to almost dare her to say something, ensuring, in fact, that she will say nothing. Simultaneously, her attention is pulled away by the dauphine, who also dares her to admit what she is looking at. Nothing is actually said directly in this rather cinematic, long passage (only the narrator reporting that the dauphine asks the princess what is distracting her), further highlighting the delay of action and narrative *durée*.

In spite of Valincour's objection to this scene,[39] it would have been impossible to casually ask Nemours to pass her the portrait so she could examine it, or to make light of his having held it, because in this moment she realizes for the first time—although it takes, in fact, her husband to jokingly accuse the princess of having given the portrait to a secret lover for her to fully realize it—her deep and requited love for Nemours. To disrupt that speechless *durée* would collapse the effect of the long gaze and tacit understanding, uncomfortable though it is, that the princess and her would-be lover share. It also would disallow the opportunity for the narrator to report to the reader, again, using the language of agency, that the princess "found that she was no longer in control of her words and of her face."[40] Unable to speak because of everything she has seen, she falls victim to

---

[38] "Madame de Clèves aperçut [...] Monsieur de Nemours [...] prenait adroitement quelque chose sur [la] table. Elle n'eut pas de peine à deviner que c'était son portrait. [...] La Dauphine remarqua qu'elle ne l'écoutait pas et lui demande tout haut ce qu'elle regardait. Monsieur de Nemours se tourna à ces paroles; il rencontra les yeux de Madame de Clèves, qui était encore attachés sur lui" (202–3). For a very different reading of this scene, see François, who writes that when the princess "is not avowing to disavow desire [...] she is passively assenting to it, but so passively as to make her 'yes' weightless" (69).

[39] Jean-Baptiste-Henri de Valincour, in his *Lettres à la marquise de *** sur "La Princesse de Clèves,"* which appeared only months after the publication of Lafayette's novel, addresses the episode of the portrait: "there were a hundred ways to get it back from him without making a scene and without letting anyone suspect the love he felt for her. [...] She could have asked him for it right out loud [...] She could have asked him for it in an amused way and pretend that he had been trying to hide it as a prank" (Trans. John D. Lyons, Norton Edition 127). These ideas, though inspired, would have required a far less naïve and innocent spirit than Madame de Clèves.

[40] "trouva qu'elle n'était plus maîtresse de ses paroles et de son visage" (204).

the recursive narrative patterns of analytical fiction. And by not knowing what to think or say, the princess remains for some time longer an inscrutable object to be observed, while also an observer herself.

The much-written about avowal scene also particularly illustrates the way in which the search for impossible knowledge functions in analytical fiction. While I cannot hope to provide an entirely new reading of Madame de Clèves' confession to her husband that she loves another man, my goal is to relate it to the larger idea of the *roman d'analyse* to illustrate how the famous *aveu* is incomplete and hindered by silences and misunderstandings, and is full of self-deception and lack of self-knowledge. I also wish to highlight Nemours' involvement in the episode, since he is spying on the couple as Madame de Clèves confesses. The scene begins when the princess tells her husband that she wishes to withdraw from the court and live at Coulommiers, the Clèves' country estate. Clèves is immediately suspicious, and pressures her to tell him what secret she is hiding: "for a long time, the prince besought her to tell him the reason" (66).[41] In truth, the princess says very little. She admits only that her behavior is "innocent" and that she never succumbed to any "weakness" that she may fear. She merely begs her husband to allow her to stay away from Paris. Ultimately, the princess only half confesses, because not only does she refuse to tell her husband the name of the man with whom she is in love, she never utters the words "love" or even "man." It is her husband who supplies the details with his own imagination while the princess implores him to stop asking questions. In this way, the avowal is both preceded and followed by silence and by the prince's frustration at his wife's refusal to speak. That is not to say that the avowal hardly exists; on the contrary, it is very real and causes a great deal of damage. The "confession's" essence, however, is in itself a troubling and enigmatic absence that the prince can only fill in with jealousy and fear. At this point in the novel, however, the princess has already made up her mind about rejecting Nemours. As she tells him at the end, "this avowal will have no consequences, and I shall follow the rigid rules that my condition imposes" (102).[42] The princess's husband, in fact, never does find direct evidence of the princess's infidelity. But it does not matter. The infidelities of the court confirm the prince's fears, without the need for his wife to actually be culpable. In many ways, she is guilty merely by association and by the misprision that he had already formed in his mind, regardless of her.

---

[41] "Il la pressa longtemps de les [raisons] lui apprendre sans pouvoir l'y obliger" (239–40).
[42] "enfin cet aveu n'aura point de suite, et je suivrai les règles austères que mon devoir m'impose" (303).

As to the role that Nemours plays in this scene, his lack of knowledge of the princess's heart is what leads him to misunderstand her avowal. He believes, in fact, in typical analytical fiction-style, that she must be speaking of yet another, *a third man*, since he assumes that he has many rivals. The narrator claims that he heard every word the princess said, and yet these words: "made him quite as jealous as it made her husband" (67).[43] In this way, Nemours, even being on the outside of the conversation, cannot see anything differently or more correctly than Clèves. Nemours, who, by his spying becomes part of the scene and yet remains outside of it (since his name is also integral to the confession, although it is never spoken), is burning with curiosity. The narrator reveals that Nemours stands there, furious with the princess's husband for not insisting that she tell him the name of the man with whom she is in love. Were Nemours less self-deceived, he could potentially enjoy this experience, rather than taking on the same role as Monsieur de Clèves, that of a jealous husband dying to know about his wife's infidelity. Like the relationship between Anselmo and Lotario, their mutual curiosity and desire actually pairs the two men against the princess.

Nemours' misreading of the princess's words adds another layer to what François calls the "uncounted [...] undoing, unthreading, unraveling with which narrative itself has come to be identified" (13) in the *aveu* scene. For François, the princess's avowal "would 'disclaim' or 'un-claim' love (claim it so as to leave it untouched) and still not amount to disavowal in the sense of a denied, unconscious, or evasive affirmative" (13). In the same way, Nemours "disclaims" or "un-claims" the very possibility of the princess's love for him which is embroidered into her avowal. He misses the point of it, ignores the confession's true significance for himself, and renders himself even more self-deceived than even the princess's husband. Nemours's self-deception is representative of the analytical mode in general, characterized by these misread signs that cyclically affirm and deny themselves, such that the impossibility of knowledge is a foregone conclusion. Moreover, this self-deception serves to distance the would-be lovers even farther apart, at just the moment that should act to bring them closer together in mutual knowledge and intuition.

Something very similar happens in the park scene, another episode of unilateral spying. The princess notices that she can see her own window through that of a silk merchant's shop opposite her garden. The merchant tells her that

---

[43] "ne lui donnait guère moins de jalousie qu'à son mari" (242).

a man often sits in the back room of the shop sketching the houses and gardens that can be seen from the window. The princess's imagination automatically inserts the figure of Nemours into this scene, and while of course she cannot be sure, the silk merchant's words immediately conjure for her an image of her love-object. In both the cabinet and park scenes, the princess blames her overactive imagination for inventing a vision of Nemours. In a realistic novel, this sort of imagining would probably be just a psychologically significant accident of thought; Nemours would not actually have to be there for the princess to daydream about him. On the contrary, in *La Princesse de Clèves*, the ghost- or fantasy-Nemours is really present, although the princess convinces herself that the truth was only an illusion. The princess, full of the image of Nemours spying on her from the silk merchant's window, goes out into a garden in the hopes of being alone. But there, she sees none other than Nemours. She stops and watches him, but he does not notice her, while he lies on a bench, deep in thought. As in the cabinet scene, while the princess is gazing at Nemours (though now it is the real man, rather than merely his portrait) who is lost in his thoughts of her, the scene represents both hope and possibility of intimacy. At the same time, understanding and consummation fail, because, like the avowal, there is "point de suite," there is nothing more. Just as the princess is gazing at Nemours, her servants suddenly make a noise that wakes him from his reverie. Without noticing the princess, Nemours stands up and walks away. Nemours leaves the place without investigating whether it might possibly be a noise made by the very woman about whom he was just thinking. While it is clear that she was the object of his daydreaming, the scene holds less of the promise of potential intimacy than the cabinet scene, since Nemours is scared away without, as far as the reader knows, imagining that he had actually seen the princess. But then, Madame de Clèves finds her love rekindled for Nemours (she realizes she loves him for his "respecting even her grief; trying to see her, without himself being seen" ([99],[44]) but these thoughts are quickly overturned by other, darker ones, in which she remembers that this very love in fact had been the cause of her husband's death.

After the park scene, the narrator tells us that Nemours, when he is finally alone again, "dreamed about devising ways of seeing her."[45] Just as in the avowal scene, after he has overheard the princess's confession, he wonders whether

---

[44] "[être] respectant jusqu'à sa douleur, songeant à la voir sans songer à en être vu" (298).
[45] "songea aux moyens dont il devait se server pour la voir" (299).

"what he had heard hadn't been a dream, so unlikely did it appear" (70).[46] The repetition of the verb *"songer"* ("to daydream" or "to wonder") is intended to mean something similar to *"envisager"* ("to imagine"), but the word also carries the implication of reverie and represents, according to Michel Glatigny, a break with the real ("être enfermé dans ses pensées" [54] ["to be locked up on one's thoughts"]). In addition, as opposed to a *rêve,* a *songe* can have the implication of a false vision with which the imagination deceives us. These parallel scenes, in which the princess and Nemours recreate each other in their mind's eye, actually move from greater intimacy to lesser intimacy, as if the narrator is purposely trying to keep them apart. In the portrait-stealing scene, the two are aware of each other, and send each other signs of mutual understanding before the princess begins to despair at her situation. In the avowal scene, Nemours is physically present, but his misreading ends in an almost-missed connection. In the cabinet scene, the princess is at first convinced that she has seen Nemours before she talks herself out of that true-false impression. And finally, in the park scene, which takes place close to the end of the novel, Nemours does not even look for the source of the noise that disrupts his daydream, and the two would-be lovers are once again separated by a wide gulf of misunderstanding. The possibility of the princess and Nemours expressing to each other their mutual love, and moreover, the possibility of their acting on it, is forever delayed. Even when they are both in the same place at the same time, the narrative causes them to deny the other's presence.

## The End of Love in the Novel's Ending

In her final conversation with Nemours, after her husband has died, the princess famously claims that the nature of love is so fickle that she fears that if they marry his love would wane. She rhetorically asks Nemours: "do men keep their love in these permanent unions? Ought I to expect a miracle in my case [...]?" (103).[47] But the princess acknowledges that the reasons for her self-imposed exile, namely duty, propriety, and her desire for "repos," are merely constructs:

---

[46] "ce qu'il avait entendue n'était point un songe, tant il y trouvait peu de vraisemblance" (248).
[47] "les hommes conservent-ils de la passion dans ces engagements éternels? Dois-je espérer un miracle en ma faveur [...]?" (306). This question mirrors Anselmo's deathbed confession, when he writes that Camila "was not obliged to perform miracles" (370) by resisting such an aggressive seduction by Lotario.

"I am sacrificing a lot for a duty that exists *only in my imagination* (emphasis added)."[48] She admits that she distrusts her own self-control and her own thoughts, and that her sense of duty is artificial. She realizes how deeply in love she is with Nemours, and how difficult it is for her to master that passion and sublimate it into anything else. In fact, one major difference between *La Princesse de Clèves* and the tenth novella of the *Heptaméron* is the absence of a divine realm in Lafayette's text. Although Florida is able to repress her love for Amador and redirect it to Jesus Christ (as we saw in the previous chapter), the princess is left entirely on her own. She blames, instead, *bienséance* or "etiquette" for her and Nemours' requisite separation. But there is something hesitant in Madame de Clèves' invocation of *bienséance* in light of her admission that she and Nemours are both "libre" and that the public would have nothing for which to reproach them. As François writes about the *aveu*, "the open secret asks that one accept as sufficient and real facts that may never become operative, and of which one may have no direct, empirical evidence" (76). Although she invokes duty, scruples, and *bienséance*, Nemours knows that the princess is asking him to accept as truth an insubstantial and irrational argument. She will not act on her passion, but not on reason either. The princess's own unique, if irrational, design of "duty" becomes motivation enough for her to withdraw from love.

Although Nemours never betrays the princess, she feels deceived and disappointed by love in general, no less for having been exposed to the negative examples of behavior throughout the novel. The princess fears that she will continue to love and to pursue Nemours in spite of herself. She feels overwhelmed by her love for him, as if it is greater than herself, and she says that it is liable to carry her away if she is not scrupulously diligent in denying it to herself. As in other works of analytical fiction, in this discourse on love we see more pain than pleasure, and that pain renews itself, cyclically. Madame de Clèves' *repos* has been interpreted as a mark of the princess's (or Lafayette's) Stoicism, and as an attempt to break the cycle and to pull herself away from what her mother previously called, in Jansenist terms, a steep precipice. In the end, though, *repos* becomes, like for the Jansenists, "a rational universal goal that man, a hopeless victim of passion, cannot realize" (Stanton 86). The princess realizes that the danger in loving Nemours is the danger of losing herself. The only way out of the entanglement of repetition and revision of painful love is to remove herself from the story. While some characters remain all too-readable in the novel, at the end,

---

[48] "je sacrifice beaucoup à un devoir qui ne subsiste *que dans mon imagination*" (247, emphasis added).

when the princess hovers near death, she manages only to close herself off more completely and to make herself illegible.

Madame de Clèves never truly learns to master her emotions. Instead, she merely abnegates them by living a habituated, detached, and unhappy existence. The princess, in rejecting life, also rejects a world in which all endings are arbitrary and relationships can be capriciously terminated and revived. Although the text gives her the possibility of undergoing several reversals (the death of her husband being the most significant), the princess does not truly change or discover anything substantial about herself or the people around her. Yet, she understands that the human heart is not comprehensible or rational, and that true movement forward may not even be possible. In this way, "repose" provides her rest and inaction only on the most literal level, since it does not bring peace. She lives her last days in isolation and self-imposed punishment as if she is afraid that something ambivalent and unresolved could resurface at any moment. Ultimately, *La Princesse de Clèves* relies less on the question of whether the heroine herself attains enlightenment, and more on the lesson learned in other *romans d'analyse* as well, that we must all learn to live with our own self-deception.[49]

---

[49] A version of the last few paragraphs of this chapter are drawn from my article "'[La] plus Jolie [de] Toutes Celles Qui Avaient Jamais Été Écrites': Madame de Thémines's Letter as Proto-Psychological Fiction in La *Princesse de Clèves*." The French Review, vol. 91, no. 3, 2018, pp. 56–69.

# 4

# Self as the "Grand Misleader" in Richardson's *Clarissa* and *The History of Sir Charles Grandison*

> *"But self here, which is at the bottom of all we do, and of all we wish, is the grand misleader"*[1]

*Clarissa, or, The History of a Young Lady* (1748) and *The History of Sir Charles Grandison* (1725) demonstrate the affinities between the fiction of sensibility in what McMurran describes as a constructed, nationalistic "domestic novel" "as a specifically English product" (114) and what I am calling analytical fiction. Despite efforts to view Richardson's novels (although this applies more to *Pamela* than the two later ones) as "a national allegory for readers abroad through its anticosmopolitan heroine[s]" (McMurran 24–25), the publication of Richardson's second novel introduced "the unworldliness of *Clarissa* [that] provoked an idealized cosmopolitanism. In other words, the *Clarissa* event unleashed both the acceptance of the English novel in a new nationalized novel system and a form of cosmopolitanizing in which the literary form captured the universal 'human heart'" (123). In this chapter, I wish to highlight one particular aspect of this perhaps unintentional "worldliness" (to repeat the use of Brooks's term, as McMurran does) in *Clarissa* and *Grandison* through a comparison with *La Princesse de Clèves*. As we will see, there are strong links between the pessimistic view of love taken in *La Princesse de Clèves* and the anti-romantic stance regarding marriage evidenced in Richardson's last

---

[1] *Clarissa, or the History of a Young Lady; In Four Volumes* 2:378–79. For quotations from *Clarissa*, I use Angus Ross's Penguin edition in one volume, unless otherwise noted. For *The History of Sir Charles Grandison*, I cite Jocelyn Harris's 1972 three-volume edition, unless otherwise noted.

two novels. While Richardson makes this connection explicit with a reference to Lafayette's work in *Grandison*, anti-romanticism as a motif also highlights Clarissa's self-deception and ambivalence about marriage and her ultimate withdrawal from a world that increasingly becomes regulated by entrapment and enclosure.

Like *La Princesse de Clèves*, and all analytical fiction, Richardson's novels explore the impossibility of mapping the psyche and the subjective nature of attempting to analyze the thoughts and actions of others. Whenever characters believe that they understand how another's mind works, what another character's motivations are, they become lost "in a sort of wilderness" (*Grandison* 1.284) or "in a wilderness of doubt and error" (*Clarissa* 565). Knowledge is controlled and limited by what gets put into letters and by who is privileged to read them, and even when honesty is continuously touted as a goal (as in *Grandison*) the letters themselves evidence more hiding and dissimulating than frankness. Thus, the characters in Richardson's novels are just as self-deceived and confused about how to read themselves and one another as are the characters in any other work of analytical fiction.

One of the first comparisons of Richardson's work to French literature was made by Denis Diderot, who gushes over *Clarissa* (which he had read in the Abbé Prévost's incomplete translation) in his *Éloge de Richardson*. He offers the English author the ultimate praise, that he thinks and writes like a Frenchman: "everything that Montaigne, Charron, La Rochefoucauld, and Nicole wrote in the maxim, Richardson has rendered into action. [...] [In Richardson] I have heard a real discourse on the passions; I have seen the mainsprings of affection and of self-love depicted a hundred different ways."[2] The encomium compares Richardson's insights to those of some of the most influential moralists of seventeenth-century France, but in a way that, like *La Princesse de Clèves*, transforms the maxim into narrative. According to Diderot, Richardson makes the tradition of *moralisme* come to life in a new century and across the Channel. He reads it as a sentimental work, modeling his own ebullient encomium on the style with which Richardson's characters write, legitimizing the novel of thought and feeling as a new literary form.

---

[2] "Tout ce que Montaigne, Charron, La Rochefoucauld et Nicole ont mis en maxime, Richardson l'a mis en action. [...] [In Richardson] J'avais entendu les vrais discours des passions; j'avais vu les ressorts de l'intérêt et de l'amour-propre jouer en cent façons diverses" (213).

# Richardson's Novels and *La Princesse de Clèves*

*Clarissa* was a bestseller in France, but French novels were also exceedingly popular in England throughout the seventeenth and eighteenth centuries. *La Princesse de Clèves*, which came out in its first English edition in 1679, only a year after its publication in France, was widely read, imitated, and cited in English fiction and drama. Although it is unlikely that Richardson read French literature in the original,[3] his references to French plays, to *La Princesse de Clèves*, and to the letters of Madame de Sévigné suggest that a critical reexamination of his interest in French writing is long overdue. As James Munro pointed out more than forty years ago, "criticism has looked [...] at the drama, at the relationship between Richardson's characters and his own unconscious mind, [and] at the overall development of western culture as a whole" for a source for Richardson's drawn-out explorations of the workings of the psyche; "what has not been sufficiently explored is the possibility [that Richardson drew from] [...] seventeenth-century romances, the most influential and best known of which were French" (752). The majority of studies that comment on Richardson's reference to *La Princesse de Clèves* compare Lafayette's novel to *Clarissa*. Munro, who looks at the "surprise of love" motif that overtakes Richardson's characters, only mentions the reference to *La Princesse de Clèves* in *Grandison* as some "disparaging remarks" (757) about Lafayette's work. Eaves and Kimpel also mention the reference once and conflate Mrs. Eggleton's condemnation of the novel with Richardson's own opinion of *La Princesse de Clèves* (583–84), while Mildred Sarah E. Greene comments on the reference to make connections between Lafayette's heroine and Clarissa and identifies that "Richardson's character [...] seems to be purposefully misreading the princess's psyche" (226), a view with which I agree.

Many critics have pointed out the possible influence of *La Princesse de Clèves* on *Clarissa*, whose heroine resembles Lafayette's in her self-deception and ambivalence as she withholds her true feelings from herself and from Anna Howe, her only confidante. Clarissa is similar to the princess in that she chooses

---

[3] Thomas O. Beebee and Richardson's biographers, T. C. Duncan Eaves and Ben D. Kimpel, reject the idea that Richardson would have read many French novels (Beebee 10 and Eaves and Kimpel 194 and 583). Richardson himself claimed—somewhat disingenuously—that he was "not acquainted in the least either with the French Language or Writers" (from an April 14, 1748, letter to William Warburton, who had written a preface to *Clarissa* insinuating that Richardson had been influenced by Prévost and Pierre de Marivaux) (Eaves and Kimpel 583).

early on in the narrative to abstain from love, although her true feelings about Lovelace remain unclear for perhaps half of the novel. There are other striking similarities between the two works, such as the often intrusive and overbearing role of parents in a woman's decision to marry, and the two heroines' penchant for the pastoral (Campbell points out that Madame de Clèves often withdraws into an "inner garden"—as well as into a real one ["The Cloud of Unknowing" 402], while Clarissa is, at the beginning of the novel, intent on using her inherited estate for a dairy house and living out a calm life as a milkmaid, although, when she actually does manage to escape from her parents' house and later from Sinclair's brothel, manages only to run into Lovelace and further into self-doubt). As Paula R. Backscheider writes, Clarissa and the princess in Lafayette's work both "are completely unsuited for the societies in which they live, and both reject a series of compromises available in their societies" (Backscheider 44). There are similarities between the men in the two books as well. As Anne Callahan points out in her article, "Mediation of Desire in *La Princesse de Clèves*, in *Approaches to Teaching Lafayette's* The Princess of Cleves," "the feminine hero first appears as the courtly lover in medieval romance, then again in the Renaissance as the *galant* [ ... and] reappeared in the next century as the rake, whose femininity is aptly evoked by the very name of Richardson's Lovelace" (168).[4]

But there are even more similarities between Nemours and Sir Charles. Both are highly respected, sought-after bachelors torn between two potential liaisons (Nemours renounces a possible marriage to Elizabeth of England in favor of pursuing the princess, who is already married, and Charles must break with Clementina—she actually rejects him because of the difference in their religions—in order to marry Harriet). Harriet and the princess are threatened with "foreign" rivals, each of whom also represents a potential religious taboo (Clementina as a Catholic whose family objects to Charles's Protestantism and Elizabeth as a Protestant who was to marry the Catholic Nemours). Even as the threats of foreign marriages are looming, Harriet and the princess both live with or spend a considerable amount of time with Charles and Nemours. Of their own volition, they participate in a salon-like environment (Harriet at

---

[4] It is interesting to note that as early as the late nineteenth century, critics were making references to Richardson's blurring of traditional feminine and masculine traits. George Saintsbury, in the introduction to his abridged *Clarissa*, calls Richardson himself "too thoroughly feminine to forgive" (xv) Henry Fielding for his satires of Richardson's works (although this may just be misogyny on Saintsbury's part), and Terry Eagleton notes that "for a man [Lovelace] spends too much time writing" (46) whereas "Clarissa's letters are signs of a unified self [...] whose relationship to writing is dominative and instrumental" (53); Clarissa is "the 'phallic' woman" (60) according to Eagleton.

Colnebrook and the princess in the apartments of the reine dauphine, Mary Stuart). In both cases, these are actually ambivalent spaces, where relationships between young people develop, but they are also where conflicts of jealousy and misaligned emotions arise.

In this chapter, I argue that *Grandison* as well as *Clarissa* not only echo the philosophical drive of Lafayette's novel, namely that we are unable, incapable—and ultimately reluctant—to know ourselves, but that they incorporate the sensibility of analytical fiction into almost every letter exchanged. As we have seen, the tension between inimitability, exemplarity, and negative behavior is central to this study of analytical fiction, and it is exactly this tension that drives Richardson's last two novels, though in different ways. Moreover, in both Richardson and Lafayette, there is always something sinister in the idea of love that repels the characters.

## *Clarissa* as *roman d'analyse*

The connection between Clarissa Harlowe and Robert Lovelace, as well as the countervailing opposition between them, is obvious from the very beginning of Richardson's second novel. As the narrative goes on, Clarissa's letters deny that she loves Lovelace, while he writes that he wishes to trap Clarissa and catch her secretly loving him. At other times, Lovelace desperately confesses his ambivalent feelings about Clarissa and suggests that he in fact may truly be in love with her (his confidant John Belford writes, "Poor Lovelace! Caught in thy own snares!" [964]). Despite the animosity between Lovelace and her family, Clarissa continues to correspond with her sister's former suitor.[5] Still wishing to enrich his fortune, James orchestrates for Clarissa a marriage to Solmes, a man Clarissa finds detestable. Clarissa's controlling parents and sister support the marriage to Solmes, but Clarissa, fearing this wedding, allows herself to be "rescued" by Lovelace. Lovelace tricks Clarissa into eloping with him; he takes her to London and hides her in a number of hostile environments, including a brothel, whose regular inhabitants Lovelace dresses up as respectable ladies. Lovelace hopes to restrain Clarissa's desire to remain single and free, and also

---

[5] Lovelace is initially a viable suitor, as well as a step up, socially speaking, for the Harlowe sisters. But after Arabella rejects Lovelace's less-than-enthusiastic marriage proposal, Clarissa—the real object of his affections—continues to communicate with him (as Eagleton puts it, Lovelace "perceives that the mere event of correspondence outweighs the 'innocence' of its content" [47]) and that he interprets Clarissa continuing to write as a positive sign.

wishes to avenge himself on the members of her family who have "mistreated" him. Throughout the novel, Clarissa refuses Lovelace, whose attempts to seduce her grow increasingly desperate, and clings to the hope that she can both heal the rupture with her family and avoid marrying Solmes. Her unbending family, however, is less than amenable to bargaining with their daughter.

Eventually, with the help of Mrs. Sinclair, the brothel owner, along with her employees, Lovelace drugs and rapes Clarissa. According to Frances Ferguson, the events leading up to the rape signify an epistemological split between Clarissa and Lovelace, wherein rape "dramatizes a problematic about the relationship between the body and the mind; although a rake like Lovelace may imagine that carnal 'knowing' includes knowing someone else's mind, a character like Clarissa—virtuous even in her violation—suggests that one knows about mental experience as much in despite of the body as through it" (99). However, in the immediate aftermath of the rape—and this is in no way intended to lessen Clarissa's incontrovertible status as victim—Lovelace recognizes that he has not gained any new knowledge or power by his heinous act: "Lovelace, having followed out the logic of his plottings and his plot, sees them as having resulted in the annihilation of the affair" (Ferguson 101). Suddenly, his epistemological superiority is thrown into question when he no longer knows what he thought he knew, and must ask "what it was that he meant" (Ferguson 102).[6] By believing that he provides a closure of possible future action by the rape (he merely famously reports to Belford that he "can go no farther. The affair is over" [883]), Lovelace attempts to recast *Clarissa* as a different sort of novel. However, the affair is by no means over, as the rape happens just about halfway through the text, and Clarissa and Lovelace's narrative continues on in a cyclical, analytical power struggle of perpetual resurrections of the effects of the rape. And the attack does not lessen Clarissa's resolve to return home to the Harlowes. Rejected by them once again, she falls physically and mentally ill, and begins to slide toward death.

*Clarissa* has been written about from just about every conceivable angle, with a particular emphasis on Clarissa's rape and subsequent slow and meticulously planned death and funeral. Criticism of *Clarissa* from 1982 and after demonstrates a renewed interest in Richardson's second novel (1982 being

---

[6] Ferguson shows that Lovelace initially mitigates the blow to his ego by rationalizing Clarissa's being drugged during the rape as only a minor point; her lack of consent being merely "a deficiency that will be retrospectively repaired" (Ferguson 103) when she, Lovelace imagines, agrees to marry him. But ultimately, Clarissa's mental degeneration and persistent refusal of marriage negate Lovelace's newfound confidence.

the year in which Terry Castle published *Clarissa's Ciphers*—in which she writes that "Clarissa's fall is [...] an orchestrated movement into increasingly incoherent realms. Through 'Art,' Lovelace destroys Clarissa's sense of 'Nature' itself, her ground of meaning. He systematically violates her faith in the essential legibility of experience" (83)—and Terry Eagleton published *The Rape of Clarissa*, cited below). In the remaining part of this section, I only wish to highlight a few scenes from *Clarissa* that are intensely analytical in their narration, and do not spend any time discussing, for example, Clarissa's preparations for her death and funeral.[7] In making these choices, I realize that I must inevitably downplay not only these pivotal and significant scenes but also many other aspects of the later part of the novel. However the cyclical aftermath of Lovelace's physical violation of Clarissa represents the ultimate reenactment of other analytical scenes that foreshadow it.

Most critics of Richardson agree that his second novel is unwieldy, and the "letters concede yet withhold physical intimacy in a kind of artfully prolonged teasing, a courtship which is never consummated" (Eagleton 45). Other critics like to point out that *Clarissa* is also a novel of anticipation and suspension. As Valenza writes, *Clarissa* is "a novel of prolepsis. [...] Richardson seals off exits, denies Clarissa escape routes at every turn. Our sense of the uncanny in reading *Clarissa* derives from what seems to be Clarissa Harlowe's occasional glimmers of knowledge of what will befall her" (232). And yet, Clarissa lacks control of this knowledge; she falls into ignorance and necessary self-deception. Valenza's interpretation also reinforces the idea that Richardson's characters inhabit a closed society of their own making (or really, for Clarissa, of Lovelace's making). Karin Kukkonen points out that the plot of *Clarissa* is even irrational for a tragic novel: "the ending of *Clarissa* challenges all principles of poetic justice" (67). For John Richetti, both Clarissa and Lovelace as characters "are defined by a process of constant introspection" (102), and Erich Kahler calls it "the Puritan fondness for poking into the recesses of the soul" (151)—though, it must be reiterated that whatever insights Lovelace and Clarissa make deliver no stable truth either to themselves or to one another. Richardson's polyphonic narrative in *Clarissa* structures the novel so that certain passages and episodes work in repeating structures that keep Clarissa

---

[7] For a fascinating analysis of these subjects that is off the beaten path of Richardson studies, see Jolene Zigarovich's chapter "Courting Death: Necrophilia in Samuel Richardson's *Clarissa*" which articulates Lovelace and Clarissa's shared affinity for the "sexual taboo [...] [of] death-in-sex" (112).

and Lovelace at arm's length from each other, misreading each other's signs, and desperate to know for certain what the correct signs are.

Imagination and misreading each play an important role in Richardson's second novel, as Clarissa, at least early on, invents and reinvents much of the drama with Lovelace through the act of writing, while he encourages this imaginative misreading by throwing at her a number of false signs. As soon as she sets her impressions about him, about Solmes, about her family, Clarissa's view becomes distorted, and she suddenly sees outside forces weighing down upon her and forcing her in undesirable directions. The moment one threat is mollified, another appears. (Similarly, as we will see, Harriet's ability to declare her love for Charles is delayed by a number of potential rivals and interruptions.) Lovelace even claims in one of his early letters to Clarissa: "if a man could not make a woman in courtship own herself *pleased* with him, it was as *much* and sometimes *more* to his purpose to make her *angry* with him" (17), and so he manipulates her field of vision to keep her at least irritated with him. Lovelace knows, from the very beginning, how to attract Clarissa, how to compel her to write to him, even when she has previously claimed that she will stop. Patricia Meyer Spacks calls this tension "two kinds of self-splitting: a woman's conscious choice, a man's confused endurance. The woman resists, the man indulges self-love. Social pressures and assumptions impede self-knowledge for both" ("The Grand Misleader" 7). As in other works of analytical fiction, the obsessive struggle and desire for knowledge and certainty take center stage, but knowledge and certainty are never achieved, or they are never allowed to be achieved by various forces within the text, at times by Lovelace, and at times by the implicit narrator, the author-"editor" of the letters.

The drama of *Clarissa* is alternatively heightened and suspended, seemingly infinitely. Even Clarissa's death scene is prolonged so that her actual death is subordinated to the dilation of her deterioration. Throughout, the focus on motivation, thought, and error are central. In this way, suspension makes up the very plot of *Clarissa*, with the major sections and episodes—from Lovelace's increasing influence over Clarissa's thoughts and behavior in the Harlowe household to his orchestration of her flight, to her captivity, escape, recapture, rape, and second escape from Lovelace, to her death—only providing a structure on which the suspense rests. As Theresa Ann Sears writes, "plot itself becomes a strategy to both bring about the satisfaction of erotic desire and, conversely, to stave it off, as if in inchoate and futile recognition of its inevitable end" (23).

In *Clarissa*, as in *La Princesse de Clèves*, and as in, in fact, all of the works examined in this book, marriage is not represented as a happy state. Sears argues similarly about sentimental literature in general, including Lafayette's novels, that they "question the very possibility of 'sanctioned satisfaction' of desire, and in several instances even invert or vacate the meaning of the conventional marriage plots. Rather than moving *towards* the safety and repose of marriage, the characters move *away* from that secure haven into the perilous world of uncontrolled desire" (18). There are, in fact, almost no happy marriages represented in *Clarissa*—even Anna and Hickman's marriage at the end of the novel is fraught because Anna has seemed so dissatisfied with him throughout her letters. Only Belford's marriage to Charlotte Montague, which he reports at the very end, serves as a counter-point to the treatment of marriage in the rest of the novel. Ironically, this last, happy marriage by a reformed rake, Lovelace's former partner-in-crime, highlights the alternative pathway that Lovelace and Clarissa might have taken if they had been the main characters in a different sort of novel (*Pamela* perhaps). Because there is no finality in happiness, stability, or marriage for the central couple, the narrative remains uncertain until the last, when death becomes, for Clarissa, "one common point, in which all shall meet, err widely as they may. In that I shall be laid quietly down at last: and then will all my calamities be at an end" (566); death is the only way out of the cyclical, unstable, and uncertain narrative.

Initially, Clarissa acts as a go-between for one of her uncles, who wishes to pass on Lovelace's stories about his travels to a young friend. Clarissa admits that Lovelace is a skilled and seductive writer, and she innocently enjoys his correspondence. Although we never read a physical description of Lovelace, beyond his being young and handsome, we learn that Clarissa's brother loathed him because he was always very successful at school, and excelled at literature and writing. Moreover, a servant on Lovelace's estate reports to Clarissa's aunt that he is a *bon vivant* and an *enfant terrible*. The reader may also be struck with the juxtaposition between Lovelace's skill at writing and his wild living: "he [...] was a great plotter, *and a great writer*: [...] he lived a wild life in town" (20, emphasis added). It seems that it is Lovelace's writing that continues to attract Clarissa, who herself illustrates love of and skill in composition through her letters. When she rejects the idea of marrying Lovelace, for reasons that include her brother's longstanding quarrel with him, and because she fears that it would be damaging to her sister, Lovelace writes to her that he will persist in pursuing her. After Clarissa's brother challenges Lovelace to fight him in a duel and is injured, Lovelace continues to visit their house, feigning to apologize to the family, and, with the backing of his uncle Lord M., continuing to court Clarissa. Because of the delicate balance of social and economic forces, Clarissa's family cannot definitively force Lovelace to end his calls. Lovelace uses this fact to his advantage to continue to pay "amicable visits" (31) to the family, and to remain present in Clarissa's psyche, whether this presence causes her pain or joy.[8]

As the princess's mother points out in *La Princesse de Clèves*, if one were to judge based on appearances, one would often be mistaken. This pronouncement, which sets the tone for the entirety of Lafayette's narrative, also encapsulates epistemology in Richardson's novels as inherently distrustful and prone to error in judgment. Clarissa's letters to Anna reveal her self-doubt, and it becomes evident that Clarissa is a far less reliable translator of her heart than she claims:

> Yet I can tell you how, I believe—one devious step at setting out!—that must be it:—which pursued, has led me so far out of my path, that I am in a wilderness of doubt and error; and never, never, shall find my way out of it. […] But I, presumptuous creature! must rely so much upon my own knowledge of the right path!—little apprehending that an ignus fatuus with its false fires […] would arise to mislead me! (565–6)

Clarissa attributes her becoming irremediably lost in the wilderness to "one devious step at setting out."[9] She also laments that she has only herself to rely on to tell her what is the right course of action with Lovelace—should she believe him, or should she try to flee? Is she really in love with him and doesn't know it?—but that the only truth she can discover within herself is that she is never correct in her judgment. As Meyer Spacks puts it, "her letters, taken all together, convey a persuasive pattern of vacillation, confusion, and ambivalence" ("The Grand Misleader" 106).

Clarissa's impulse is to flee from Lovelace and from her family as well, and her language evokes wandering and movement; Lovelace's implies caging and immobility. But they come to the same thing. The more she tries to run away from Lovelace, the more she runs straight into him. Faced with Lovelace as an enigma, a sometimes monstrous, sometimes attractive, force, Clarissa is metaphorically

---

[8] She claims, in fact, that she is completely indifferent to him, although her insistence fails to convince her brother and sister. James Harlowe calls her attitude toward Lovelace "ap-*pa*-rent indifference" (58). Emphasis and ellipses are Richardson's unless otherwise noted.

[9] This phrase parallels Lovelace's philosophy: "I have known a bird actually starve itself, and die with grief, at its being caught and caged—But never did I meet with a lady who was so silly" (557).

trapped as much as she becomes physically trapped. Richardson provides a way in to Clarissa's mind through the very confusion she is describing, and passionate emotions are mediated by confusion, fear, and self-deception.

The senses and reason engage in mutual deception quite clearly in *Clarissa*, perhaps most notably in the abduction scene. Here, Richardson's heroine reports that all was "amaze and confusion" (380), and that her own imagination (aided, unbeknownst to her, by Lovelace's servant who helps orchestrate the scene) propels her to run away from home and into Lovelace's waiting arms: "expecting a furious brother here, armed servants there, an enraged sister screaming and a father armed with terror in his countenance, more dreadful than [...] those I apprehended [...] calling out to others, whom I supposed he saw [...] whom I imagined to be my brother, my father and their servants" (380). Clarissa's vocabulary, namely the verbs "to expect," "to apprehend," "to suppose," and, finally, "to imagine," is significant. Clarissa illustrates how very impressionable the mind can allow itself to be as she imagines that she saw her father's face as more terrifying "than even the drawn sword which I saw or those I apprehended" (380). At the moment of her narration to Anna, she has been disabused about the plot, and has more or less figured out that Lovelace has tricked her: "and so, to save [...] an *apprehended* rashness, I have rushed into a *real* one myself" (380), she concedes. Clarissa admits that she could not see what was actually happening because of the garden wall, but the scene that she created in her mind—that of an enraged and also armed family coming after her—is more vivid than reality.

## Deception and Delusion

Another example of the ways in which Clarissa is duped by Lovelace's tricks, but which also serves as an example for the ways in which Lovelace fundamentally cannot understand Clarissa, is the ipecacuanha episode. Here Lovelace tests Clarissa by feigning illness: he takes medicine to make himself vomit, and he uses chicken blood procured from a butcher to pretend he has burst a blood vessel. Lovelace's justification to Belford for this charade is that he wants to "catch" Clarissa loving him. He claims that he will not even need to speak the words, for "if she has *love* [...] it will [...] come forward, and show itself [...] in every line of her sweet face" (673). Lovelace relies on Clarissa's physiognomic signals to tell him the truth. As in the spying scenes in *La Princesse de Clèves*, Lovelace imposes himself not only into Clarissa's physical space, but into her psychological space as well. She can never be entirely sure of whether he is being truthful or untruthful, while he believes that he can perfectly read her psyche. But how could Clarissa possibly not show affectation at this plot? Anna points out, much earlier, in teasing Clarissa: "don't you find at your heart somewhat unusual make it go throb, throb, throb [...] It is your *generosity*, my love!" (71).

Nevertheless, Clarissa manages to deceive Lovelace as well in this scene, as her goodness—to which the rake can never become accustomed, since it is so far from his own nature—becomes baffling to him. The episode shows that *Clarissa* is a study of unrequited expectations; the characters are distant and protean to each other, they watch and attempt to understand what the other is thinking and going to do, and they wish to penetrate each other's thoughts. But they always fail in their attempts. Indeed, Lovelace is duped—even to the verge of tears—by Clarissa's goodness, fundamentally inconsistent with what he had previously considered the nature of women. While Lovelace's plots are convincing to Clarissa—such as when he brings the counterfeiter McDonald to pose as "Tomlinson," a man who is supposed to be her family's neighbor, in order to reconcile her with them—her reaction is so very genuine and innocent that Lovelace himself is drawn into the charade and becomes affected by it. In the episode with Tomlinson, Lovelace cries when he sees Clarissa's tears, even though he knows full well that he is merely furthering his "trial" of her chastity and virtue:

> Then drying her tears with her handkerchief [...] she retired to her chamber with precipitation; leaving me almost as unable to stand it as herself. [...] In short, I was—*I want words to say how I was*—my nose had been made to tingle before; my eyes have before been made to glisten by this soul-moving beauty; but so very much affected, I never was—[...] I *audibly* sobbed. (695)

Richardson shows how indeed every now and then Clarissa manages—unwittingly—to produce in Lovelace some human feeling. Moreover, his emotion is so strong and so uncontrolled that he even hesitates to find words to describe it. Earlier in the novel, Anna had congratulated Clarissa on being unique in being able to transform love "into a lap-dog" (73); she is capable of piercing Lovelace's misleadingly attractive surface: "but were he deep, and ever so deep, you would soon penetrate him, if they would leave you to yourself" (75). Thus, Lovelace—who boasts that he is so skillful in deception—is duped by his own trick and is rendered speechless by it.

In this way, Lovelace misreads Clarissa, his mistake being that he cannot conceive of someone (or, perhaps, of a woman) whose emotional range goes beyond the extremes of love and hate. Because Clarissa's reactions do not always fall into these categories, Lovelace is propelled to continue his trials, perhaps even out of frustration. Citing Ariosto (one of the sources for Cervantes's trial of Camila in "El curioso impertinente") Lovelace, just like Anselmo, asks, "for what woman can be said to be virtuous till she has been tried?" (430). He orchestrates so many tests, one after another, that Clarissa falls victim to his plots. And yet, he is never satisfied. Clarissa's reactions to his tests are sensitive and generous, but never cause her to submit fully to him. His trials are malicious, but also incompatible with Clarissa's nature. The ipecacuanha scene, in the end, only frustrates Lovelace. While he garners the hoped-for reaction from Clarissa, the signs of concern that she gives him end up not satisfying his desire to conquer her. The citation of Ariosto's magic cup that reveals to the lover if his beloved is faithful provides a clue to interpreting Lovelace's relentless testing of Clarissa. It is possible that Lovelace is actually jealous. Although he has no real rivals, the constant possibility of Clarissa's departure, the very tenuousness of their relations, his distrust of her nature, all fit with the jealous lover model that we have seen so often in analytical fiction, in which, again, it is not necessary for a real infidelity to occur; the lover's imagined infidelity is enough to make him doubt.

The interpretation of Lovelace's jealousy is supported by Clarissa's attempted escape toward the middle of the novel. Her departure and what Lovelace perceives as her indifference launch him into a renewed passion for Clarissa, and he admits to Belford that he begged her for forgiveness. He says that he feels remorse, that he admitted to having been wrong to try to trick her, and calls their interaction after she returns a "soul-penetrating conversation" (853). But Lovelace becomes obsessed with the fact that Clarissa half-rejects him. He asks Belford, "why will she break from me, when good resolutions are taking place?" (853) That is, he feels like they are getting somewhere, since he is so deluded by his own self-love and perceived power over Clarissa. And yet, he wonders that Clarissa cannot declare her love to him: "the red-hot iron she refuses to strike—O why will she suffer the yielding wax to harden?" (853) Lovelace's metaphor underscores the push-and-pull of their cyclical relationship, his own jealousy, and, moreover, the cyclical nature of the novel. Not unlike in other works that we have already examined, it is precisely because Clarissa alternatingly shows concern for Lovelace (again, only because his tricks are often so devious and difficult to identify as tricks) and then turns away from him that the rake constantly looks to test her. Clarissa is not merely being indecisive, however. Instead, she is kept suspended between acts of Lovelace's deception and her own doubts about whether his intentions are honorable, and this uncertainty is ingrained in the cyclical narrative.

For much of the novel, Lovelace becomes the creator of a whole false universe for Clarissa, pulling all the marionette strings in a world that repeatedly and implacably challenges the title character's sense of right and wrong, illusion and reality: "Ovid was not a greater master of metamorphoses than I" (412), he says. In another passage, he describes himself as protean. And yet, when Clarissa manages to escape from him the first time, just before he rapes her, Lovelace accuses Clarissa of being a "plotter." "This plaguy sex is *art* itself" (737), he exclaims. The metaphorical form that knowledge takes in *Clarissa* is the idea of closure, which is never achieved. For Lovelace it would come in the form of conquest and subduing Clarissa's spirit, while the closure that Clarissa desires is escape and solitude. Yet, outside of death, these two goals are completely incompatible. The contrast between Lovelace's desire to contain Clarissa and her insistence on abstaining from love is too strong. Moreover, as is always the case in analytical fiction, knowledge and closure are nearly impossible to achieve; the very narration (in this case, the way that knowledge is disseminated and contorted through letters) prohibits a true ending.

In Lovelace, we see a feature that we have not witnessed nearly so overtly in characters of analytical fiction: he is a liar. Even his name conjures images of intricate woven patterns that mirror the ways in which he invents stories. Yet, as Lisa Zunshine points out, Lovelace does not always seem to know that he is a liar, and the first time one reads the book it may take five hundred pages or more "to realize that one of the narrators of the story is misleading not just Clarissa but also himself" (86). Thus, Lovelace's dissimulations and deceptions work so well that he occasionally manages to fool himself, and to forget where the truth ends and the lie begins. Like other analytical characters, Lovelace collapses the limits between appearances and reality, to the point that they are conflated and indistinguishable.

The two main characters, of course, are diametrically opposed: Clarissa is supposed to be goodness, honesty, virtue, and Lovelace is diabolical, plotting, and deranged, and yet their distinct voices share certain features: humor, cleverness, pride, misguided and erroneous confidence, and, eventually, self-doubt and desperation. Lovelace himself writes that they are quite similar, with one significant difference: "my charmer, I see, has a pride like my own: but she has no *distinction* in her pride" (449). As Kahler puts it, "the fact that Clarissa's resistance is not due to another man, but to sheer indifference to his charms, offends his vanity just as much as it increases his ardor" (Kahler 159). As much as Clarissa views Lovelace as a monster and herself as an angel, the rake "is not cold enough to be a sheer devil; […] The tricks of the dandy, the Don Juan, the master of intrigue fail him; the bravado becomes desperation, the seducer a hounded, suffering human being. But it takes, to produce such a development, an antagonist as narrow-minded and unfeeling as Clarissa, utterly obsessed with family and propriety" (Kahler 160). Throughout the central part of the novel, after Clarissa has flown from her family, Lovelace begins to feel as if he is just as much confined as Clarissa; he is trapped by his inability to read Clarissa properly. Because she is not interested in participating in Lovelace's games (and like the princess in Lafayette's novel, a withdrawal from both life and love is far more appealing to Richardson's heroine), Lovelace feels frustrated and thwarted. Thus, Clarissa ends in also trapping Lovelace in the same kind of inaction that she suffers throughout the novel.

## The Epistemology of Love in *The History of Sir Charles Grandison*

The same elements of the closed and controlled society, the same deceptions and misreadings, also predominate in Richardson's *History of Sir Charles Grandison*. Nevertheless, two connected views prevail among modern Richardson scholars about *Grandison*: first, that the novel is primarily a conduct book and, second, that because of its didacticism the novel lacks interiority.[10] And yet, Richardson's other novels are credited with the power of mining the recesses of the human psyche. Samuel Johnson famously remarked on Richardson's attention to psychological analysis in *Clarissa* and on the way in which the author "enlarged the knowledge of human nature" (*The Yale Edition* 153). But did any early readers find Richardson's third novel psychologically compelling? Richardson's friend Thomas Edwards identifies, if obsequiously, that *Grandison*'s author is possessed of a "ceaseless diligence, to guide the mind/In the wild maze of error wandering blind/To virtue, truth, and honour" (*Grandison*, Ed. William Lion

---

[10] For a full literature review, see my article "Lost 'in a Sort of Wilderness'" (427).

Phelps xl).[11] In this chapter, I am more interested in the "wild maze of error" in which *Grandison*'s characters find themselves "wandering blind" than his desire to guide the reader to virtue and truth. Indeed, as we will see, Richardson puts psychological analysis center stage in his last novel, creating interiority, psychological depth, and conflict between the lovers in order to continue to explore the complex, unruly epistemology of love and the darker side of romance that he began in *Pamela* and *Clarissa*.

About half of the letters in *Grandison* are written by Harriet Byron, a wealthy young woman from Northamptonshire, to her cousin Lucy Selby. Unlike Clarissa, Harriet has been given the freedom to choose her own husband. As a result, she at one point has seven different suitors simultaneously, none of whom she wishes to marry. (Like the princess at the beginning of Lafayette's novel, she has not yet experienced love. Harriet writes of herself: "she is too good to *hate any-body*; and as for *love*, her time seems not to be yet come" [1.104]). In the first volume, Harriet is kidnapped by the rake Sir Hargrave Pollexfen, but Sir Charles Grandison hears Harriet's calls for help from Pollexfen's carriage; he disarms and injures the rake, then brings Harriet to safety. At Colnebrook, the house of Grandison's sister and her husband, Lord and Lady L., Harriet befriends the Grandison family, and becomes especially attached to Charlotte Grandison, Charles's younger sister. This family adopts Harriet as their own, the women calling her their and Charles's third sister. Soon, Harriet falls in love with Charles, but it is months before she can admit it to herself. Lucy and the rest of her family, as well as the Grandison sisters, in fact identify Harriet's inclination long before she does.

Sir Charles, whose feelings about Harriet remain unknown until much later, has his own secret: many years before, in Italy, he had become attached to Lady Clementina della Poretta. Clementina's family refused to sanction their engagement because of the difference in religion, and Charles agreed to leave Italy and return to England. However, Clementina grows desperately ill after their separation, causing her family to change their minds and accept Charles's Anglicanism. In the middle of the third of seven volumes of *Grandison*, Charles is recalled to Italy to attempt to save Clementina and

---

[11] Several editions of *Grandison* are prefaced by a sonnet written by Edwards. According to Jocelyn Harris, a thousand copies of the second edition (in which Edwards's poem first appeared) were printed in octavo and published simultaneously with the first edition in 1754 (*The History of Sir Charles Grandison*, Ed. Jocelyn Harris xxvii). Harris does not include Edwards's sonnet as a paratext, nor does she mention it in the introduction to her authoritative edition of the novel in three volumes.

possibly marry her. When he arrives, it is Clementina who refuses to marry him—on the grounds of religion—and so Charles is free to wed Harriet. They marry, but the novel does not end. Instead, Clementina visits the Grandison family in England, and the majority of the seventh volume revolves around whether or not she will marry the Count of Belvedere or return to Italy to join a convent.

Richardson enjoyed keeping readers on their toes with the various twists and turns that *Grandison*'s narrative allows and did not seem committed to any one trajectory of the plot, at least not at first. For a long time while he was writing, the author claimed that even he was unsure of who—Harriet or Clementina— would be the actual star of his third novel. Saintsbury comments that as readers, "we are left to ourselves to find out whether Harriet or Clementina is the heroine, as well as to discover the precise moral which the fortune or misfortune of each is to point" (xxviii). Richardson wrote, in a letter from October of 1751 to William Duncombe, that

> Clementina's fate is not yet come to my Knowledge. I have been hinder'd from enquiring after her; in other words, from pursuing her story. But I think she rises upon me. And as I know not what to offer next, being too irregular a scribbler to be able to write by a plan, I seem to be at a loss, to know what to do with her, or to fetch up Harriet again, and make her the principal Female character. (quoted in McKillop 128)

Then, however, in another letter to Lady Echlin on May 17, 1754, Richardson writes

> Will I give you Leave to think, that Harriet is superior to Clementina? Indeed I will. I have owned the Superiority to our dear Lady B[radshaigh]. And have reflected upon the Judgment of those who are struck with the Glare of a great Action, which was owing principally to a raised Imagination. Your beloved Sister [Bradshaigh again] is of Opinion with you, madam, in preferring Harriet: And I will not choose for my Judges of the Work, any of those, who are of a contrary one. (McKillop 129)

In this way, it seems that there was never a specific plan to make Harriet marry Charles. Instead, Richardson deferred to his female friends and patrons as to the outcome of the novel. The identities of the characters, if we can use this term, were certainly not fixed from the beginning.

*Grandison* is the only one of Richardson's three novels in which a hero and heroine of equal social status find true love and happiness together.[12] But while their marriage should be a foregone conclusion, Harriet and Charles cannot acknowledge their feelings nor avow them either to themselves or to each other for much of the novel. In fact, Harriet's self-knowledge is deferred until almost the very end of the book, while Clementina's certainty is put off indefinitely. *Grandison* truly ends *without* a marriage between Clementina and Belvedere. As Martha J. Koehler points out, "*Grandison* [is] literally interminable, without any final release or resolution" (317), while Albert J. Rivero interprets Clementina's story as a foreign element that must be expunged from the novel in order to allow romance to triumph for Harriet and Charles and for Charlotte Grandison, Charles's witty and secretive sister, and Lord G. (209–25). *Grandison* incorporates intercalated stories of infidelity and inappropriate matches as negative examples purportedly intended to teach its heroines (and, to a point, its heroes) about how to think about love. But this Horatian aim is also frustrated by the characters who, like Charlotte, "[make] it a rule […] to remember nothing that will vex her" (2:264), that is, she makes up her sense of self as it is convenient to her and not in any reliable manner. And indeed, she asserts to Harriet that "some of us are to be set up for warnings, some for examples: and the first are generally of greater use to the world than the other" (2:264) (she identifies herself squarely on the side of warnings). Some interpolated stories—such as Lucy's disastrous love of Captain Duncan (which is alluded to very early in the novel), the story of Lord Grandison, Sir Charles's father, the story of Sir Charles's rakish cousin Mr. Grandison, and almost all of the Italian episodes—implicitly function to build interior drama, but also as warnings against passionate, romantic love.

On the contrary, knowledge for Harriet deepens quite slowly, often moving one step forward and two steps back; the truth is constantly doubted and revised. Harriet knows that she must "keep a *look-out* … upon [her]self" (1.233) so as

---

[12] Marriage is, of course, the first subject of *Grandison*. As Martha J. Koehler points out, "Richardson's third novel focuses extensively (in plots both major and minor) on questions of choosing one's spouse" (319) in the wake of Hardwicke's Marriage Act of 1753, which placed strict limitations on how and when weddings could be conducted. Wendy Jones explains how "the middle-class recoding of aristocratic values" functioned to create an ideal of "sentimental love as a fully mutual, erotic response to moral excellence" in the wake of the newly "privatized" marriage in England (298; 315). For Richardson's position on the 1753 law, see Mary Vermillion (395–412). Apparently, "Richardson explicitly advocated parents' rights to veto the marriage choices of their children who were still minors" (Vermillion 396). *Grandison* sidesteps this issue because Harriet Byron, the novel's heroine, is over twenty-one.

not to reveal too much, or suffer too greatly from love. Yet, she does suffer. The "look-out" acts as a sort of self-censorship, an inhibition that manifests itself in her letters when she is trying to penetrate the problem of Charles's "divided or double Love" (3:76). Throughout the novel, Harriet must learn to banish her own doubts, as well as comparisons to the many negative examples with which she is presented, and to decide definitively that she is in love. But Harriet is self-deceived about her own feelings for Charles, and their union is threatened both by the plot (Charles's indecision) and by the "cruel suspense" (3:76) that the analytical epistolary narrative imposes. Harriet suffers from the symptoms of romantic love: inhibition, jealousy, and self-doubt, and yet, as we will see, she takes a decidedly prosaic view of marriage and is impeded from admitting her love to herself. Her inclination is actively to deny the more impetuous love that she feels for Charles, while her letters and physiognomy reveal, accidentally, how she truly feels.

It is true that *Grandison*'s letters are not forged as in *Clarissa*, but they are circulated, translated, interpreted, and reinterpreted by the members of the Grandison and Selby families. Yet, the idea of "frankness" is often touted in the novel as an ideal. As Tita Chico points out, all the characters are expected to read each letter received out loud (52). The quasi-public nature of all the letters in *Grandison* has also been interpreted by Rebecca Anne Barr as a sign of the novel's authoritarianism concerning the dissemination and dissimulation of knowledge (393; 396). But even this idea of *Grandison*'s epistemology being controlled by a central authority—either the Selby or Grandison households—is turned on its head by Harriet's frequent insertions to Lucy, who is instructed to keep Harriet's avowals to herself, hiding secrets in plain view. In truth, as much is withheld from characters' letters as is expressed; knowledge is always tentative and inhibited. Joe Bray writes that there are many moments in the novel that resist "openness," in which, on the contrary, "reserve" is privileged. These are episodes in which "it is better not to speak out; to keep one's private thoughts hidden [...] [which] encourages the exploration of [...] past thoughts" (62) in the form of deliberation and self-questioning.

Harriet faces a number of obstacles to her love that encourage her to continue to hide it, even from herself: "How often [...] did I turn my eye *to* myself, and *from* myself [...]!" (1.168), she exclaims at one point early in the novel. A little later, Harriet writes to Lucy, "and O, thought I, now-and-then, as I looked upon him, Sir Charles Grandison is a man with whom I would not *wish* to be in love" (1.209) on the grounds that she would have too many rivals.

Indeed, one of the first epithets that is used about Charles—and it is repeated throughout the novel—is that of heartbreaker; were he to get married at least half a dozen women would suffer. At some point, Lord L. bungles this formula and claims that it would be half a score. This can only serve to increase Harriet's disquiet. The omnipresence of Emily Jervois, Charles's young and pretty ward, seems to threaten the happiness of the potential match between Grandison and Harriet as well, even though Harriet claims to love Emily like a sister. The arrival of two other potential rivals for Harriet, Lady Anne and the Italian Lady Olivia, increases the drama and suspends Harriet's happiness yet again on two other occasions.

Because each character has multiple potential love interests, when aspiring lovers appear—either for Harriet, Charlotte, or Charles—they come with the predisposed anxiety that the character they desire may already be promised to someone else. Thus, there is a question of attachment, whether a character is "absolutely disengaged." The word "disengaged" is used in no fewer than twenty-five unique episodes in the novel, and the word "engaged" dozens of times more. Before she hears the full story of Charles's Italian travels—that is, the story of how he fell in love with Clementina—Harriet begins to loathe the mysteries they hold. When her would-be lover receives some letters one day, she bursts out to Lucy: "Foreign Letters, I doubt not!—I wish this ugly word *foreign* were blotted out of my vocabulary; out of my memory, rather. I never, till of late, was so narrow-hearted—But that I have said before, twenty times" (2.110). Matters become even more ambiguous when Charles seems to be simultaneously engaged and disengaged; Harriet collects some phrases from one of Dr. Bartlett's letters and jumbles them together in her fearful uncertainty: "'Issue hidden from himself.' 'Engaged in some affairs at Bologna and Florence, that embarrass him'—[*Is, or was* so engaged, means the Doctor?] 'Sir Charles not reserved; yet reserved'" (1.464, brackets and emphasis in original). These fragmented lines confuse the clear-cut boundaries of taken and not taken that the characters in *Grandison* are so intent upon knowing. Harriet risks losing control over herself (she loses control over forming complete sentences) when faced with a jealousy inseparable from love. Even after she has for the most part overcome the Clementina problem by marrying Charles herself, Harriet is troubled by Clementina's unhappiness and does not feel permitted to feel pleasure ("I know not how to describe what I felt in my now fluttering, now rejoicing, now dejected heart" [3.18]).

It is no wonder that characters probe for faults in their potential matches. When Harriet paints the portrait of Charles for Lucy, she attempts to discover some imperfection. She writes, "he has too many personal advantages for a woman who loved him with *peculiarity*, to be easy with, whatever may be *his* virtue" (1.182). She acknowledges that she is searching for something amiss to prove to Lucy that she could not really be in love with him, while accidentally revealing how ideal she thinks he is: "I want [...] to find some fault in his outward appearance" (1.183). Later in the same letter, she revises her impression and writes that it is impossible that anyone could be faultless, and even misreads the situation in saying that Charles could not possibly be as honest as Charlotte is. Harriet is not wrong in finding fault with his potential to keep secrets (although Charlotte arguably keeps more secrets than anyone else in the novel). A few pages later, Harriet is still preoccupied with what may be wrong with Charles: "I wonder why a man of a turn so laudable, should have *any* secrets? [...] Can he have, *so many* love-secrets [...]?" (1.189). After all, "it is very difficult," writes Harriet in the same letter, "to know one's self" (1.189), let alone anyone else.

Harriet is skeptical about love because everyone keeps secrets in *Grandison*, and no one is ever straightforward about the person she or he loves.[13] But Harriet promulgates secret-keeping herself when she writes to Lucy that women need to manage the effusiveness of their passions: they "suffer a great deal in the apprehension, at one time, of disgusting the object of their passion, by too forward a Love" (1.423). The only characters who overtly declare their passion are the impetuous Italians (like Olivia, who at one point threatens Charles with a knife if he will not love her), and the worst of Harriet's suitors, Pollexfen, who ironically expresses the greatest amount of forthrightness about his intentions for her. Even to Lucy, Harriet seems scared to reveal too much of herself lest the affection she feels for Charles be unrequited, misunderstood, or inappropriate. She ends up relating to Lucy not her true feelings, but her self-deception.

Thus, *Grandison* incorporates the foundation of the analytical novel, which is driven entirely by fear, self-doubt, and self-preservation, manifested in shame—that "apprehension [...] of disgusting the object of [...] passion" cited above—and the inhibition of desire. Harriet even asks Lucy, "have I [...] any [secret] to reveal? It is, I hope, a secret to myself, that never will be unfolded, even *to* myself" (1.386) that she is in love with Charles, who at this point in the novel has not confessed his love to her. Thus, the need to hide the truth begins

---

[13] At the same time Charles is hiding the secret of his attachment to Clementina (although he castigates Charlotte for "love[ing] to puzzle, and find out secrets where none are intended" [1.394]), Charlotte is hiding her secret contract with Captain Andersen that prohibits her from marrying without his consent, and later is reticent about whether she feels inclined to marry Lord G.

the process of leaking it. Harriet has certainly begun to take cognizance of her feelings for Charles, even though it is difficult for her to declare it openly. Similarly, Harriet writes, "If this should end at last in love, and if I should be *entangled in an hopeless passion*, the object of it would be Sir Charles Grandison" (1.219). Here, Harriet admits her love only circuitously and frames it in a subjunctive clause, attempting to preempt a bout of uncontrollable feeling by naming it in advance. In refusing to tell Lucy that she loves Charles directly, Harriet shows that she is deceiving herself, trying to protect herself against her growing passion.[14] Although Richardson's characters are joined together into an "affective community" of siblings, cousins, and friends, the epistemological drive of the novel still tends toward secrets and lies and thus a mistrust of the possibility of self-knowledge.[15]

Indeed, despite the novel's insistence on "frankness," letter-writers in *Grandison* are actually "less spontaneous and frank than those in [Richardson's] first two novels […] [and they] allow their past, experiencing selves, a fuller expression" (Bray 66). Harriet knows that she revises her feelings: "I am not generally so much affected at the moment when any-thing unhappy befalls me, as I am upon reflexion, when I extend, compare, and weigh consequences" (3.173). And her mind often lags behind her heart: "what a *rememberer*, if I may make a word, is the heart!—Not a circumstance escapes it" (2.299). So while Harriet desires to interpret her feelings and motivations in the moment, she knowingly, even purposefully, falls short. Knowledge and reality are not stable entities in this novel, because meaning and understanding are only as old as the most recent letter read, the most recent insight and counter-insight made. All it takes is for Harriet to receive a letter from Sir Charles that is vague in some way, and she begins to doubt everything, creating a *dédoublement*, a doubling-back. Harriet quickly learns that she cannot trust herself and her insights.

---

[14] On the contrary, Charlotte claims that she will never marry the rather boring Lord G., whom she teases mercilessly, because she is seeking a romantic and passionate story, and she refuses to settle for anyone whom she deems too conventional. In a meta-literary exchange, Charlotte contrasts herself with Anna Howe and Mr. Hickman, Anna's initially uninspiring suitor in *Clarissa*, whom she ends up marrying. And yet, Charlotte protests too much, and she *does* become Lady G. (and Anna Howe ends up with Mr. Hickman), although Charlotte claims that she is unwilling, even jokingly so, on her wedding day. They marry, she gives birth to a baby girl, and seems to live in uncomplicated, domesticated bliss with a man whom she continues to mock unsparingly. But if Charlotte ends in relinquishing her romantic ideal and embracing the man her brother wishes her to marry, her domestication is not entirely credible. For more on this ambiguous ending, see Emily Friedman (651–67).

[15] Chico defines an "affective community" as an honest and open environment of friends and family in which there is a "*mutual* admiration bound by duty" (47, emphasis in original).

"Self, my dear Lucy, is a very wicked thing," writes Harriet; it is "a sanctifier, if one would give way to its partialities, of actions, which, to others, we should have no doubt to condemn. Delicacy, too, is often a misleader. [...] It should be called *Indelicacy*" (2.1). Here, Harriet implicitly cites Clarissa, who, in the third edition of Richardson's second novel, claims, "*Self* here, which is at the bottom of all we do, and of all we wish, is the grand misleader," a quotation that serves as the epigraph for this chapter.

*Grandison*'s narrative is focused on, even obsessed with, analyzing whether and in what manner Harriet and Charles know they are in love, and as an ironic consequence, their love is deferred. We see this when Harriet recalls to Lucy how she felt in the presence of Charles, before she is quite able to comprehend her true feelings for him: "I'll tell you how the Fool, the maiden Fool, looked, and acted. Her feet insensibly moved to meet him. [...] And then, finding my hand in his, when I knew not whether I had an hand or not [...] and I sighed for one reason [...] and blushed for two" (1.245). Here Harriet's body is acting separately from her will, as her unconscious movements react faster than her words or thoughts. She reports that she feels that she is under "obligation" to Charles, referring to the heroic rescue from the clutches of Sir Hargrave. But her other reason for blushing because she had no idea what to say to him—so arrested is she in inaction when faced with this man whom she both admires and to whom she is grateful—indicates that she has deeper, unconscious feelings for her protector. The moment in which she realizes that they had been holding hands without her being aware of it is a particularly beautiful one; the unconscious position of her hand, her sigh, and her blushes embody Harriet's growing feelings in a way that words and thoughts could not. In this way, Harriet does not yet *know* she is in love, though her movements do.

Several pages later, Harriet takes stock of her feelings but begins by actively denying love. She uses very similar language to that which Clarissa uses when she explains to Anna that she had been tricked by Lovelace into escaping her family's home, though, of course, Harriet is in no physical danger here. She writes, "I am in a sort of wilderness. [...] But it cannot be from *Love*: [...] [you said] there was a sort of you-know-not-what of *pleasure* in sighing [...] yet that it was involuntary?—Did you not say, that you were ready to quarrel with yourself, you knew not why?" (1.284) Harriet "quarrels" with herself, illustrating her divided consciousness in the act of deliberating. She is afraid, it seems, of conflating a feeling of love with a sense of obligation to Charles for rescuing her. Yet, her ignorance of her own motivations is significant: she cites the *je ne sais quoi* feeling of pleasure in having accidentally, involuntarily sighed in Charles's presence, and again, a feeling of not knowing her own mind. Harriet is concerned with not seeming "far gone in a certain passion" (1.292), what she considers to be "so *vehement* a folly" (1.293) from which there is no return. Harriet seems determined to not know she is in love. She never allows herself to get swept up in the articulation of love without a thorough reexamination of it later in her letters to Lucy. This reexamination, the act of reporting her actions and thoughts, attempts to undermine and check her passions.

We can see other instances of Harriet's self-deception from early in the text. For example, she writes to Lucy that she has determined to be careful to distrust any man's flattery, since intense passion can never last. She does not want a man who praises her too much or who seems overly attached, since she knows that such affairs are short-lived. She would prefer, she says, a man who has "gratitude" and "principle" and "whose love is founded in reason" (1.109–10) rather than in physical attributes or overt passions. Harriet's emphasis on reason, mind, gratitude, and resolution, contrasted with haste, fluttering, and violent passions shows that her ideal is a dispassionate love. Using the language of reason and anti-romanticism, she attempts to banish the possibility of passion *before* she feels it in order to protect herself against the pain it inevitably produces. But it is clear to the reader that she is, indeed, in love, and hiding that fact from herself.

Why are characters in *Grandison* so frightened by and ashamed of the idea of love? As a narrator of her own story Harriet is trying to avoid a negative outcome. It is not an ethical dilemma that Harriet faces but one of fear that is concomitant with the sensibilities of analytical fiction, where love is aligned with distrust and lies rather than honesty and joy. "I don't know whether," Harriet writes, "while [love] is in suspense, and is only on one side, it be not the parent of jealousy, envy, dissimulation; making the person pretend generosity, disinterestedness, and I cannot tell what" (1.387). According to Koehler, the word "suspense," which appears ninety-five times in *Grandison*, is a kind of "state of mental torture" (317). Harriet is even still ambivalent about her feelings after she is sure that she and not Clementina will marry Charles. Recognizing the uneasiness of her love, the heroine of *Grandison* claims that passion is "a narrower of the heart" (1.387 and 2.131), diagnosing the very problems with which novels like *La Princesse de Clèves* are preoccupied.

Lafayette's novel acts in *Grandison* as a negative example of dangerous romance in which knowledge is often misinterpreted and doubted and in which love is concomitant with dissimulation, jealousy, and fear. In the scene in which the French novel is mentioned, Harriet's cousins, as well as her aunt Selby and her grandmother, Henrietta Shirley, talk about unrequited and jilted love, sparked by accounts of Clementina's suffering after Charles marries Harriet (although Clementina is notably absent from the party). Clementina's story—which consumes almost a third of the overall narrative and most of the seventh volume—depicts a calamitous alternative to the happy marriages of Harriet, Lucy (to Lord Reresby at the very end), and Mrs. Shirley, when Clementina defers her marriage to Belvedere, who would be a very good match for her. Although several of her own letters are included throughout the novel, in the seventh volume, Clementina's conversation is narrated mostly in Harriet's letters to Lucy, which Chico reads as "Clementina's epistolary silence [that] opens the way for Harriet's narrative control" (61). Harriet deceives herself when she continuously champions Clementina at the end of the novel as an "inimitable example" (Charles calls her an "inimitable woman" [2.567] in the fifth volume), to borrow the famous epithet from *The Princess of Clèves*: "O Lucy! you will be delighted with Clementina: You will even, for a while, forget your Harriet [...] never did a young Lady do more honour to her sex" (2:163). But even this ebullient praise of Harriet's former rival signals a threat hanging over the heroine's happiness; it reveals that she still sees Clementina as an opponent that needs to be watched closely. This is, perhaps, because Clementina may still be in love with Charles, even after his marriage to Harriet.

Clementina often blushes when the issue of a second love comes up in conversation, which could be interpreted as an enduring inclination for Charles. While there are a number of successful second-love marriages that occur in this novel, Clementina intermittently refuses to marry Belvedere, which leaves the question of whether or not the marriage plot in this novel completely triumphs at the end.[16] In this context, Lucy's young cousin Kitty Holles describes Clementina's "struggles" in quite romantic terms that she is torn between duty, family, her passion, and that her parents absent in the novel, but who wield power over her, inducing her to marry rather than to remain single or to enter the convent, as she professes that she wishes to do (3:394). In response, Mrs. Shirley tells the story of how she almost rejected Mr. Shirley, a man for whom she felt esteem but not

---

[16] As far as whether Charles may still be in love with Clementina, Chico writes: "While raising suspicions about Clementina's feelings for Sir Charles, Harriet willfully denies that Sir Charles harbors any lingering and inappropriate affection for the Italian. Harriet reads Clementina's studied avoidance of Sir Charles as a sign of her desire for him, but refuses (as does the novel) to speculate on the other side of the amorous coin" (62).

love (but for whom a love would eventually grow). "Suppose," said the young Henrietta to her friend Mrs. Eggleton, a woman whose first lover had died and whose second had left her at the altar,

> after I had vowed love to a man quite indifferent to me, I should meet with the very one, the kindred soul, who must irresistibly claim my whole heart? [...]
> 
> A Duke de Nemours! said [Mrs. Eggleton], taking up La Princesse de Clèves, that unluckily lay on my table—Ah, my Henrietta! Have I found you out?— That Princess, my dear, was a silly woman. Her story is written with dangerous elegance; but the whole foundation of her distresses was an idle one. To fancy herself in love with a mere stranger, because he appeared agreeable at a ball, when she lived happily with a worthy husband, was mistaking mere liking for love, and combating all her life after with a chimera of her own creating. (3:399–400)[17]

Although Kitty seems to think that Clementina's resolution to remain single sounds romantic, for the older generation, this notion is an irrational and destructive idea, symbolized by the figure of the chimera—an unknown and terrifying specter—that Mrs. Eggleton cites in the passage above. Mrs. Eggleton reads *La Princesse de Clèves* as a relic of medieval courtly romances, which, through the image of the monstrous chimera, warns its heroine of the dissimulation, jealousy, pain, and, ultimately, loneliness that attend passionate romantic love. By reporting Mrs. Eggleton's advice to the younger women, Henrietta, now older and wiser, and indeed happier for having married Mr. Shirley, cautions them (and the reader) not to fall into romantic traps that could lead to improper matches or, even worse, to no match at all.

In this scene we see Mrs. Eggleton playing the role of Madame de Chartres, warning her daughter against the dangers of courtly love. Mrs. Eggleton urges the young Henrietta to marry Mr. Shirley because it would be an "advantageous" match that would benefit all of Henrietta's family. Mrs. Eggleton continues to say that "gratitude" and "duty" will soon transform into warmer attachment, and that this kind of dispassionate, sensible regard is "the only sort of love that suits this imperfect state" (3:398). Mrs. Eggleton

---

[17] It is interesting to note that Richardson classifies Mrs. Eggleton's speech under the heading "Fancy. Imagination. Romances," in his *Moral and Instructive Sentiments*, emphasizing that passionate love was not the ideal kind that he imagined for his characters (262). Everyone in *Grandison* seems to have read *La Princesse de Clèves*. Perhaps they believe it threatens to catalyze a Quixotic decision by Henrietta—and later Clementina—to emulate the princess's adulterous passion.

ends in encouraging Henrietta to "condescend to be happy" (3:398).[18] Similarly, Madame de Chartres urges the princess to consider the world of difference between "the domestic miseries which illicit love-affairs entail" (8)[19] and a happy existence that comes with marrying for duty rather than for love. Madame de Chartres wishes more than anything to protect her daughter from entering into an infidelity, a behavior that does not seem so much morally problematic (since everybody in the novel practices it) as emotionally dangerous. Madame de Chartres deliberately and overtly warns the princess about letting her passions overtake her and cites the "tranquility," "virtue," and a feeling of "elevation" that she could achieve by avoiding temptation. She wants to teach her daughter

> [what] peaceful happiness [follows] a virtuous woman's life [...] [and] how hard it was to preserve this virtue without extreme care, and without that one sure means of securing a wife's happiness, which is to love her husband and to be loved by him. (8)[20]

Madame de Chartres insists that the only way to protect oneself from the harm of entering into an extramarital affair is constant self-doubt ("une extrême défiance de soi-même"). Tranquility and freedom from "trouble"—which, as we saw in the previous chapter, is used many times throughout the French novel as a synonym for *agitation, intrigue,* and *passion*—requires, for the princess at least, self-effacement and a complete withdrawal from public life. Clementina's desire to enter a convent—a resolution she makes periodically throughout the seventh volume of *Grandison*—would reflect the fate of the princess in Lafayette's novel were she to go through with it.

In *La Princesse de Clèves*, love is always tied to the danger and fear of being deceived by others and by one's senses and to a loss of control over oneself. The princess cannot shake the bitter pains of having felt the "the cruel repentance

---

[18] Interestingly, the Countess of D. gives Harriet very similar advice when she is trying to convince her to marry her son, Lord D., a match which would be socially beneath her. She tells Harriet that it is silly and romantic to expect "adoration" and absolute perfection in a husband, and claims that in most cases, a "preferable choice" will serve well enough (2.547). The same advice coming from such an unreliable source may lead one to distrust Mrs. Shirley's advice as well.

[19] "les malheurs domestiques où plongent les engagements" (248).

[20] "quelle tranquillité suivait la vie d'une honnête femme [...] [et] aussi combien il était difficile de conserver cette vertu que par une extrême défiance de soi-même et par un grand soin de s'attacher à ce qui seul peut faire le bonheur d'une femme, qui est d'aimer son mari et d'en être aimée" (248).

and mortal anguish that are inseparable from love" (64)[21] when she believes Nemours is in love with another woman. Even after she has been disabused of this notion, she cannot be happy because she realizes that it is not possible for her to be secure and satisfied (to "love confidently" as Venus tells Fiammetta to do in the *Elegia*) in any kind of passionate entanglement. She realizes that it is not within her nature to love easily. The princess recognizes that the danger in loving is the danger of losing control over her emotions and herself. So she convinces herself that it is impossible that Nemours could love anyone with "a sincere and lasting attachment" (64).[22] These very same sentiments are mirrored in Harriet's letters to Lucy out of a sense of self-protection.

When Mrs. Shirley warns the younger women that they must not "set out with false notions of happiness; gay, fairly-land imaginations; and when these schemes prove unattainable, sit down in disappointment and dejection" (3:395), she cites exactly the ending of the princess in Lafayette's novel. In *La Princesse de Clèves*, Madame de Clèves retreats into ascetic self-denial and then dies. She gives up any hope of love, resolution, or self-knowledge. Throughout *Grandison*, Harriet, Charlotte, and Clementina all grapple with understanding their own hearts, and whether or not what they feel, as Mrs. Selby tells Harriet, is love, in a world in which first impressions are often deceiving: "young women in a beginning love are always willing to conceal themselves from themselves; they are desirous to smother the fire, before they will call out for help, till it blazes" (1:212). Although Mrs. Selby's prescription for Harriet to know herself is intended playfully, the metaphor of fire invokes a real danger to the self in any work of literature that involves romance or the pursuit of marriage.

For Harriet, the specter of losing herself in an unrequited love haunts the initial six volumes of *Grandison*. Love is both idealized and feared in the novel, and the passionate expression of love is considered downright dangerous. The attraction is counteracted by the simultaneous potential of rejection. The problem the characters in *Grandison* face is, therefore, one of fear and potential shame, not morality. Harriet escapes the princess's and Clarissa's fate because the narrative shifts toward the resolution of a marriage plot at the end of the novel, and we are told that the balance between passion and virtue in Harriet and

---

[21] "cruels repentirs et [...] mortelles douleurs que donne l'amour" (237).
[22] "un attachement sincère et durable" (236).

Charles's union sanctifies their love.²³ And yet, the difference in the outcomes for the heroines does not save Harriet from the psychological ordeals and the tortures of suspense through which Richardson has put her nor the fact of having had to confront the limitations of her own self-knowledge. The reference to *La Princesse de Clèves* yokes *Grandison* to the analytical novel, even if the difference in Harriet's and the princess's endings shows us how far, narratively, from Lafayette's novel and from the tragedy of *Clarissa* Richardson has come. Yet, *Grandison* remains unresolved, re-opening doubt and indecision at the end of the novel because of Clementina's abstention from love. Despite all of Harriet's anti-romantic protestations, there is a shadow of sadness that hangs over the renunciation of passion and romance in Richardson's last novel. We are, perhaps, in *Grandison*'s ambiguity, invited to romantically hope that Clementina will keep holding out for someone who, as Henrietta calls the duke de Nemours, is "the very one, the kindred soul, who must irresistibly claim [her] whole heart."

As I hope is evident enough, this chapter had a double aim. On the one hand, to demonstrate the affinities between Lafayette's novel and Richardson's last two books in terms of their pessimistic, anti-romantic philosophies and persistent epistemological drive toward rejecting love, rather than embracing it. On the other hand, I also intend to show—following Chapter 2 on Marguerite and Cervantes, and in anticipation of the following, final chapter of this study, on Austen and Stendhal—that the field of comparative literature—which take as a given that literary texts from multiple national traditions can and should be read together to find both shared themes and ideologies, as well as intertextuality and analogous social and psychological concerns—offers readers interpretive tools to more deeply understand the complexities of analytical fiction. When we read these texts together, we not only are able to explicate more or less straightforward intertextuality, as exists between *Grandison* and *La Princesse de Clèves*, *Grandison* and Austen's novels, and *La Princesse de Clèves* and Stendhal's work, we are able to identify patterns of literary expression that illuminate the deeper structures of each text and, moreover, of the sub-genre. In this way, analytical fiction transcends the French tradition, as its mood and sensibility are encountered across temporal and national boundaries.

---

23 They have transcended the false starts and self-deceptions (primarily Charles's sense of duty to Clementina and Harriet's anti-romanticism) to finally arrive at what Jones terms a "'sentimental love,' a dialectical resolution of reason and passion, which [...] became an acceptable basis for marriage" (296) in the second half of the eighteenth century.

# 5

# Silence and the Cruel Gaze of Society: Austen's *Persuasion* and Stendhal's *Armance*

> *The reaction of the past and of the future on the present brings unhappiness [...]. What I have suffered no longer exists, what I shall suffer does not exist, and I am alarmed, I am tormented, I am destroyed by these two nothingnesses! [...] What stupid reasoning [...]. what stupid, metaphysical irrationality, wouldn't you say?*[1]

Stendhal's first novel, *Armance* (1827), and Austen's last novel, *Persuasion* (1817), have been compared at least once before, by J.F.W. Hemmings, who notes that *Armance* reads like "a rather darker *Persuasion*, the situation between the lovers being, in a sense, reversed" (73). Stendhal's novel, like Austen's, is a novel of manners, investigating the language, behavior, and unwitting motivations of its characters. Though one ends tragically and the other happily, *Armance* and *Persuasion*, I argue, both hinge on a troubling and loaded silence that undermines almost every intimate scene involving the main characters. Particularly evident in these nineteenth-century novels is the role that the representation of setting (be it familial or societal)—always closed, suspicious, and judgmental—plays in understanding analytical fiction. In this chapter, I elaborate the ways in which the gaze of society within the novel can help to fuel the silences that simultaneously hide and reveal as well as the ways in which silence functions alternatively to bring about and hinder intimacy between the central couple in each work. The refusal to provide the full story also manifests itself as a form of reluctance or inhibition in the narrators, who struggle to gain knowledge about characters' states of mind, beliefs, and motivations.

---

[1] "C'est la réaction du passé et de l'avenir sur le présent qui fait le malheur. [...] Ce que j'ai souffert n'est plus, ce que je souffrirai n'est pas, et je m'inquiète, je me tourmente, je me crève, pour ces deux néants là! [...] quel sot calcul. [...] quel sot déraisonnement métaphysique, direz-vous?" (Benjamin Constant, in Rudler 337).

## A Fragile Society in *Persuasion*

*Persuasion* begins where most other works of analytical fiction end: with a renunciation of love. Put another way, *Persuasion* is a work of analytical fiction told in reverse, or, it is at once a perversion of analytical fiction and the apotheosis of analytical fiction. It begins with the denial of love and ends with the mixture of pain and pleasure that love bestows. The novel tells the story of Anne Elliot, an unmarried twenty-seven-year-old woman who lives unhappily with her father and sister. Years before, Anne had been in love with Frederick Wentworth, a naval officer whom she had renounced because her godmother, Lady Russell, disapproved of him. Eight years later, Captain Wentworth returns, wealthy and triumphant from the Napoleonic Wars. By a coincidence, Frederick's sister and brother-in-law, Admiral Croft, a much wealthier man, but not a gentleman, rent Kellynch-Hall, the manor house of Anne's father Sir Walter, while Anne's father and sister settle in Bath for the winter, leaving Anne to move in with her younger sister, Mary, and Mary's husband. Suddenly thrown together with Frederick, Anne struggles simultaneously to cope with and hide her rekindled feelings. Although Anne and Frederick believe that they are adept at reading each other's thoughts, she becomes convinced that he is attached to her sister-in-law, Louisa Musgrove. At the same time, Frederick becomes increasingly jealous of Anne's supposed engagement to her cousin and heir to the Elliot title, William Elliot, of whom everyone in the family except Anne is very much enamored. Nevertheless, Anne and Frederick engage throughout the novel in an almost accidental and silent courtship that, while not totally unthreatened by jealousy and social and familial strain, is the closest we have come in this examination of analytical fiction to intimacy.

Like *Armance*, which takes place during the Restoration of the monarchy in France, *Persuasion* is set in a fragile social milieu, with Anne's family desperately holding on to an archaic and degenerating idea of aristocracy, while the middle classes flourish around them. In fact, the impetus for the drama is that Sir Walter, who is consumed with his lineage and who reads nothing but his *Baronetage*, can no longer afford the lifestyle to which he is accustomed. Ann Elizabeth Gaylin describes Anne's situation as "in between homes, social circles, and marital status" (43), and this interstitial position underlines that "the narrative is set at a transitional moment, when the values of the landed aristocracy are giving way to those of the commercially based middle class" (Gaylin 43). This outer social and political frame helps to define the setting of *Persuasion* (as well as of *Armance*, as we will see) as bordered by sweeping, encroaching social and economic changes in nineteenth-century England and France. But as in other works of analytical fiction, the secondary characters in these two novels are wrapped up in their own tightly closed society, while the main characters create yet a third, though much smaller, society of their own, and which transcends the other two. The world of Sir Walter Elliot, deliberately exclusive and contemptuous of lower social classes, is self-conscious and self-selected, but Anne does not entirely inhabit this world. She is enclosed within her own thoughts and her own questioning of what she knows and whom she loves, just like any heroine of analytical fiction.

Austen's darkest courtship novel is ambiguous, straddling romance and realism, at once mediating the harshness of the Napoleonic Wars and depicting a quietly blossoming intimacy between two characters who had already given up on love.[2] The bleak social, economic, and political forces weighing heavily on the characters, whether explicitly or implicitly, contrasted with the small personal triumphs and excitements that punctuate the text, create a tension that pulsates throughout the novel. *Persuasion* opposes, to use the narrator's words from the end of the narrative, "moments, marked by returning hope or increasing despondence, [which are] [...] dwelt on with energy" (162). It is haunted by the way in which, as Adela Pinch puts it, Anne Elliot "is always 'resuming an agitation', [...] experiencing a 'revival of former pain'" (150). And Janet Todd notes that "Anne is represented as correcting her attitudes with intense and occasionally ironic awareness" (131) and is "bewildered" (138) by the confusion of inner and outer worlds, pleasure and pain. Even though Anne and Frederick are reunited and married by the end of the novel, Austen's narrative creates a pattern of affective contradiction, an emotional back and forth between happiness and anguish. These affective contradictions systematically undercut the heroine's sense of joy with competing feelings of fear, hopelessness, and isolation, so that Austen paints an unsentimental view of human nature that belies the traditional marriage plot narrative.

Certainly, the novel's pessimism and its focus on the cruelty of society are evidenced even before Frederick returns. Anne's sisters perpetrate a kind of "motiveless malignancy" (as Coleridge famously describes *Othello*'s Iago) against her, although they have no reason to be jealous of Anne, since her "first bloom" has faded and they consider her quite useless. After she discovers that Frederick's sister will be renting the Elliot family house, Anne's thoughts immediately turn

---

[2] Jocelyn Harris's book *A Revolution Almost Beyond Expression* points out the ambivalence of Austen's subject, which recounts both a world haunted by war and "a tale of a woman who regains her lost bloom in a second spring" (20).

to the eight years that have passed since she rejected him. The latent pain of this memory is revived, and yet, she must pretend that she is little affected by it, since her sisters deny the fact that Anne had rejected Frederick's marriage proposal against her better judgment (21). Moreover, Mary is "perfectly unsuspicious of […] inflicting any peculiar wound" (41) as she reports to Anne that Frederick had not recognized her, because she is "so altered" (41). As in all of analytical fiction, indifference is never really naïve. Rather, it is a studied dissimulation of passivity and calm, and in this case, a calm that intends to wound. Whether or not the Elliots are consciously aware of their cruelty toward Anne, the result is a poorly disguised contempt for her feelings and for her status in the family. Their indifference to Anne's feelings eventually reaches a point where it can be nothing but conscious affectation when, in Bath, Elizabeth snubs Frederick in the street. The resulting silence is overwhelming. In another example, toward the end of the book, when Anne and Frederick are speaking to each other at the White Hart Inn, they are all of a sudden interrupted by her family, when the door is thrown open and Elizabeth and her father walk into the lobby:

> Anne felt an instant oppression, and, wherever she looked, saw symptoms of the same. The comfort, the freedom, the gaiety of the room was over, hushed into cold composure, determined silence, or insipid talk, to meet the heartless elegance of her father and sister. (150)

The room falls silent as Elizabeth and Sir Walter enter in the almost comically dramatic passage above. The general chill, the oppression, the cold composure: all of these words contrast with the previous warmth, comfort, freedom, and gaiety of the scene that the Elliots interrupt. There is a vividness to the sudden change of air in this scene. One can hear the silence and feel the stifling chill flood the room as the door is thrown open. Displaced from their manor by (very) relative poverty, Elizabeth and Sir Walter wish to make their perceived power felt across all the different classes of people with whom they interact. Their arrival at the inn is a rather pathetic attempt to wield that power, although it also serves for Anne and Frederick, who are finally speaking to each other, as an interruption to their nascent rekindled familiarity.

## A Game of Hide and "See"

Never having found her place in her family, Anne becomes the foremost observer in the novel who remains mostly silent and fades into the background.

She is introduced very slowly, and does not even emerge as the protagonist until chapter 4 when she is often relegated to the role of witness, left out of conversations, and forgotten by her family. At the same time, this outsider status places Anne in a position to comment on and appraise those around her. As Alliston puts it, connecting *La Princesse de Clèves* with Austen's work, "as in Lafayette [...] [there is an] interplay and competition among observers who are also constantly observed" (241). In *Persuasion*, as in scenes of spying and being spied in Lafayette's text, the vocabulary of seeing and seeming indicates a desire to know and learn (although it does not always succeed). Since the voice of the narrator is combined with Anne's, seeing—that is understanding— is elevated to a third degree. For example, at one of the Musgroves' parties, Anne plays the piano hoping that no one—particularly not Frederick—will notice her. Of course, he does: "she felt that he was looking [...]—observing her altered features, perhaps, trying to trace in them the ruins of the face which had once charmed him" (48). Anne is troubled by Frederick's surreptitious glance. Having heard from her unfeeling sister that he considers her "altered beyond his knowledge" (41), Anne does not want to know she is being looked at with the judging and demoralizing gaze of a man who not only still blames her for abandoning him but also finds her aged and no longer attractive. Later in the story, his looks take on a different dimension, as Frederick watches an amorous William Elliot watching Anne. Now Frederick notices how attracted he is to her (he attributes her flushed cheeks to the wind, though it is more likely their reconnection that makes Anne blush): "he gave her a momentary glance,—a glance of brightness, which seemed to say, 'that man is struck with you,—and even I, at this moment, see something like Anne Elliot again'" (70). Although it is Frederick's thoughts that are central in this passage, they are being guessed at by Anne, who mediates and interprets them. Anne perceives that a man (she does not know it is Mr. Elliot, nor does she know that he knows who she is) sees a beautiful woman in the road, but she is looking at Frederick when William is looking at her. While at first one might think that Anne is rather passive in the passage above, she is really an active participant in this game of watching and discovering.

Anne is even more active in another scene that takes place in Bath, although this one is far less consequential. Anne is walking with Lady Russell, but she is actually looking for Frederick, when she—quite coincidentally—sees him walking in the street. Anne is convinced that Lady Russell must see him, too. She notices that Lady Russell is staring in Frederick's direction:

> She looked at her however, from time to time, anxiously; and when the moment approached which must point him out, though not daring to look again [...] she was yet perfectly conscious of Lady Russell's eyes being turned exactly in the direction for him, of her being in short intently observing him. (118–119)

This dizzying description of Anne's nervous double watching—at once for Frederick and then for Lady Russell's reaction to a Frederick whom, in fact, she never actually sees—signifies the culmination of the desire for knowledge and certainty in the novel. In the passage above, Anne also seeks confirmation of her suspicions that Frederick may be in Bath for her sake, and also to hasten the reunion between him and Lady Russell. She would like to act, to speak to him, to at least tell Lady Russell that she sees him, but for characters in analytical fiction, action becomes a game of chance, and it is almost always forestalled. This scene ultimately fails to produce any such knowledge, when it turns out that Lady Russell has been looking at some window curtains in that same general direction (or so she claims).

## Duty and Persuasion

Eight years before the action of the novel begins, Anne "was persuaded to believe the engagement [to Frederick] a wrong thing—indiscreet, improper, hardly capable of success, and not deserving it" (19). As Tony Tanner puts it:

> The story of [Anne's] life consists precisely in having had her own way blocked, refused, negated. One might almost think of the book as being about dissuasion, for she is urged or forced not into doing something which she does not want to do, but into *not* doing something which her whole emotional self tells her is the right thing." (233)

The term "persuasion" means a few different things in this novel. According to Kenneth L. Moler, "a parental attempt to influence a child's choice of a matrimonial partner was frequently described as 'persuasion'"(193).[3] Once in the novel, the word "persuasion" is used to signify Frederick's jealousy of Mr. Elliot, and at other times it means "belief" or "conviction." It is also a false impression that Frederick has convinced himself is true ("the same unfortunate persuasion" [147]), in other words, a misreading and self-deception. More often

---

[3] Moler points out that "in *Sir Charles Grandison*, for instance, the term is often used in connection with the matrimonial controversy between Lady Clementina and her parents" (193).

than not, however, the "persuasion" in question is a reference to Anne's rejection of Frederick before the beginning of the novel. Anne's past was governed by this kind of "persuasion," in which she had to normalize a denial of her desires. This leaks into her confrontation with the present upon Frederick's return. *Persuasion*, then, is a meditation on reading and rereading the self, past and present. It is a work of analytical fiction because of the self-doubt and revision inherent in coping with "persuasion." Frederick uses the term "persuasion" in this negative sense when he reflects that Anne "had given him up to oblige others. It had been the effect of *over*-persuasion" (41, emphasis added). Similarly, it is Frederick again who recollects at the end of the novel, when he is explaining the jealousy he felt at seeing Anne, William Elliot, and Lady Russell at a concert, how he had deceived himself because of his lingering feelings of loss and pain. He imagines that Anne is in love with William, and the presence of Lady Russell disturbs him and reminds him of "the indelible, immoveable impression of what persuasion had once done" (163).

Frederick has persuaded himself that Anne was weak-willed in her decision to renounce his love; he is "totally unconvinced and unbending [...] feeling himself ill-used by so forced a relinquishment" (19). Since he had made the decision to love and marry Anne, Frederick saw no barriers to their union. Anne, on the other hand, tries out a number of explanations for her persuasion by Lady Russell when she was nineteen. In part she felt that it was her duty to obey the woman who acted like a mother to her, in part she convinces herself that she was doing what was best for Frederick (and in fact, at the end of the novel, the now reunited and married couple's happiness is flawed to an extent by Anne's family, which gives a sense of what kind of protection Anne was considering in her youth). But Anne merely believed that she was being prudent, while the text points out that it was "self-denying" (19) that caused her misery. Though at the end of the novel, Anne argues that she does not entirely regret what had happened—had she not heeded Lady Russell's advice eight years earlier, she would have felt too guilty to be happy. As Pinch points out, this story is not exactly *Clarissa*:

> The duties to which Anne submits herself belong to the scheme of things outlined in the Baronetage her father loves to read—the preservation and perpetuation of the landed gentry through marriage. Anne submits, however, under no terrors, no parental threats and prohibitions. She gives in under the gentler ministrations of a friend [...] who compensates for her family's indifference to her." (139)

Anne's nature makes it so that she is "glad to have any thing marked out as a duty" (23), so on first reading it may seem perfectly correct that Anne is thwarted by obligation to her family. She claims as much several times, that breaking her engagement to Frederick was what she thought she ought to do as her filial duty. Anne's sense of responsibility of course recalls Lafayette's princess, who also is glad to relegate her behavior to the realm of *bienséance* or "propriety." Each of these women attributes to outside forces what is, in fact, an internal restriction. The claim of "duty" or "propriety," thus, acts merely as a cover for much more complex and irrational, inexplicable feelings.

Austen's novels tend to center on the motif of women's education, and a woman's learning to "read" to greater effect as the novel progresses. But *Persuasion* is different. The novel illustrates "a reversal of a woman's *Bildung*" (Vranjes 179); Anne must *un*learn a "prudent" decision she had been persuaded to make in the past, and instead learn romance: "the natural sequel of an unnatural beginning" (*Persuasion* 21). In this way, she must unlearn pessimism and the skeptical philosophy that had governed her early adulthood, and she must begin to live in the moment and follow her instincts rather than deliberate and analyze. But *Persuasion* never becomes a romance, per se, because Anne never fully stops dissecting and doubting her own thoughts and the motivations of others (nor does the narrator). Anne's use of the vocabulary of seeing and seeming and her relegation to the background as constant observer (as well as a persistent interpreter) underscore the idea that she had abandoned Frederick because the barrier was within herself. Over the course of the novel, Anne learns to overcome her silence and meets Frederick halfway between skepticism and romance.

Anne and Frederick's initial engagement is described as a short "period of exquisite felicity" (18), although the narrator is not satisfied to provide any true unadulterated happiness: they fall in love, in large part, because they are lonely and bored ("he had nothing to do, and she had hardly any body to love" [18]), and "it would be difficult to say which had seen highest perfection in the other, or which had been the happiest; she, in receiving his declarations and proposals, or he in having them accepted" (18). This less-than-passionate courtship seems, in fact, mostly predicated on a mutual desire in the lovers to escape their respective predicaments—Anne her family and Frederick his bachelorhood. Thus, as Tanner points out, there is a mini-romance, as if a "first novel" is embedded in *Persuasion*. But this story, "told in telescopic brevity" (Tanner 234), is a tragedy. As is typical of an analytical novel, two people who are perfectly suited to each other cannot be together, at least not without a lot of agitation and trouble to begin with. It is inevitable that Anne and Frederick should have to separate, and to have many obstacles put between them. After the disappointing break, Frederick's stubbornness, which is a facet of his romanticism, is evident when the narration folds into his thoughts which reveal that he is still angry with Anne for having "used him ill; deserted and disappointed him" (41). He deliberates to no longer love her—despite the fact that it never occurred to him to try to marry anyone else—because he deceives himself. It is clear that he must still feel passion for Anne when he asserts that he would never want to see her again ("her power with him was gone forever" [41]), "*except from some natural sensation of curiosity*" (41, emphasis added). But were Frederick truly finished with their love, he would neither feel "curiosity" to see her again nor hold a grudge.

In analytical fiction, the presumption of knowing one's own motivations, rather than bringing about self-knowledge, leads characters astray and into self-deception. Frederick believes he fully understands Anne (as well as his own effaced love for her), but he is, at the same time, mired in his own inability to forgive her. In this way, it is not only Anne who must change and grow in the novel. According to Claudia L. Johnson, Frederick also must learn to forgive and to love more generously:

> Wentworth's determination is generally considered to mark him as a 'new man,' temperamentally as well as ideologically opposed to the way of life Sir Walter represents. But like his gallantry towards women, his steadfastness to the point of inflexibility actually aligns him with Sir Walter, and he must mitigate his self-will before reconciliation is possible. (157)

Thus, just as Anne has "learned romance" from Frederick's departure, he must learn, over the course of the novel, to be both less rigid and less romantic, to allow himself to be persuaded by Anne—who in turn must learn to assert herself, to herself—that not all hope is lost.

Anne, on the other hand, is more aware of her self-doubt; she questions her own and other characters' motivations, and she maintains an anti-romantic belief, if not the *inevitability* of the end of love, then at least, in its possible negative consequences. At the end of the story of the original persuasion, the narrator reveals that Anne actually merely concedes to Lady Russell's opinion of Frederick because it is far easier than continuing to fight. At such a young age, "such opposition, as these feelings produced, was more than Anne could combat" (19). And so she gives in to Lady Russell when it is time to decide whether or not to marry Frederick. Throughout the novel, she continues to feel the asphyxiating weight of that original story, and, the reader imagines, the regret at having given in so easily. As the narrative moves from one episode to the next, in which she comes into closer and closer contact with Frederick, Anne must contend with the memory of the past. But she must also learn romance in order to relegate the past to a distant memory and accept Frederick's renewed love, as soon as he is able to acknowledge it himself.

## Intimacy, or as Close as We Can Get

So far, we have seen a number of novels that critique romance and demonstrate how passionate love is a dangerous and inconvenient matter. Except for *Grandison*, which, in fact, ends in debilitating doubt for Clementina, even if Harriet and Charles's love is resolved, none of the stories about love examined in this book manage to truly become love stories. *Persuasion*, however, follows a slightly different pattern. Chronologically, it begins with the mini-novel described earlier about Anne and Frederick's almost-perfect love that too-quickly disintegrates, and dispels romance with Lady Russel's persuasion of Anne that she should not marry Frederick. The novel then recreates, from the ashes of an extinguished youthful desire, a warm, knowing intimacy that lies somewhere between romance and skepticism as the narrative progresses. Anne and Frederick's love for each other, which is evidenced throughout the novel, is a more mature passion, preternaturally aware of the other's psyches and folded into the other's feelings and consciousness (Anne is certainly the oldest female protagonist of any examined in this book; although Florida is probably just a bit younger at the end of the *Heptaméron*'s tenth novella). Even the Crofts, who perhaps are modeled on Lord and Lady L. in *Grandison*, are shown as still being very much in love fifteen years after their marriage. Austen's last novel in this way presents characters profiting from second loves, though with the distinction of having loved and lost each other in the first place. Thinking about what may happen with Frederick, were she given a second chance, Anne tries to make herself into a romantic too: "how eloquent could Anne Elliot have been […] against that over-anxious caution" (21). If only that qualifying "could […] have been" were absent, Anne would, indeed be able to open herself to a constant love whose expression does not ebb and flow cyclically. But her caution, her anxiety, her fear of error, all keep her from acting, and it is clear that the centuries of abandoned or potentially abandoned women behind her influence her sense of self-governance. Anne is not an intertextual character, per se, but the narrative mode of this novel precedes her. Like the protagonists in other *romans d'analyse*, Anne is cautious, fearful, and skeptical of love in ways that keep her and Frederick apart.

Early in the novel, Anne wonders what it will be like to meet Frederick again after so many years: "she would have liked to know how he felt as to a meeting. Perhaps indifferent, if indifference could exist under such circumstances. He must be either indifferent or unwilling" (39). This imaginative rumination which, of course, foreshadows the real reunion can be read as an attempt on Anne's part to forestall whatever disappointment Frederick may give her when they see each other again. She imagines that Frederick has forgotten her, although her second thought—the afterthought—represents the true insight: he is unwilling to see her because he has not forgiven her. We see this explicitly in a few different scenes, including when Mary's two-year-old son begins to climb on Anne's back and refuses to desist. Without being fully conscious of why or how, Anne unexpectedly feels relief, and she just knows that it is Frederick who has removed the child. But the kind action renders Anne speechless, she is unable even to thank him (54). John Wiltshire finds that the little boy's "unruliness is a metonym for the pressures that are present in the room" (79). Indeed, none of the adults there are willing to speak to each other. Charles Haytner, who is sitting on the sofa, picks up the newspaper when Frederick goes over to him, and as this scene takes place fairly early in the novel, Frederick is still refusing to speak to Anne. Unlike in the scene quoted above at the White Hart Inn, the lack of communication in this case is truly an absence; a deeply felt, painful, and debilitating silence that threatens to keep Anne and Frederick apart. While Harris posits that the scene with Anne's nephew is imbued with an "impressionistic, erotic charge [that] enters the narrative when their bodies almost touch" (Harris 25), Anne's inability to speak and Frederick's continued refusal to directly acknowledge Anne render the scene at least a partial failure of communication.

Something similar happens when Frederick helps Anne into the carriage at Lyme, when they are returning to Uppercross after Louisa is injured. Here again, the sentences are fragmented and impressionistic, and Frederick's act is accomplished in silence. One can read this scene in two ways, as either a completion of an intimate, but unspoken action between the would-be lovers, or as a failure of communication:

> Yes,—he had done it. She was in the carriage, and felt that he had placed her there, that his will and his hands had done it. [...] She understood him. He could not forgive her,—but he could not be unfeeling. [...] It was a remainder

of former sentiment; it was an impulse of pure, though unacknowledged friendship; it was a proof of his own warm and amiable heart, which she could not contemplate without emotions so compounded of pleasure and pain, that she knew not which prevailed. (61)

Here the references to understanding, desire to give relief, sentiment, friendship, warmth, amiability, and pleasure (feelings that amplify and intensify as the passage goes on) are contrasted with lack of forgiveness, condemnation, resentment, and pain. François, when interpreting this passage, focuses on the "Yes,—he had done it." The critic notes the "suspensive dash at once lengthening and completing the pause of breathlessness produced by the perfectly executed [...] act [...] even if the sentences immediately following this one both thicken and trouble the basis of Anne's psychological contentment with Wentworth" (15). But the "pure" friendship is mitigated by the qualifying "though unacknowledged" that hovers dangerously in between. In the end, this scene is mired in painful ambivalence. The phrase "she could not contemplate without emotions so compounded of pleasure and pain" captures the mood of analytical fiction in its insistence on rumination and affective contradiction. Pleasure can never exist without pain, as we have seen throughout *Persuasion* and throughout all the texts examined in this study. The cycles of difficult recognition of love, the attendant jealousies, regrets and condemnation for past grievances can go on indefinitely. Even when characters are momentarily contented, another impetus that will disrupt their happiness is never far away.

*Persuasion* can be read as a celebration of rekindled love—or of love that was never truly lost—but it is simultaneously loaded with references to that painful beginning. The past and the present not only remain inseparable, more so in the beginning of the novel, but when they meld, they create silence. When Anne is introduced properly in the fourth chapter, the reader learns that "her attachment and regrets had, for a long time, clouded every enjoyment of youth; and an early loss of bloom and spirits had been their lasting effect" (19–20). This deadening effect, highlighted by the novel's taking place in autumn and winter, metaphorically silences Anne in her adulthood. Her first meeting with Frederick is a non-meeting, and the language is strangely fragmented and scattered, echoing Anne's own disconnected impressions: "her eye half met Captain Wentworth's; a bow, a curtsey passed; she heard his voice—he talked to Mary, said all that was right. [...] The room seemed full—full of persons and voices—but a few minutes ended it. [...] 'It is over! It is over!' she repeated to herself [...] in nervous gratitude" (40). Thus, the reunion is over before it even happens. All of the anticipation and questioning, the self-doubt and fear about how the meeting will go are flattened into silence and inaction.

Although there are no interpolated tales in the novel, there are instances where Austen hides references to Anne and Frederick's enduring love in a seemingly unrelated part of the story. The scene in which Anne plays the piano for the Musgroves demonstrates how Frederick and Anne's love is redirected through another conduit:

> She knew that when she played she was giving pleasure only to herself; but this was no new sensation: *excepting one short period of her life*, she had never, *since the age of fourteen*, never since the loss of her dear mother, known the happiness of being listened to, or encouraged by any just appreciation or real taste." (32, emphasis added)

On first reading, the emphasis seems to be placed on Anne's too-brief relationship with her mother. Lady Elliot, we learn, was the only person who spoke to and listened to Anne, she had "just appreciation and real taste," both for music and conversation. It is easy to overlook, then, the phrase in the middle of the quotation: "*excepting one short period of her life*," as a reminder of Anne's engagement to Frederick. Although he is not named in the passage above, it is implied that he is the only other person in the world who took Anne's opinions seriously, and who found her to be interesting and talented. Mediated through the memory of her mother, Anne is thus allowed to think fondly of Frederick, without any overt allusions to their painful separation. But the memory of him, which she sanctions to herself only hidden in a memory of her mother, couples rejection and death, creating a double pain of remembering.

Another kind of sublimated conversation or hidden intimacy is evidenced in each of the eavesdropping scenes, one of which takes place on the long walk from Uppercross to Winthrop. Anne happens to overhear a conversation between Frederick and Louisa, who is in love with him. Frederick says to Louisa that her character is decisive and firm. He is speaking implicitly of Anne (whom he considers weak-willed) by contrasting her with this idea of Louisa. Rather, it seems more likely that he is referring to himself, and to his own philosophy of love. We are reminded in his speech of his own feelings after Anne breaks off their engagement. He considers her irresolute and himself decisive. Unlike Louisa, who is flattered by Frederick's compliments, Anne, eavesdropping, can read him correctly, and it causes her to interpret "a great deal of very painful import [...] which [gives] her extreme agitation" (59–60). Frederick's speech is tied to the past in the act of remembering parting with Anne so many years earlier. The past and the future are embedded in his speech to Louisa, in the sense that Frederick seems to be reaffirming that he will not entertain the idea of rekindling his love of Anne. But of course he is self-deceived; it is unclear whether he is deliberately speaking loudly enough for Anne to hear him, or if this is a coincidence. In any case, Frederick's very return to Uppercross signifies the possibility of reopening what he insists is closed.

## Psyche and Insight[4]

*Persuasion* meditates on characters' faculties of intelligence, understanding, perception, and penetration. While Anne is silent throughout much of the novel, she is always reading and interpreting other characters. Several times in the text, we learn that Anne has uncommon insight into Frederick's mind: "Anne felt the utter impossibility, from her knowledge of his mind, that he could be unvisited by remembrance any more than herself" (42). For example, the passage in which Sir Walter and Elizabeth burst into the inn to invite all the Uppercross and Lyme connections to an evening party demonstrates how Anne and Frederick are capable of reading each other when no one else can. With an incredible use of free indirect style here, the narrative moves in and out of Anne's mind, interspersing her insight into Frederick's thoughts with Mary's (Mary insisting that Frederick's inability to put the invitation card away must illustrate his delight in being asked to join the party). Whereas Anne

> *knew him*; she saw disdain in his eye, and could not venture to believe that he had determined to accept such an offering, as atonement for all the insolence of the past. Her spirits sank. [...] Anne caught his eye, saw his cheeks glow, and his mouth form itself into a momentary expression of contempt. (151, emphasis added)

Having gotten used to each other's presence again in the several months that they have been reacquainted, Frederick and Anne exchange a look so meaningful that no explanations are necessary, and their mutual insight renders the false

---

[4] This subtitle is borrowed from an article by André Aciman, "L'Esprit de pénétration: Psyche and Insight" (1997).

interpretations of the other characters laughable. Anne senses immediately that her sister and father think that Frederick will feel "gratification" and "delight" because of this invitation, whereas it is truly surprise and "polite acknowledgement," and finally, as he processes it more, "contempt" (151). The two do not speak to each other in this scene but they communicate volumes through their looks.

By the end of the novel, it seems that Frederick is able to fully express this longing to rekindle the relationship with Anne. The most famous scene of listening in is found in the penultimate chapter, as Anne and Captain Harville are discussing whether women or men are more constant in love, which Frederick overhears while he is writing a letter. The scene is also important because it is the first in which Anne is the central figure, being granted agency to articulate her opinions. Anne claims that men love "as long as [they] have an object" (157) while women's love is eternal, even after "hope is gone" (157). While Anne is speaking, however, she is distracted by a noise; it is Frederick dropping his pen. He is secretly listening to her, and he has lost his train of thought while writing. As Rachel Brownstein has noted, Anne's argument "shows she is not thinking of Benwick [the inconstant man in question] at all, but of Wentworth" (87). When Frederick drops his pen, it is a sign that he has understood Anne's coded message. He also begins to write a new letter, this one to her, a beautiful and touching love letter that reveals and offers to her his entire heart. The symmetry of the scene is striking and elegant (Brownstein 88). He explains to her that although he feared her lost, he could never give up loving her beyond all others. Unlike other analytical characters who do the same thing, only surreptitiously or unconsciously, Frederick deliberately wishes to reopen what he had long considered past hope, just as in her speech Anne implies that she is still in love with him. With this letter, Frederick intends to break their silence, to invite her to speak to him again, and to acknowledge what they have both known for quite a while, that they still love each other.

And yet, the ending of *Persuasion* returns to the sort of ambivalence that is witnessed in most other passages in the novel. Anne's total happiness is tainted by the same kinds of gnawing fears that we will also see in the following section on *Armance*, the re-encroachment of the outside world on the possibility of individual happiness. François's analysis of the end of *Mansfield Park* applies equally to *Persuasion*: "whatever Fanny's final satisfaction with such enclosure, there is a sideways glance to the world at large here, which, were it her own, would betray a cynicism in her prudence" (221). At the conclusion of *Persuasion* Anne and Frederick are married, but, as the narrator tells us, Anne's happiness is still not without "alloy" since she has no family that will accept Frederick as her husband. She ends in marrying him without fully persuading her father and sisters that it is the right choice; "there she felt her own inferiority keenly" (167), the narrator reports. Although Frederick's family is loving and accepting, harmonious, respectable, and full of good-will, having her own family continue to refuse to acknowledge Frederick "was a source of as lively pain as her mind could well be sensible of, under circumstances of otherwise strong felicity" (167). And again, in the last paragraph of the novel:

> Anne was tenderness itself, and she had the full worth of it in Captain Wentworth's affection. His profession was all that could ever make her friends wish that tenderness less; the dread of a future war all that could dim her sunshine. She gloried in being a sailor's wife, but she must pay the tax of quick alarm for belonging to that profession which is, if possible, more distinguished in its domestic virtues than in its national importance. (168)

By contrasting the navy's "domestic virtues" and its importance on a national scale, Austen provides a split-paned view of what Moler characterizes as—not unlike in *Clarissa*—the spheres of "Art" and "Nature" (191) (where "Art" is represented by the Bath set—Sir Walter, Lady Russell, Lady Dalrymple, and Colonel Wallis—because both their behavior and their self-image are artfully constructed and the group associated with "Nature" are the Uppercross and Lyme sets, the sailors and middle-class Musgroves, as well as Frederick. Anne, who moves fluidly between these two sets, is, for Moler, the symbol of their reconciliation at the end of the novel). Throughout the novel, the two worlds synthesize in Anne and Frederick, but part of what haunts the narrative is their occasional re-splitting. Moreover, when they split apart again, the reader is witness to the most dangerous and unpleasant properties of each, namely the Elliots' malevolence and the naval captain's perpetual likelihood of being called to war. Like Stendhal's warning that in moments of intimate happiness, society "devait se venger" (208) ("will seek its revenge") that governs *Armance*, as we will see in the next part of the chapter, in the passages above, each happiness is also undermined by a stipulation or contingency, a "sideways glance at the world at large," as François puts it. Whether it is characterized by Anne's lack of a proper family or her fear of Frederick's profession, this vacillation between the comforts of an intimate world of two and the larger world outside creates feelings of "inferiority," "lively pain," "dread," and "quick alarm." In both *Armance* and *Persuasion*, the danger is largely external, but the characters internalize these fears, creating inhibition. Thus, the anxiety in *Persuasion*, which throughout the novel had emanated from the past, is now projected onto the future, such that, as the epigraph to the chapter notes, "the reaction of the past and of the future on the present brings unhappiness."

## Troubling Silence in *Armance*

No motif is more prominent in *Armance*, Stendhal's first novel about a fragile, young Parisian aristocrat, Octave de Malivert, and his improbable love for his cousin, Armance de Zohiloff, than silence. The reader observes Octave's determined silence about a mysterious problem, an affliction to which he refers over and over to excuse his failure to speak to his beloved. Armance, too, suffers an almost perpetual inability to express her love to Octave.[5] Moreover, the most prominent silent "character" in the novel is the narrator himself, who is complicit in keeping silent about the motivations behind Octave and Armance's enigmas. Even in the preface, a fictitious paratext in which Stendhal attributes the novel to a "femme d'esprit" (45) ("a woman of character" [ix]) and writes falsely modest words about the book's inadequacies, Stendhal converts what should be an explanatory, and thus, communicative, text into an incommunicative one. The preface ends in aposiopesis, rather than in an elucidation ("and such a subject, too! ... " [xi]).[6]

---

[5] Little has been written about Armance's inhibitions, with at least one critic claiming that "the character of Armance is in a technical sense accessory to that of Octave. [...] Her shyness and her doubts, borrowed from *La Princesse de Clèves*, are just there to keep the novel going" (Wood 58). Although Hemmings notices that Armance's "frigidity matches [Octave's] incapability" (72).

[6] "d'ailleurs, un tel sujet! ..." (47). *Armance* is modeled on Claire de Duras's *Olivier ou le secret*, a novel about a physically impotent man, but the very existence of the secret itself—and the fact that the reader is never sure what is being alluded to—keeps the reader reading. Gide was perhaps the first to claim that "to make the reader guess this impotence is, we might say, the very subject of the book, and I know of no other that requires a more subtle collaboration of the reader" (264). Other critics also recognize that "explaining" the novel is a danger: "En transportant l'explication à l'intérieur de l'œuvre, on détruit l'énigme mais du même coup on détruit l'intérêt et le sens du roman" (Mouillaud 526) ["by transporting the explanation within the work, we destroy the mystery, but at the same time we destroy the value and meaning of the novel"]. And Charles O'Keefe asserts that Stendhal "wanted to write a story about a young man hiding his impotence but that he had very good artistic reasons for paying more attention to the hiding than to the impotence" (580) and argues that "the elusiveness of truth constitutes one of the major themes of *Armance* and that this subject, emphatically exemplified in several different ways throughout the novel, makes it only appropriate that Octave's secret should ultimately perplex and tease the reader" (580). This sort of "lacune," Genette writes, "l'interruption du texte, n'est pas une simple absence, un pur non-texte; c'est un manque, actif et sensible comme manque, comme inécriture, comme texte inécrit" (176) ("the interruption in the text is not a simple absence, a pure non-text; there is an active and tangible lack, like *inécriture*, like an unwritten text"). The style of narration refracts truth presented as a motif, and "encourages us [...] to understand the narration as a form of language whose function is to make palpable the silence which divides us from the scene" (Preston 262).

Throughout the novel, the narrator refuses to reveal the secrets of his characters, replaying the motif of indescribability found in *La Princesse de Clèves* and other works of analytical fiction.[7] At the same time, this silence highlights the analytical motif of the search for knowledge, to which, as Tzvetan Todorov puts it, "the entire plot of [*Armance*] is, in fact, subjugated" (159). The search itself becomes a form of impotence, rendered rhetorical through the narrator's complicity in writing an inhibited text. Octave and Armance are caught in a double-bind in which dissimulation and revelation equally frustrate and cause unease and disunity with their environment and with each other. Their secrets and lies constantly double back and create more frustrations and misunderstandings between the couple.

Octave and Armance's overanxious, Restoration-era society shapes the inhibited affective environment of the novel, which is, of course, necessarily ignorant of the coming 1830 Revolution. Despite the fact that many of this society's members believed in the Restoration as a sort of resurrection of the *ancient regime* that could erase the bloody, shameful past (Amoss 44), the restored aristocracy's power was quite tenuous, and the factions within it—it is unclear in the text whether Octave is an ultra-royalist (i.e., the far-right party who supported even increasing the restored monarchy's power), but it is possible—make it even more unstable. In this Restoration-era society in which Armance and Octave live—and of which Stendhal himself was a critic—every speech act is subject to the most acute scrutiny. In *Armance*, moreover, the text and the characters are also subjected to Stendhal's acerbic politicization. Both Armance and Octave's families are victims of the 1789 Revolution, émigrés who could only return to France after 1814 with the restoration of Louis XVIII as monarch (when Octave and Armance would have been nine and seven years old, respectively). Charles O'Keefe notes that the milieu in which Armance and Octave live is a society plagued by "gnawing fears and anxieties" and "haunted by bloody memories of the guillotine" (581). In this way, the silence that pervades the narrative also reflects a calculating, frightened, but ultimately self-deceived society that is terrified of change and evolution. In this novel, the language of feeling and the

---

[7] According to Stendhal's journal (quoted in Armand Hoog's edition of *Armance*, which is the one I use in this chapter for the French text; the English is C.K. Scott Moncrieff's translation), in an entry dated June 6, 1828, the author had Lafayette's text in mind when he wrote *Armance*: "ce roman [...] n'a de ressemblance qu'avec des ouvrages très anciennement à la mode, tels que *La Princesse de Clèves* [...] Quoi de plus simple?" (*Armance* 273) ("this novel [...] resembles only very old works that used to be in style, like *La Princesse de Clèves*. [...] What could be simpler?"). Later on the same date he wrote that his novel "semble délicat comme *La Princesse de Clèves*" (*Armance* 274) ("seems delicate like *La Princesse de Clèves*").

feelings elicited by an ever-present historical trauma are intertwined; and the focus on hiding public fears in private places redoubles in narrative withholding, inhibiting the young characters' consummation of their love.

Octave is remarkable for having "a certain somber air" (1)[8] about him, a "profonde mélancolie" (50); he "would have created a sensation had he been in the habit of talking" (1),[9] but he "seemed to have turned misanthrope before his time" (2).[10] The narrator reminds us repeatedly that Octave "was given to fits of somber ill-temper which he found difficult in concealing" (224),[11] and that he has a "fatal secret," something whose nature is never revealed, but that makes him "un *monstre*" (239). But Armance, too, harbors her own parallel "fatal secret," her love for Octave, which she feels must be unrequited. She is often left suffocated by tears,[12] and wishing to "erect an eternal barrier between Octave" (65) and herself.[13]

At the beginning of the novel, the two characters are described as being very much indifferent to one another, and thus they are able to converse with complete frankness. And yet, even at the start, an unspoken tension between them belies and threatens the intimacy the narrator claims exists. Armance realizes that she is in love with Octave early in the novel, but she is unable to recognize that he is in love with her, too. At some point, Octave apprehends that Armance feels a strong passion for him, but he is not able to name this feeling within himself.

Octave and Armance are, after all, excellent dissimulators. Octave feigns liking his room, chess, horses, and walks with his uncle, just to keep up the appearance of being a good son and nephew. Armance, to make Octave jealous, pretends that she has a fiancé, and in turn, Octave pretends to be indifferent to her, and makes it seem that he is in love with another woman, Madame d'Aumale. O'Keefe writes that the very form of *Armance* is constituted of "obstacles to truth": "lies are not merely frequent, and lack of mutual understanding does not merely help to move the story along. Rather, they and other obstacles to truth constitute the very bulk and substance of this novel" (582). In this way, all the other lies function as a cofactor to Octave's secret. As in the other works we have examined, Stendhal's narrative continuously puts off the possibility of honest communication between

---

[8] "quelque chose de sombre" (49).
[9] "eût fait sensation s'il eût eu l'habitude de parler" (49).
[10] "semblait misanthrope avant l'âge" (50).
[11] "avait des accès d'humeur noire qu'il pouvait à peine dissimuler" (236).
[12] "les larmes [...] la suffoquaient" (102).
[13] "élever une barrière éternelle entre Octave" (102).

the characters. But whereas in the typical *roman d'analyse*, pretending that you are not in love with someone is almost always a ruse to make that person love you more, throughout *Armance*, the characters' fears remain impenetrable, and their anxieties frustrate the narrator as well as the reader.

Even though moments of mutual understanding and love exist in the novel (Michael Wood goes so far as to write that "Octave and Armance have the moments all Stendhal's lovers have, their instants of perfect comprehension, and they have no more and no less of them than the others" [57]), intimate moments are always fraught with melancholy. Octave's complaints "interested Armance. […] She, without clearly explaining it to herself, felt that Octave was the victim of that sort of unreasoning sensibility which makes men wretched and worthy to be loved" (30).[14] The words "victime" ("victim") and "malheureux" ("wretched") underline the same kind of affective contradiction that we see in *Persuasion*, where each happiness is undercut by painful emotions or thoughts (and the "worthy to be loved" is rather a surprise). Later, understanding and fear are conjoined when Octave thinks to himself at the end of the novel, "Armance has always frightened me. I have never approached her without feeling that I was appearing before the ruler of my destiny" (245, translation modified).[15] Octave's hyperbole reveals that he is afraid of being found inadequate; only by faking his disinterestedness in her can he hope, in this case, *not* to win her love and approval. Moreover, the narrator warns the reader not to fall under the spell of beauty and romance during any particularly happy moment in Octave and Armance's relationship when the lovers "had an air of caring singularly little what society might think. It [society] was bound to have its revenge" (190).[16]

## Public Fears in Private Places

The restitution of money from the Revolution and the social status that it can restore are major sources of unease in *Armance*. When Octave's family receives an indemnity of two million francs, and Octave becomes wealthier than Armance, the money becomes the subject on everyone's lips at Madame de Bonnivet's next

---

[14] "intéressaient Armance. […] Elle, sans se le bien expliquer, sentait qu'Octave était la victime de cette sorte de sensibilité déraisonnable qui fait les hommes malheureux et dignes d'être aimés" (72).
[15] "Armance m'a toujours fait peur. Je ne l'ai jamais approchée sans sentir que je paraissais devant le maître de ma destinée" (252). Perhaps this is why Hemmings calls Armance "a virgin of terrifying purity" (73).
[16] "avaient l'air de fort peu songer à la société. Elle devait se venger" (208).

party. The narrator offers a subtle, implicit commentary, presenting the would-be lovers as impotent victims of society's malice: "at this moment, [Madame de Bonnivet's] interest in Octave was plain to the eyes of several malicious watchers; for they were being watched" (55).[17] Those who are watching Armance and Octave "indulged in the most rash judgments" (55).[18] As François Landry puts it, "it is under this disturbing sign that Octave makes his entry into society."[19] And another critic writes, Octave "is a male protagonist whose sexual conduct becomes subject to the merciless scrutiny and censure that the nineteenth century typically applied only to women" (Counter 164). Armance fears that the money has changed Octave, that his soul has become base because of it. The anxious silence that falls between the two provides the other party guests an irresistible opportunity to gossip, their "aristocratic silliness [serving] as only the skimpiest of masks to hide [their own] […] fears" (O'Keefe 581) about money and status. Suddenly the whole salon is talking about Octave and his money, but they are scrutinizing Armance, too. Since it appears to be common knowledge that Armance loves Octave, the Duchesse d'Ancre in particular seems poised to expose it. She sits down near where Octave and Armance are sitting and whispers loudly to her friend that Armance is envious of Octave's fortune. Just as Octave was starting to feel a greater closeness with Armance, because of a few overheard words—and moreover, words that were explicitly designed to injure him—he begins to believe that Armance's silence is explained. Feeling distanced from her, he begins to burn for reconciliation, even as he begins to worry, in a reversal of Armance's fears, that it is she who cares too much about money. Here the narrative, cataloging the surreptitious perceptions of the characters, what is meant to be heard and by whom, and what anxieties are the effect of all these indirect speeches and looks, creates an environment mired in paranoia.

The misunderstanding over Octave's newfound wealth drives Octave and Armance apart, as Armance's sudden realization that she is now too poor for Octave also makes her confront that she loves him. They spend several weeks in mutual silence. Finally, the two find themselves alone in Armance's garden. Octave tries to apologize to her and win back her friendship. Octave does not know what he is asking; she is too timid and anxious about their financial differences now to reveal her love:

---

[17] "en ce moment, son intérêt pour Octave fut évident aux yeux de quelques observateurs malins, car ils étaient observés" (93).
[18] "se livraient aux jugements les plus téméraires" (93).
[19] "C'est sous ce signe inquiétant qu'Octave fait son entrée dans le monde" (231).

she still remained silent for a long time. […] 'I have forfeited your esteem,' he cried, and the tears trembled in his eyelids. […] It was no longer possible for her to pretend, her tears overpowered her, and she wept openly. She was afraid lest Octave might go on and say something that would increase her discomfiture, and make her lose what little self-control she still retained. Above all, she was afraid to speak. […] 'You have all my esteem,' she told him. (62)[20]

She is grateful that a maid enters, and she runs from the garden. Octave too is crying; he is rendered immobile, although the narrator tells us that it is unclear whether it is because he wishes to rejoice or to mourn. At the same time, he is puzzled at what he perceives as Armance's coldness. Back in her bedroom, Armance suffers from confusion and trouble; she realizes that her reaction was unwarranted, and yet, she takes comfort in calling herself only "demi méprisable" (102) ["half-despicable" (65)] since she does not confide her "fatal secret"—that is the fact that she loves him—to Octave. Her language parallels his, indicating that they are quite equal in the novel. Thus, it is not only Octave's impotence that will render their love impossible; Armance's reserve acts as an obstacle as well. Here, neither the characters' speeches nor the narration betrays Armance's secret word, love, or why it is fatal.[21] Instead, the narrator presents the reader with another enigma, a frustration parallel to the one we have already been told about Octave. For Stendhal, encouraging the reader's curiosity about the secret becomes the only type of device that can propel forward so recursive a narrative.

Remarkably, Madame de Malivert, Octave's mother (and we have seen how significant a role mothers can play in *romans d'analyse* already in the countess of Aranda, Madame de Chartres, and Clarissa's mother), the one person who should be able to mediate between the two lovers, also cannot bring herself to speak to her son about his relationship with Armance. We are told that Octave's mother often "gazed at him without venturing to address him" (11).[22] Although she cannot speak to Octave, Madame de Malivert tells Armance that she would like to arrange the marriage. Yet, she cannot help but notice the extreme reticence

---

[20] "elle se tut encore pendant longtemps. […] J'ai perdu votre estime, s'écria-t-il, et les larmes tremblaient dans ses yeux. […] Il ne lui fut plus possible de feindre, ses larmes la gagnèrent et elle pleura ouvertement. Elle craignit qu'Octave n'ajoutât quelque mot qui aurait augmenté son trouble et lui aurait fait perdre le peu d'empire qu'elle avait encore sur elle-même. Elle redoutait surtout de parler. […] Vous avez toute mon estime, lui dit-elle" (98–9).

[21] Later, when Armance is called upon to explain her bizarre behavior, she lies to Octave and tells him that she is engaged to another man. This scene is set at the tomb of Abélard and Héloïse, a location symbolic of Octave and Armance's ill-fated love.

[22] "le regardait bien plus qu'elle n'osait lui parler" (57).

of both young people, and she recognizes that the "assurances of Octave's love were excruciating to Armance" (100).[23] Octave's mother becomes "extremely anxious" (100)[24] when she realizes that Octave has in fact not professed his love for his cousin and that he is so timid. But rather than addressing the problem with her son, the Marquise instead chooses to lie to Armance, claiming that Octave had indeed spoken to her about an affection for her, thus putting the onus on the shy and fearful girl to precipitate the relationship.

Hemmings suggests that Octave also falls in love with Armance when he is desperate to recover respect in her eyes: "His colourless life is thus temporarily orientated towards the reconquest of her *esteem*, and, being forced to concentrate his attention on his cousin, unwittingly he falls in love with her" (75). Wishing to get close to Armance, Octave begins spending much of his time at the house of Madame de Bonnivet, Armance's guardian, but it seems that he has no real idea why he is there. The narrator reminds us in this moment that he had taken many vows against love and that "hatred of that passion was the main object of his life" (51).[25] For her part, Armance tries to hide her love through carefully dissimulating indifference in her speech, but it is all too obvious to everyone else. However, her loaded words escape Octave's comprehension: "any one but Octave would have been able to read in them an expression of the warmest passion. He enjoyed without understanding them" (108).[26] Octave clearly suffers from a lack of insight (the word in French is, ironically, *pénétration*, a reminder of Octave's implied physical disability). He has sworn so many times that he will not fall in love that he is incapable of realizing that the very thing he is so afraid of has already happened.

In turn, Armance fabricates a number of excuses to abstain from love, none of which is convincing: she worries that if they were married, "every day would be poisoned by the fear that Octave might come to think that I had chosen him because of the difference in our fortunes" (104),[27] or she invokes the same noncommittal reason that the princess gives to Nemours: "marriage is the grave of love" (103),[28] and that "to see love perish in the heart of a husband

---

[23] "[les] assurances de l'amour d'Octave étaient déchirantes pour Armance" (132).
[24] "fort inquiète" (132).
[25] "la haine de cette passion était la grande affaire de sa vie" (89).
[26] "Tout autre qu'Octave eût su y voir l'expression de la passion la plus vive. Il en jouissait sans les comprendre" (138–9).
[27] "chaque jour serait empoisonné par la crainte qu'Octave ne vînt à penser que je l'ai préféré à cause de la différence de nos fortunes" (136).
[28] "le mariage est le tombeau de l'amour" (135).

whom she adores is the greatest of all misfortunes for a person" (104).²⁹ Even after she inherits a fortune of her own, which would make her perfectly financially matched to Octave, Armance shrinks away because she fears he may love another woman. When Octave becomes ill, she rushes to his side, but she remains silent. She steels herself against a possible rejection: "she felt for the second time in her life the assault of a sentiment that is terrifying. [...] 'I must keep a strict watch over myself' she said to herself" (203).³⁰ Armance also attributes her fear of speaking to Octave to a fear of what society would think; she becomes paralyzed by the gaze of the society around them. She becomes jealous of Madame d'Aumale, observing that this woman possesses all of the self-confidence that Armance lacks. In fact, Madame d'Aumale and Armance are opposite characters, almost as if they are from different novels. Madame d'Aumale belongs to the social world and to the world of realism, while Armance is an analytical character. When an extreme jealousy attacks both Armance and Octave, they renounce their love rather than try to combat it, although it is extremely painful. But even when they are happy together, Octave mistakes and misreads, attributing the "look of happiness in her eyes" to a cause that threatens to serve as "the confirmation of all his fears" (106).³¹ The truth is that Armance is happy because she is near Octave, while Octave thinks that she must appear happy because she is thinking of another man. He imagines that the opposite of what is true, that the cause of her change could not be but in spite of him. Octave's rejection of any other more obvious or local explanation for Armance's happiness highlights his obstinacy and self-deception.

**The Fatal Word**

Octave puts off recognizing and naming his real feelings for Armance for as long as possible. He "had not the slightest idea that he was genuinely in love with Armance. He had bound himself by the strongest vows to resist that passion, and as what he lacked was penetration rather than character,

---

²⁹ "voir l'amour s'éteindre dans le cœur d'un époux qu'on adore, est le plus grand des tous les malheurs" (136).
³⁰ "elle sentit pour la seconde fois de sa vie les atteintes d'un sentiment affreux. [...] Je dois veiller sur moi d'une manière sévère" (218).
³¹ "il y avait tant de bonheur dans ses yeux qu'Octave prévenu y vit la confirmation de toutes ses craintes" (137).

he would probably have kept his vows" (71).³² And yet, at the height of their jealousy, the reader comes across one of the most beautiful and passionate scenes in the novel. Armance and Octave share a moment of near-perfect harmony and mutual understanding, although it is a silent scene and the word "love" is never uttered between them. The two young would-be lovers take a walk in the woods together (though Madame d'Aumale and others are walking within earshot of them), at the Malivert's country house in Andilly. In this scene, their silence takes on a new dimension, causing (mostly) pleasure rather than pain:

> [Armance] had not the courage to resist the happiness of seeing herself so dearly loved. She leaned upon Octave's arm, and listened to him as though in an ecstasy. [...] Octave gazed into Armance's open eyes which were fastened on his own. [...] [Her words] would have enlightened any one but Octave as to the passion that she felt for himself. But he was so astonished by what was going on in his heart, so disturbed by Armance's shapely arm. [...] He was beside himself, he was tasting the pleasures of the most blissful love, and almost admitted as much to himself. (126–7)³³

This intimate, erotic moment, in which Octave is described as "hors de lui" [Moncrieff translates it as "beside himself," but "outside of himself" is more literal] (a reference to the sublime) is marred only by one word: *presque*. Octave *almost* admits to himself how much passion he feels for Armance. This one word from the narrator undercuts the passion that could be, but is not, the center of this passage. Instead, the word *almost* steals the focus and serves to heighten Octave's lack of self-knowledge.

---

³² "n'eut pas la moindre idée qu'il aimait Armance d'amour. Il s'était fait les serments les plus forts contre cette passion, et comme il manquait de pénétration et non pas le caractère, il eût probablement tenu ses serments" (107).

³³ "elle n'eut pas le courage de résister au bonheur de se voir aimée ainsi. Elle s'appuyait sur le bras d'Octave et l'écoutait comme ravie en extase. [...] Octave regardait les grands yeux d'Armance qui se fixaient sur les siens. [...] [Les] mots si simples, eût appris à tout autre qu'Octave toute la passion qu'on avait pour lui. Mais il était si étonné de ce qui se passait dans son cœur, si troublé par le beau bras d'Armance. [...] Il était hors de lui, il goûtait les plaisirs de l'amour le plus heureux, et se l'avouait presque." (155) Mouillaud writes, surprisingly, that "on chercherait en vain dans *Armance* cette attirance-répulsion pour la 'chair' si répandue chez d'autres auteurs du XIXè siècle. La chair n'y est ni triste ni impure parce que la notion même de chair est absente" (527) ("one searches in vain in *Armance* for this attraction-repulsion for the 'flesh' so common in other writers of the nineteenth century. The flesh is neither sad nor impure because the notion of flesh is missing"). Although the references to physical attraction are few and far between, they still exist, as the rather erotic scene above demonstrates, and at other times as well, Armance's figure or the feeling of her hand clearly attract Octave.

But, in truth, all it will take to completely destroy even this *almost*-happiness is the declaration of the real fatal and impossible word: "love." As soon as he realizes his true feelings, Octave plunges into a state of total despair. It is, in fact, Madame d'Aumale who pronounces it unequivocally, just after the beautiful and intimate scene described above: "you are in love with that pretty cousin, do not attempt to deny it; I know" (128).[34] Unlike Octave or Armance, Madame d'Aumale is not afraid to say it, and in fact, she utters the last part, "je m'y connais" ("I know") in a voice loud enough for Armance to hear. Though perhaps Madame d'Aumale does not realize the extent to which this observation will cause Octave harm (or she does not care, since she is jealous of Armance), its directness rings with a truth that destroys all of Octave's self-protective dissimulation:

> [the word] fell on him like a thunderbolt. […] That frivolous voice seemed to him a pronouncement of fate, falling on him from the clouds. The sound of it seemed to him extraordinary. This startling speech, by revealing to Octave the true state of his heart, dashed him from a pinnacle of bliss into a frightful, hopeless misery. (128)[35]

At this moment, there is nothing more terrifying for Octave than having cataleptically been forced to take cognizance of and face this terrible knowledge. Becoming aware of his love for Armance feels like a failure to his sense of duty, not unlike the way in which the princess in Lafayette's novel invokes "bienséance."[36] Here, the narrator hyperbolizes and mocks Octave with an example of narrative refusal that again evokes the style of *La Princesse de Clèves*: "words fail me if I am to give any idea of the grief that overpowered the poor wretch" (131),[37] says the narrator. Octave finally admits it himself: "'I am in love,' 'Great God!' and with throbbing heart, parched throat, staring eyes raised to heaven, he stood

---

[34] "vous êtes amoureux de cette belle cousine, ne vous en défendez pas, je m'y connais" (156).
[35] "Le mot […] fut un coup de foudre pour lui, car il portait sa preuve avec lui, il se sentit frappé. Cette voix frivole lui sembla comme un arrêt du destin qui tombait d'en haut. Il lui trouva un son extraordinaire. Ce mot imprévu, en découvrant à Octave la véritable situation de son cœur, la précipita du comble de la félicité dans un malheur affreux et sans espoir" (156).
[36] Emile J. Talbot provides a thorough analysis of Octave and Armance's sense of duty. Though I disagree with some of the ideas in this account, one of Talbot's theses resonates: "in lying to each other, each believes he/she is being faithful to the code of honor. The lie becomes necessary in order to maintain the code. As Armance puts it, 'this lie constitutes all my strength against him.' […] The pleasure of a sustained human relationship is prevented because it is outside the confines of an ethic that, forcibly turned in on itself, must have recourse to deception" (39).
[37] "les expressions me manquent pour donner quelque idée de la douleur qui s'empara de ce malheureux" (159).

motionless, as though horror-stricken. [...] Unable to hold himself erect, he let himself fall against the trunk of an old tree" (131).[38] Having uttered the fateful words, Octave also loses control over his body; it contracts and completely fails to enact the motions—or the emotions—that his words require, almost negating the "j'aime!" which he had earlier acknowledged to himself. Even more upsetting than having admitted the truth and betraying his vow to never love, Octave now realizes his self-deception and is destroyed by the fear of self-knowledge. He laments that he had ever thought himself a philosopher, when he was merely a hypocrite; he berates himself for his ignobility; he feels grief, torment, despair; he compares himself to a criminal and feels only contempt for himself for having forgotten all of his former oaths and for allowing himself to feel love. Thus, Stendhal reveals a paralyzed world, in which both truth and lies cause irrevocable damage, but also in which silence and speech are equally scrutinized. It would have been better, perhaps, to remain deceived.

The only thing Octave can muster, after regaining consciousness, is to flee Andilly, go back to Paris, and plan a trip to Greece, where he intends to commit suicide after proving his courage and fulfilling an ancestral duty by going to fight in the Greek War of Independence. Before he goes, however, Octave encounters Armance by chance. He is cruel to her. She tries to speak, but merely collapses. Octave is struck by her figure for a moment, and whispers that he loves her (although she does not hear him), before taking his leave for Paris. At Andilly, Armance tries to understand Octave's actions. She locks herself in the attic and she imagines that Octave's sense of duty prohibits him from revealing his plans to her. In Paris, everything reminds Octave of Armance. The silence of his room amplifies his own apprehensions about her. The narrator jumps back and forth between Paris and Andilly, engaging Armance and Octave in a silent, long-distance dialogue of which, of course, the characters are unaware.

As luck would have it, Octave is given the chance to reenact his ancestral prowess sooner that he expected, though the heroic scene becomes a caricature due to Stendhal's ironic descriptions. While in Paris, Octave is challenged to a duel by a fop, the marquis de Crêveroche, a comic character who becomes desperately jealous of Octave when they meet in Madame d'Aumale's box at

---

[38] "'J'aime!' [...] Moi aimer! Grand Dieu! et le cœur serré, la gorge contractée, les yeux fixes et levés au ciel, il resta immobile comme frappé d'horreur. [...] Incapable de se soutenir, il se laissa tomber sur le tronc d'un vieux arbre" (159). It is easy to interpret Octave's action as an inversion of a confession scene. Like Augustine and Rousseau, Octave has his great realization and takes shelter by a tree. Except there is no real conversion that follows; as in Fiammetta's confession, the repentance and conversion remain unconsummated.

the Théatre-Italien. Octave's spirits instantly brighten at the thought of this challenge, and although Crêveroche cuts the figure of a less-than-worthy rival (he invites Octave and his second over for tea before the duel, and at the fight appears even more of a dandy than usual), the prospect of pistols at dawn revives Octave from his depression. Octave had been ready to commit suicide just a few hours before, but now, brought back to reality, he is ready to fight. Octave kills Crêveroche, and himself is wounded. He is taken to the house of a peasant, where, on what he believes is his deathbed, he wishes to write a letter to Armance.

The letter, which one should think would be a love letter, is an utter failure. Although it confesses nothing of his love, Octave consoles himself with the idea that he could always burn it if he feels better later.[39] During this pathetic scene, the narrator cannot stop himself from mocking Octave, and simultaneously refers back to silence in the process, when he asks, "dare we confess it? Octave was so childish as to write with his own blood, which continued to ooze from the bandage on his right arm" (164).[40] The narrator's posture here is almost as cruel as that of the ladies in Madame de Bonnivet's drawing room. By redirecting the reader's attention from Octave and his love for Armance to the narrator's judgment of Octave's immaturity, Stendhal deflects the question of love, postponing and denying it.

Octave and Armance are only able to speak openly about their love as soon as Octave's life is in danger. Finally, Armance admits that she never loved another man, and Octave explains what had happened to him in the woods before he disappeared. Armance also admits her fear that Octave will abandon her again, which mirrors Octave's fear of being alone from earlier in the novel. This new spirit of openness is conditional, however. Armance makes Octave promise that they will never marry, so that they can, she believes, remain as good friends as ever. This condition being agreed upon, the narrator tells us that "Octave's self-esteem had nothing now to keep secret from Armance, and these two young hearts had arrived at that unbounded confidence which is perhaps the most charming thing about love" (187).[41] They cannot but notice how willing they

---

[39] Martine Reid notes that "writing, and in it the portrayal of feelings, is experienced as an eminently dangerous act. Speaking is 'frightful,' but writing is even more so" (189).
[40] "Oserons-nous l'avouer? Octave eut l'enfantillage d'écrire avec son sang qui coulait encore un peu à travers le bandage de son bras droit" (186).
[41] "l'amour-propre d'Octave n'avait plus de secrets pour Armance, et ces deux jeunes cœurs étaient arrivés à cette confiance sans bornes qui fait peut-être le plus doux charme de l'amour" (206).

are to confide in each other now that they renounce the possibility of marriage, whereas in the months before they had imposed restraint on themselves.

But at the same time, they cannot admit that this mutually agreed upon self-deception reopens the possibility of jealousy and more deceit, quickly returning them to the state of anxiety that had governed them throughout the novel. They are blind to the fact that this vow of friendship, which precludes any romantic relationship, is also a lie. Sooner rather than later Octave begins to suspect the Chevalier de Bonnivet of being Armance's suitor, and as quickly as they acknowledged their love for each other, they are plunged again into mutual fear and silence, "tormented by dark suspicions" (198).[42] Having been injured already by Octave's disappearance after the scene in the woods, Armance recoils the next time he tries to kiss her cheek.

Yet, silence and fear do not only discourage action in *Armance*, they also sometimes, though by pure machination of plot device, motivate it. At the height of Armance and Octave's suspicions about each other's fidelities, Armance creates a situation in which her reputation is compromised. Octave's malicious uncle, M. de Soubirane, who vehemently dislikes the girl, discovers Armance hiding in a closet in Octave's room as she tries to learn whether Octave is entertaining Madame d'Aumale there.[43] Desperate because she perceives that Octave has made a sign to someone outside—presumably to this other lady, but actually to one of his servants—Armance does not realize that M. de Soubirane is in the hallway when she emerges from the closet. He sees her leaving Octave's room and is ecstatic to find a way to discredit her. Armance runs to Madame de Malivert and confesses what has happened. In turn, Octave's mother explains the situation to her son, who, completely out of character, declares that the only remedy to this ill, which will compromise both young people, is to marry Armance immediately.

Octave's decisive move, which makes his mother so very happy, is undercut by Armance's misgivings, which serve to nullify any sense of romance or love. When he proposes, she tries to talk him out of it; she claims that he is not in love with her, that there must be some other reason besides love that propels him to marry her, and she reminds him that he "used to have a horror of marriage" (214).[44] Octave insists that he loves her and wishes to marry her, but

---

[42] "tourmentés par de sombres soupçons" (215).
[43] This scene may remind us of the hiding scene in "El curioso impertinente" described in Chapter 2.
[44] "Vous abhorriez le mariage" (228).

if he seems distracted it is the fault of his uncle's vile suspicions. But in fact, Armance has a point. The narrator confirms that Octave is acting completely counterintuitively and based on self-deception, only this time the self-deception dictates to Octave that he really *does* love Armance; he only spoke the words of love because a kind of persuasion has taken over his senses, and quick deliberation causes him to convince himself that they are genuine. And, of course, not long afterwards, the specter of silence resurfaces: "Octave could think of nothing to say to her. He could not even look lovingly at her, this calm after the storm left him powerless" (215), once more, outside of himself.[45]

As soon as the prospect of marriage is again upon Octave, he begins to feel melancholy and troubled. Understandably, this causes Armance "inquiétude" (237). They attempt to talk about it, but he breaks off mid-sentence: "'I shall be able to see you and to talk to you at every hour of the day, *but*,' he went on […] and fell into one of those moods of gloomy silence which filled Armance with despair" (226, emphasis in original).[46] She urges him to speak, but he will not. He alludes only to a secret, something that makes him "un *monstre*" (239). He flees again to Paris. The next day, she receives a letter from him explaining that his secret is too shameful to admit to her, that he cannot name the lethal word, the "parole fatale" (241).

The bulk of criticism on *Armance* contends with this ineffable word. For Gide, the impotence is "revealed in [Octave's] gestures, his actions; but we could remain in doubt because the novel skillfully maintains the secret" (262), and Shoshana Felman writes that "the absence of the key itself is functional, necessary and meaningful: silence is part of the text. It is not, in fact, the missing key, but an absence that is the key. […] The ellipse, that is essential."[47] The tension between Octave and Armance after the announcement of their engagement and before they are married changes the linguistic stakes of the novel. The forbidden semantic territory transitions from "love" to a new unknown realm. Armance's imagination again wanders off in a number of directions. She fears that Octave may be a murderer. But even this, she says, she will forgive him. Armance is

---

[45] "Octave ne trouva rien à lui dire. Il ne put même la regarder avec amour, le calme l'avait mis hors de lui" (228).
[46] "je pourrai vous voir et vous parler à tout heure, *mais*, ajouta-t-il […] et il tomba dans un de ces moments de silence sombre qui faisaient le désespoir d'Armance" (238).
[47] "L'absence de la clé est elle-même fonctionnelle, nécessaire et signifiante: le silence fait partie intégrante du texte. Ce n'est pas, en effet, la clé qui manque, mais un manque qui en est la clé. […] l'ellipse qui est essentielle" (170).

willing to give Octave a year to reflect on his secret, but asks him to reveal it to her eventually. Octave allows Armance to believe he is a criminal, enacting another dissimulation that only pulls them farther apart. Octave resolves to write "la lettre fatale" (243) to Armance, and in the first café he finds, he writes her a short letter, the content of which remains unknown.[48]

The repetition of the word "fatal"—and Armance too, when she was secretly in love with Octave, called her affection her "fatal secret"—clearly evokes not only ill luck and unfortunate circumstances, but also destruction and death. Significantly, Armance also calls their marriage "cette fatale idée" (237) ["this fatal idea"], implying, at worst, that it will destroy them both if it is carried through. Nevertheless, in other instances, the narrator tells us that Armance is blissfully happy at the idea of marrying Octave, and claims she would be happier married than only loving in secret. It is possible, then, that Armance is deceiving herself when she calls their marriage a "fatal idea," and she is just looking for a way to reopen conflict, to re-complexify their affair, so as to prolong it even further.

What is ultimately fatal to Octave and Armance's love—although it seems that it could have self-destructed eventually on its own—is Stendhal's device of the forged letter—reminiscent of Madame de Thémines's letter in *The Princess of Clèves*, or perhaps of Lovelace's adulterated letters, since this one is actually written by Octave's uncle—claiming that Armance has fallen out of love. Octave's immediate reaction is entirely self-centered; rather than despairing at the idea of Armance no longer loving him, he claims that he knew it all along, and that he would need far more passion from a woman than Armance could possibly muster. Obviously, Octave has been tricked, and he is mistaken to doubt Armance. Yet, the forged letter reminds the reader of what kind of love they had felt throughout the novel, namely the kind that is thwarted at every turn, denied, held secret, and when it is finally pronounced, despaired of to the utmost degree. Perhaps there is some hidden truth in the Commander's note. Octave finds the letter in the same place, in the pot of an orange tree at Andilly, where the lovers were used to exchanging letters (apparently, that was no secret at all to the rest of the household). He is also about to place there his own letter, which reveals his fatal flaw. He rips up his letter as soon as he reads the forged one, destroying any evidence of the secret. The Commander's letter is a false avowal swapped, as

---

[48] Interestingly, *Persuasion* also ends in the writing of a letter at the White Hart Inn, as we saw in the previous section.

it were, for a real one that never comes to be. These confessions—one forged and the other shredded—are just symbols of the destructive forces of the narrative that inhibit Armance's and Octave's love once again. While the love letters that Armance and Octave had exchanged in the orange tree may be tender and meaningful, they are ultimately rendered inconsequential by the false and torn up ones. The only meaningful letter in the novel is the forged one, about which Armance never knows, as it destroys forever Octave's resolve to tell his lover about his secret. The letter expresses feelings of inconstancy on Armance's part and, as if holding up a distorted mirror to what she had previously feared about marriage in general, a loss of love equal to that which Armance had feared in Octave. The forged letter reiterates the fears that Armance had already expressed herself throughout the novel.

Inexplicably, Armance loves Octave still more constantly, even as he begins to behave in stranger and stranger ways. Indeed, as Octave's life becomes more shrouded in mystery, Armance, on the contrary, grows happier. The accusations of somberness in the letter exacerbate that condition in Octave and amplify his anxieties. Once again, Octave doubles back to his earlier melancholic state, one which punctuated his behavior throughout the novel, just as Armance becomes more honest and tender. The marriage as a symbol of regeneration of the aristocracy is also bound to be a failure here, when the impotent Octave functions himself as a personification of his degenerated class. Yet there is a wedding; like the vote on the bill of indemnity itself, a formal ceremony to be gone through. (And Stendhal, in a letter to Mérimée, was concerned that the reader would be able to discern enough "spice" in the text regarding their honeymoon). But throughout their days-long marriage Octave still fears that Armance is merely dissimulating happiness, although it is unclear whether he really believes that she is feigning or whether he desires her to do so in order to avoid having to face his own inadequacy. After the marriage is celebrated, Octave still believes that Armance is playing a part.

The lie Octave believes has infected his love forever. He resolves again to kill himself. This time, however, it is not entirely because of his own "fatal secret," but rather because he believes Armance has one herself. Armance's former secret—now disavowed and legitimized—that she loved Octave, brings her the greatest happiness. The false secret, in which is embedded all of the dissimulation and unhappiness that the characters had felt throughout the novel, remains just that—a secret—to Armance. Octave departs for Greece, leaving Armance in Marseille, where they had celebrated their honeymoon. The sublime Romantic connotations of the act of suicide, and the name of Greece, stir Octave to action. This ultimate and eternal silence, enacted in a Byronic (not to mention ironic) vision, born of all the words that they could never express to each other, represents for Octave not a final destruction, but rather a *repos*, like the princess's death in *The Princess of Clèves*. His carefully planned-out suicide recreates the thwarted flights and the near-death from which he had recovered earlier, in real terms this time, and completes the process that he had been planning from the start of the novel: in short, Octave wishes to escape from his anxieties and fears and to truly flee the world in which he and his diminished, struggling aristocratic class cannot fully participate. This death finally represents a break from the recursive self-doubt and jealousy that life comprises in the particular, and in general the incongruous new world order to which his family refuses to attempt to belong.

In *Armance*, the secondary characters speak freely and bring about many of the intrigues and plot twists of the novel. Conversely, every intimate scene between Octave and Armance is stalled by silence. Octave, Armance, and Madame de Malivert almost never speak openly or directly to each other, and they all lie and dissimulate. Stendhal surely presents a milieu—that of the aristocracy in Restoration France that still fears the Revolution—in which to betray too much of oneself can be dangerous, but a finely wrought malicious and untruthful phrase can work to one's benefit. However, just as in *Persuasion*, in which Anne's fear of war and her lack of family recast the ending of the supposed marriage-plot novel as far less optimistic than a fairy-tale ending, the silence that overwhelms the characters of *Armance* surpasses public fear, and becomes internalized. This inhibition renders Stendhal's narrative as yet another distrustful and pessimistic work of analytical fiction, which denies the possibility of self-knowledge and true love.

It is not that analytical fiction is disinterested, then, in social, political, or economic questions, since novels that are oriented toward those concerns always reveal their presence. It is more that the interior psychological states and interpretations of the characters absorb these public matters. The personal may always be political—Anne Elliott's personal fear of her husband's reentry into war can be read as representing the status of all women affected by senseless wars—but it works the other way around as well. Often in *romans d'analyse*, public concerns become projected onto the already fragile egos of the main characters, who internalize and privatize them into an overwhelming inability to act, or, as we have seen, even to speak. But we can interpret the failure of communication and introspection in analytical fiction as a broader philosophical problem. If we cannot know our own minds and hearts, let alone those of other people, what is to become of us? We remain mired in self-doubt, reexamining, re-questioning, and redoubling ourselves, collectively. We remain stuck in our own self-delusion and perplexity, not in a productive Socratic way, but, rather, in a way that perpetually forestalls action and denies truth.

# Conclusion

The metaphor of unconsummated—that is, incomplete, indefinitely delayed, or troubled—love belies an even more profound lack, that of the possibility of self-knowledge. In each instance of analytical fiction that we have seen, the faculty of communication between the characters at some point breaks down; they deceive each other or themselves (or, usually, both), and what results is what we can call an epistemology of failure.[1] Characters deflect and distance rather than grow, and true happiness is rendered an impossibility, even in texts like *Grandison* and *Persuasion*, which both end in marriages. There is always something that keeps the narrative from fully resolving. By cutting off connections between words and actions, that is, by rendering signs equivocal and lacking meaning, authors of analytical fiction effectively limit their characters' ability to trust either their senses or reason. Similarly, as we have seen, none of the many scenes of letter-writing or confession (in every novella and novel examined here) provides any kind of comfort or therapeutic power for the characters, in contrast to other, non-analytical works, in which writing and reading themselves can be curative. The body provides little relief either, as so many of the corporeal representations (limited as they are) prove either ultimately inconsequential or dissatisfying, or, in extreme cases, aggressive, destabilizing, and, indeed, violent.

That is not to say that there are not also beautiful or harmonious scenes in many of these novels. The ease with which Camila and Lotario improvise the play that dupes Anselmo into continuing his self-deception in "El curioso impertinente"

---

[1] Searching philosophical and literary texts for this term, I am surprised at how little it has been used. For example, one critic appropriates the title of Judith (Jack) Halberstam's *The Queer Art of Failure*, in which "the systems that tether queerness to loss and failure" (98) are examined through theory and popular culture, into the term "the queer epistemology of failure" to describe Halberstam's work (O. Landry 36, abstract). But the phrase does not appear again in the article.

is hilarious and thrilling. The quite famous episode in which, in Lafayette's novel, the princess and Nemours must lock themselves in a room together to recreate from memory a letter about a destructive love affair is—indeed, ironically—an intimate and beautiful scene (suffice to say that they spend more time gazing at each other than completing the required task). Similarly, the passage in *Persuasion* in which Frederick and Anne finally can acknowledge their love to each other at the White Hart Inn is slightly marred by all of the other instances of the mingling of pleasure with pain, but it is a joyful moment nonetheless. Armance and Octave walking together in the woods before Madame d'Aumale utters the fatal word, "love," is another beautiful moment. Those small, warm moments of togetherness, which pulsate with intimacy in spite of the narrative's distrust of intimacy, offer some respite before the novel returns to its usual suspicions and condemnations of human nature. But in spite of the beautiful moments, we should not kid ourselves; the condemnation is dark indeed.

Like the recursive narratives themselves, the eight major texts examined in this study, from the *Elegia* to *Armance*, do not represent a progression or an evolution in the history of analytical fiction, but rather a kind of totality of pessimistic, anti-humanist thinking about the self. Throughout this book, I have been careful to not categorize any of these texts as "love stories," despite the fact that love is the central metaphor. Instead, as I have shown, characters and narrators in analytical fiction are deeply skeptical about love. Characters deny the possibility of love, let alone the possibility of love's expression, and the narrative, in turn, denies them true insight or growth. Deliberation, analysis, misprision, and doubt supplant plot and the narratives of analytical fiction remain fixed in reexamination and uncertainty.

As this book has developed, I have become increasingly aware of the representations of the physical body in each of the texts studied, in particular the ways in which women's bodies are often objectified and essentialized. Not surprisingly, given the present moment's global focus on #MeToo, which aims in part to restore the voices of silenced women in the public and popular sphere—in fact, something that has been happening in scholarly discourse for decades through the re-publication and critical discussion of lost women's voices thanks to the now long history of feminist literary criticism—the representations of rape and attempted rape in the texts that I study have taken on an even greater immediacy for me.

Recent criticism on the topic of the body has demonstrated that, to take as an example Boccaccio, the Florentine author "hints at a poetics of the bodily emotions that will remain specific to the genre of the novella until the seventeenth century" (Albers 27). And as James C. Kriesel argues, in the *Decameron*, Boccaccio "used the immediacy of the body to teach readers to engage a complex world, by expressing love for others and for themselves" (443). But this illustrates a clear distinction between analytical and non-analytical fiction (of which the *Decameron* is an example). In the *Elegia*, the language and signs of the body convey no compassionate redemption for Fiammetta or for the narrative in general. In Fiammetta's account, unlike that of the Pygmalion story, the Word is not "made flesh."[2] The body, in analytical fiction, becomes another site of pain and self-doubt. Fiammetta's physical body is plainly seen throughout the entire narrative, both to reinforce the elegiac (i.e., lower style) qualities of the text, and, moreover, to truly ground Fiammetta's suffering to her earthly existence. In the descriptions of the motions of her hands, her face, and the ways in which she ornaments her body, later leading to contrasting descriptions of a body ravaged by lovesickness, Fiammetta is visible throughout the narrative. In the first chapter, Fiammetta describes her childhood and coming of age corporeally, linking, moreover, growing into adulthood with the causes of future suffering: "as my body grew with the passing of time, my charms, which were the specific cause of my troubles, multiplied" (3).[3] Do these words not empathically resonate with young women everywhere? Similarly, to take an example from the other end of this study's scope, how much is Anne Elliot's maturing into adulthood linked to her anxiety-inducing "loss of bloom"?

When Florida disfigures her own face with a rock, she takes Amador's sin upon herself; she attempts to expiate her would-be-lover's lust. Later, she sublimates love and marriage into a spiritual relationship with God in the convent in which she dies a nun. Physical intimacy is so terrifying to characters like Anselmo, Armance, and Octave that they destroy their own lives and the lives of those around them in order to avoid it. Richardson, in a narrative roughly the length of four long novels, has no words to describe Clarissa's rape, although the aftermath of it is protracted and Clarissa, having been drugged and unable to recall the details of what happened to her (again, Ferguson points out that this is so as to negate the question of consent since "[the rape] cannot depend upon the

---

[2] Kriesel points out some of the framing devices in the *Decameron* consist of allusions to and images of the Incarnation and the Crucifixion and connects Boccaccio's idea of compassion to Jesus's suffering (419). And Fiammetta describes herself, quite dramatically, in the *Elegia* as a "misero corpo, futuro essemplo di tutti li dolori" (199) ("miserable body that will be a future symbol of all pains" [125]).
[3] "come la mia persona negli anni trapassanti crescea, così le mie bellezze, de' miei mali speciale cagione, multiplicavano" (31).

victim's mental state" [99]), aligns "sexuality with death" (Zigarovich 114).[4] And even "Harriet Byron's narrative includes self-blame for attending a masquerade in a flimsy, shape-revealing Arcadian Princess costume" (Easton) when she is nearly raped by Sir Hargrave Pollexfen. As Celia A. Easton points out, "rape is not unknown in [...] Austen novels." Heckerling, the writer/director of *Clueless*, which I reference in the introduction to this book, sagaciously adapts Mr. Elton's "unexpected" proposal (an "aggressive presumption of Emma's affection" that he defends "with the words of a rapist, insisting he only acted because of 'the encouragement I received'" [Easton]) by having the teenager Elton attempt to rape Cher in his car as he drives her home from a party. Even in the most comical representations of analytical fiction, the specter of violence haunts the text. We are confronted simultaneously with the knowledge that none of the female characters in this study are over the age of twenty-seven; young, vulnerable, and expected to take on so much responsibility (for their sexuality, for their conduct in the face of society's strict expectations and norms, for their futures which are always attached to those of men) at such a young age, these women moreover must rely on outside signs and signals to attempt to govern their conduct in the face of possible violence.

In this way, besides the major stylistic and philosophical affinities between the works of analytical fiction that I have studied here—the pessimism and skepticism, the dilation and indefinite delaying of closure, the insistence on narratorial distance and ignorance—another element most of these texts share is their exposing of the prevalence of violence against women across historical boundaries. Despite falling within the paradigm of a sub-genre whose main philosophical drive is that of extreme skepticism about human motivations—a predominantly intellectual experience—the amount of ink expended on the representation of rape and attempted rape is jarring when one reads all of these texts together without necessarily having been looking for this particular common motif. Moreover, outside of feminist criticism, rape is not often discussed as a critical object or is insufficiently problematized, or is sometimes rendered in early modern and eighteenth-century studies as historically incompatible with our contemporary discussions of violence against women. But the trajectories of our studies are sometimes unexpected, and one must find ways of not only recognizing, analyzing, and coping with unexpected results, but growing as a

---

[4] As Katherine Binhammer notes, however, *Clarissa* is, paradoxically, the "paradigmatic seduction novel, which, of course, is technically a novel of rape" (860).

scholar, too. Having written about so many texts that include attempted rape and real rape, I no longer think that such discussions are necessarily anachronistic.

The germ of this book began many years ago in a graduate seminar (in fact, in my first semester of graduate studies) at the CUNY Graduate Center, taught by André Aciman, in which I wrote a seminar paper on the interpolated letter written by Madame de Thémines in *La Princesse de Clèves* (although the paper did not become a part of this book, it was eventually transformed into an article that I cite here). I remember very clearly André asking the students to consider what he called "psychological fiction" as a tool for attempting to know another person and as an instrument for exploring knowledge. Of course, what the students in that class found was a body of fiction of ambivalence, counterintuitiveness, narrative withholding, and opacity. Although my thinking about the *roman d'analyse* has evolved since that graduate seminar, the idea of there being a literary, rather than philosophical or psychological, language for enquiring into the self—even if that self proves to be unknowable—continues to fascinate me, as well as the idea of insight. From the perspective of narrative, what does it mean when a narrator does not trust their characters, to the point of not being capable of narrating their feelings and thoughts? I also do not think it is possible to write enough about irony, which serves as both the mainspring and the offspring of analytical fiction.

One thing I have learned from writing this book is that although analytical fiction does imply a very specific pessimistic worldview, the sub-genre has no beginning or end. Just as the characters in analytical fiction continually manage to reopen what might have previously been closed, I hope that this study in itself can act as a kind of opening. Although I have limited my own study to a relatively small range of canonical European novels and novellas, and my approach has been narrowly circumscribed by genre studies, close reading, and narratology, my intention is that this book serves for other scholars to continue the discussion of analytical fiction as a transnational and trans-historical sub-genre; I hope that others will continue the conversation about analytical fiction into other discursive realms, to other countries, and to other time periods, interpretations, and comparisons.

# Works Cited

Académie Française. *Le Dictionnaire de l'Académie française,* Première édition. Coignard, 1694. *Dictionnaires d'autrefois,* French dictionaries of the 17th, 18th, 19th and 20th centuries. ARTFL Project, University of Chicago.

Aciman, André. "L'Esprit de Pénétration: Psyche and Insight." *L'Esprit En France Au XVIIe Siècle: actes du 28e congrès annuel de la North American Society for Seventeenth Century French Literature: the University of Texas at Austin 11–13 avril 1996.* Edited by François Lagarde, Paris: Papers on French Seventeenth Century Literature, 1997, pp. 95–111.

Aciman, André. "Passions of the Mind." *Salmagundi,* vol. 87, 1990, pp. 344–53.

Aciman, André. "The Recursive Matrix: Jealousy and the Epistemophilic Crisis." *Analecta Husserliana,* vol. 32, 1990, pp. 87–102.

Albers, Irene. "The Passions of the Body in Boccaccio's Decameron." *MLN,* vol. 125, no. 1, 2010, pp. 26–53.

Allaire, Gloria, translator. *Il Tristano Panciatichiano. Arthurian Archives VIII: Italian Literature,* vol. 1, D. S. Brewer, 2002.

Alliston, April. *Virtue's Faults: Correspondences in Eighteenth-Century British and French Women's Fiction.* Stanford University Press, 1996.

Amoss, Benjamin. "Révolution et Restauration Dans Armance: La Loi d'indemnité et La Narration de Stendhal." *MILFC Review,* vol. 4, no. 1, 1994, pp. 42–52.

Andreas Capellanus. *Andreas Capellanus on Love.* Translated by P. G. Walsh, Duckworth Press, 1982.

Andreas Capellanus. *The Art of Courtly Love.* Edited by John Jay Parry, Columbia University Press, 1960.

Andrei, Filippo. *Boccaccio the Philosopher: An Epistemology of the Decameron.* Palgrave Macmillan, 2017.

Apuleius. *Metamorphoses (The Golden Ass).* Translated by J. Arthur Hanson, Loeb Classical Library, 1977.

Aristotle-Horace-Longinus. *Classical Literary Criticism.* Translated by T. S. Dorsch, Penguin Classics, 1965.

Augustine of Hippo. *The City of God.* Translated by Thomas Merton, The Modern Library, 2000.

Austen, Jane. *Persuasion.* W. W. Norton, 1994.

Backscheider, Paula R. "The Rise of Gender as a Political Category." *Revising Women: Eighteenth-Century "Women's Fiction" and Social Engagement,* edited by Paula R. Backscheider, Johns Hopkins University Press, 2000, pp. 31–57.

Baker, Mary J. "Rape, Attempted Rape, and Seduction in the Heptaméron." *Romance Quarterly*, vol. 39, no. 3, 1992, pp. 271–81.
Baragwanath, Emily. *Motivation and Narrative in Herodotus*. Oxford University Press, 2008.
Barolini, Teodolinda. *Dante and the Origins of Italian Literary Culture*. Fordham University Press, 2006.
Barr, Rebecca Anne. "Richardson's Sir Charles Grandison and the Symptoms of Subjectivity." *The Eighteenth Century*, vol. 51, no. 4, 2010, pp. 391–411.
Barthes, Roland. *Critical Essays*. Northwestern University Press, 1972.
Barthes, Roland. *Writing Degree Zero*. Translated by Annette Lavers and Colin Smith, Beacon Press, 1967.
Beasley, Faith Evelyn, and Katharine Ann Jensen, editors. *Approaches to Teaching Lafayette's* La Princesse de Clèves. Modern Language Association of American, 1998.
Beebee, Thomas O. *Clarissa on the Continent: Translation and Seduction*. Penn State University Press, 1990.
Binhammer, Katherine. *The Seduction Narrative in Britain, 1747–1800*. Cambridge University Press, 2009.
Boccaccio, Giovanni. *Decameron*. Edited by Vittore Branca, A. Mondadori, 1985.
Boccaccio, Giovanni. *Elegia di madonna Fiammetta*. Edited by Maria Pia Mussini Sacchi, Mursia, 1987.
Boccaccio, Giovanni. *The Elegy of Lady Fiammetta*. Edited by Mariangela Causa-Steindler. Translated by Mariangela Causa-Steindler and Thomas Mauch, University of Chicago Press, 1990.
Bourget, Paul. "The Evolution of the Modern French Novel." *Booklovers Magazine*, June 1903. pp. 583-89
Braun, George M. "Old French 'Dangier': A New Interpretation of Its Semantic Origin." *The French Review*, vol. 7, no. 6, 1934, pp. 481–85.
Bray, Joe. *The Epistolary Novel: Representations of Consciousness*. Routledge, 2003.
Brock, Theresa. "Subverting Seduction: Gender and Genre in Marguerite de Navarre's Heptaméron." *Women in French Studies*, vol. 26, 2018, pp. 13–26.
Brody, Annalise M. "An Experiment in the Healing Power of Literature." *Boccaccio: A Critical Guide to the Complete Works*, edited by Victoria Kirkham et al., The University of Chicago Press, 2013.
Brooks, Peter. *The Novel of Worldliness: Crébillon, Marivaux, Laclos, Stendhal*. Princeton University Press, 1969.
Brownstein, Rachel M. *Becoming a Heroine: Reading about Women in Novels*. Columbia University Press, 1994.
Burckhardt, Jacob. *The Civilization of the Renaissance in Italy*. Penguin Classics, 1990.
Burns, E. Jane. "How Lovers Lie Together: Infidelity and Fictive Discourse in the *Roman de Tristan*." *Tristan & Isolde: A Case Book*, edited by Joan Trasker Grimbert, Routledge, 2002.

Bynum, Caroline. "Why All the Fuss about the Body? A Medievalist's Perspective." *Critical Inquiry*, vol. 22, no. 1, 1995, pp. 1–33.

Calabrese, Michael A. "Feminism and the Packaging of Boccaccio's *Fiammetta*." *Italica*, vol. 74, no. 1, 1997, pp. 20–42.

Caluori, Damian. "Francisco Sanchez: A Renaissance Pyrrhonist against Aristotelian Dogmatism." *Skepticism: From Antiquity to the Present*. Edited by Diego E. Machuca and Baron Reed, Bloomsbury Academic, 2019.

Campbell, John. "The Cloud of Unknowing: Self-Discovery in La Princesse de Clèves." *French Studies*, vol. 48, no. 4, 1994, pp. 402–15.

Campbell, John. *Questions of Interpretation in La Princesse de Clèves*. Rodopi, 1996.

Caruthers, Peter. *The Opacity of Mind: An Integrative Theory of Self-Knowledge*. Oxford University Press, 2011.

Castelvecchi, Stefano. *Sentimental Opera: Questions of Genre in the Age of Bourgeois Drama*. Cambridge University Press, 2013.

Castle, Terry. *Clarissa's Ciphers: Meaning and Disruption in Richardson's* Clarissa. Cornell University Press, 1982.

Cervantes, Miguel de. *Don Quijote*. Edited by Francisco Rico, Real Academia Española, 2004.

Cervantes, Miguel de. *Don Quixote*. Translated by J. M. Cohen, Penguin Books, 1950.

Cervantes, Miguel de. *Don Quixote*. Translated by Walter Starkie, Signet Classics, 2001.

Chang, Leah. "Blushing and Legibility in *La Princesse de Clèves*." *Romance Studies*, vol. 30, no. 1, 2012, pp. 14–24.

Chapman, Raymond. "Changing Perspectives in Genre Theory." *Revue Belge de Philologie et d'Histoire*, vol. 74, no. 3, 1997, pp. 617–28.

Chatman, Seymour. *Coming to Terms: The Rhetoric of Narrative in Fiction and Film*. Cornell University Press, 1990.

Chatman, Seymour. *Story and Discourse: Narrative Structure in Fiction and Film*. Cornell University Press, 1978.

Chico, Tita. "Details and Frankness: Affective Relations in 'Sir Charles Grandison.'" *Studies in Eighteenth-Century Culture*, vol. 38, 2009, pp. 45–68.

Cholakian, Patricia Francis. *Rape and Writing in the Heptaméron of Marguerite de Navarre*. Southern Illinois University Press, 1991.

Cohn, Dorrit. *Transparent Minds: Narrative Modes for Representing Consciousness in Fiction*. Princeton University Press, 1978.

Counter, Andrew J. "Astolphe de Custine and the *Querelle d'Olivier*: Gossip in Restoration High Society." *Forum for Modern Language Studies*, vol. 50, no. 2, 2013, pp. 154–67.

Culler, Jonathan. "The Closeness of Close Reading." *ADFL Bulletin*, vol. 41, no. 3, 2011, pp. 8–13.

Culler, Jonathan. *Structuralist Poetics*. Routledge Classics, 2012.

Dallas, Dorothy. *Le Roman Français de 1660 à 1680*. Geneva: Slatkine Reprints, 1977.

Dällenbach, Lucien. *The Mirror in the Text*. Translated by Jeremy Whiteley and Emma Hughes, University of Chicago Press, 1989.

Dawson, Lesel. *Lovesickness and Gender in Early Modern English Literature*. Oxford University Press, 2008.

De Armas, Frederick A. *Quixotic Frescoes: Cervantes and Italian Renaissance Art*. University of Toronto Press, 2006.

De Armas Wilson, Diana. "'Passing the Love of Women': The Intertextuality of El Curioso Impertinente." *Cervantes: Bulletin of the Cervantes Society of America*, vol. 7, no. 2, 1987, pp. 9–28.

DeJean, Joan. "Lafayette's Ellipses: The Privileges of Anonymity." *PMLA*, vol. 99, no. 5, 1984, pp. 884–902.

Delers, Olivier. *The Other Rise of the Novel in Eighteenth-Century French Fiction*. University of Delaware Press, 2015.

Deleuze, Gilles, and Félix Guattari. *A Thousand Plateaus: Capitalism and Schizophrenia*. Translated by Brian Massumi, University of Minnesota Press, 1987.

de Mourgues, Odette. *Two French Moralists*. Cambridge University Press, 1978.

Descartes, René. *The Passions of the Soul and Other Late Philosophical Writings*. Translated by Michael Moriarty, Oxford University Press, 2016.

Diderot, Denis. *Œuvres Complètes de Diderot: Revues Sur Les Éditions Originales*. Vol. 5, Paris: Garnier Frères, 1875.

Doody, Margaret Anne. *The True Story of the Novel*. Rutgers University Press, 1997.

Eagleton, Terry. *The Rape of Clarissa: Writing, Sexuality and Class Struggle in Samuel Richardson*. University of Minnesota Press, 1982.

Easton, Celia A. "'The Encouragement I Received': Emma and the Language of Sexual Assault." *Persuasions: The Jane Austen Journal On-Line*, vol. 37, no. 1, 2016, http://jasna.org/publications/persuasions-online/vol37no1/easton/

Eaves, T. C. Duncan, and Ben D. Kimpel. *Samuel Richardson: A Biography*. Claredon Press, 1971.

Edel, Leon. *The Modern Psychologica l Novel*. New York: Grosset and Dunlap, Inc., 1964.

El Saffar, Ruth. *Beyond Fiction: The Recovery of the Feminine in the Novels of Cervantes*. University of California Press, 1984.

El Saffar, Ruth. *Distance and Control in* Don Quixote: *A Study in Narrative Technique*. University of North Carolina Press, 1975.

Fabre, Jean. *L'Art de l'analyse dans "La Princesse de Clèves."* Presses universitaires de Strasbourg, 1989.

Febvre, Lucien. *Autour de l'Heptaméron: Amour Sacré, Amour Profane*. Gallimard, 1944.

Felman, Shoshana. *La "Folie" Dans l'œuvre Romanesque de Stendhal*. J. Corti, 1971.

Ferguson, Frances. "Rape and the Rise of the Novel." *Representations*, vol. 20, Fall 1987, pp. 88–112.

Ferrand, Jacques. *A treatise on Lovesickness*. Translated and edited by Donald A. Beecher and Massimo Ciavolella. Syracuse University Press, 1990.

Fleming, John V. *The Roman de La Rose: A Study in Allegory and Iconography.* PrincetonUniversity Press, 1969.

Fontenelle, Bernard le Bovier. *Les Œuvres de Monsieur Fontenelle.* Vol. 3, Paris: François Changuion, 1744.

Foucault, Michel. *The Order of Things.* Routledge, 1989.

Fox, Cora. *Ovid and the Politics of Emotion in Elizabethan England.* Palgrave, 2009.

François, Anne-Lise. *Open Secrets: The Literature of Uncounted Experience.* Stanford University Press, 2007.

Freccero, Carla. Rape's Disfiguring Figures: Marguerite de Navarre's *Heptameron* Day 1:10. Rape and Representation Edited by Lyn A. and Brenda R. Silver, Columbia University Press, 1991.

Frelick, Nancy. "Speech, Silence, and Storytelling: Marguerite de Navarre's 'Heptameron' and Narrative Therapy." *Renaissance and Reformation/Renaissance et Réforme*, vol. 36, no. 1, 2013, pp. 69–92.

Friedman, Emily. "The End(s) of Richardson's Sir Charles Grandison." *SEL Studies in English* Literature *1500–1900*, vol. 52, no. 3, 2012, pp. 651–67.

Frye, Northrop. *Anatomy of Criticism.* Princeton University Press, 2000.

Garcia López, Jorge. "*Camila se Rindió*: Psicología en la Historia de Anselmo." *Philologia Hispalensis*, vol. 18, no. 2, 2004, pp. 137–149.

Garrett, Matthew, editor. *The Cambridge Companion to Narrative Theory.* Cambridge University Press, 2018.

Gaylin, Ann Elizabeth. *Eavesdropping in the Novel from Austen to Proust.* Cambridge University Press, 2002.

Genette, Gérard. *Figures II.* Editions du Seuil, 1969.

Gide, André. "Preface to *Armance*." *Pretexts: Reflections on Literature and Morality*, edited by Justin O'Brien. Translated by Blanche O. Price, Secker & Warburg, 1959.

Gilby, Emma. *Sublime Worlds: Early Modern French Literature.* Legenda, 2006.

Ginsburg, Warren. *The Cast of Character: The Representation of Personality in Ancient and Medieval Literature.* University of Toronto Press, 1983.

Ginzburg, Lydia. *On Psychological Prose.* Translated by Judson Rosengrant, Princeton University Press, 1991.

Girard, René. *Deceit, Desire, and the Novel: Self and the Other in Literary Structure.* Translated by Yvonne Freccero, Johns Hopkins University Press, 1965.

Glatigny, Michel. "Songe: Introduction Lexicologique." *Bulletin de l'Association d'étude Sur l'humanisme, La Réforme et La Renaissance*, vol. 23, 1986, pp. 53–57.

Gray, Floyd. "Gender, Rhetoric, and Print Culture in French Renaissance Writing." Cambridge University Press, 2000.

Green, Robert. "Lost Paradise and Self-Delusion in the Maxims of La Rochefoucauld." *The French Review*, vol. 48, no. 2, 1974, pp. 321–30.

Greene, Mildred Sarah E. "'A Chimera of Her Own Creating': Love and Fantasy in Madame de Lafayette's *Princesse de Clèves* and Richardson's *Clarissa*." *Rocky Mountain Review of Language and Literature*, vol. 40, no. 4, 1986, pp. 221–32.

Guillaume de Lorris, and Jean de Meun. *Le Roman de La Rose*. Edited by Armand Strubel, Lettres Gothiques, 1992.

Guillaume de Lorris, and Jean de Meun. *The Romance of the Rose*. Translated by Frances Horgan, Oxford University Press, 1994.

Hagedorn, Suzanne. *Abandoned Women: Rewriting the Classics in Dante, Boccaccio, & Chaucer*. University of Michigan Press, 2004.

Halberstam, Judith. *The Queer Art of Failure*. Duke University Press, 2011.

Hamlin, Cyrus. "The Origins of a Philosophical Genre Theory in German Romanticism." *European Romantic Review*, vol. 5, no. 1, 1994, pp. 3–14.

Harris, Jocelyn. *A Revolution Almost beyond Expression: Jane Austen's Persuasion*. Associated University Presses, 2007.

Heckerling, Amy. *Clueless*. Paramount Pictures, 1995.

Heinrichs, Katherine. *The Myths of Love: Classical Lovers in Medieval Literature*. The Pennsylvania State University Press, 1990.

Hemmings, F. W. J. *Stendhal, a Study of His Novels*. Oxford University Press, 1964.

Hodgson, Richard G. "Mise En Abyme and the Narrative System of La Princesse de Clèves: Mme de Themines' Letter to the Vidame de Chartres." *Madame de Lafayette, La Bruyère, La Femme et Le Théâtre Au Pouvoir: Actes de Davis*, 1988, pp. 55–61.

Hollander, Robert. *Boccaccio's Two Venuses*. Columbia University Press, 1977.

Immerwahr, Raymond, "Structural Symmetry in the Episodic Narratives of *Don Quijote*, Part One." *Comparative Literature*, vol. 10, no. 2, 1958, pp. 121–135.

Johnson, Claudia L. *Jane Austen: Women, Politics, and the Novel*. University of Chicago Press, 1988.

Johnson, Samuel. *The Complete Works of Samuel Johnson*. London: George Dearborn, 1837.

Johnson, Samuel. *The Yale Edition of the Works of Samuel Johnson*. Edited by W. J. Bate and Albrecht B. Strauss, Yale University Press, 1969.

Jones, Wendy. "The Dialectic of Love in Sir Charles Grandison." *Eighteenth-Century Fiction*, vol. 8, no. 1, 1995, pp. 15–34.

Kahler, Erich. *The Inward Turn of Narrative*. Princeton University Press, 1973.

Kamuf, Peggy. "A Mother's Will: The Princess of Clèves." *Fictions of Feminine Desire*, University of Nebraska Press, 1982.

Kaplan, David. "The Lover's Test Theme in Cervantes and Madame de Lafayette." The French Review, Vol. 26, no. 4, 1953, pp. 285–290.

Kaps, Helen K. *Moral Perspective in* La Princesse de Clèves. University of Oregon Press, 1968.

Kelly, Henry Ansgar. *Love and Marriage in the Age of Chaucer*. Eugene, Oregon: Wipf & Stock Publishers, 2004.

Koehler, Martha J. "The Problem of Suspense in Richardson's *Sir Charles Grandison*." *The Eighteenth Century*, vol. 54, no. 3, 2013, pp. 317–39.

Koppisch, Michael S. "The Dynamics of Jealousy in the Work of Madame de Lafayette." *MLN*, vol. 94, no. 4, 1979, pp. 757–73.

Kriesel, James C. "Boccaccio and the Early Modern Reception of Tragedy." *Renaissance Quarterly*, vol. 69, no. 2, 2016, pp. 415–48.

Krueger, Allison E. "Cervantes's Laboratory: The Thought Experiment of 'El curioso impertinente'." *Cervantes: Bulletin of the Cervantes Society of America*, vol. 29, no. 1, 2009, pp. 117–65.

Kudish, Adele. "'[La] plus Jolie [de] Toutes Celles Qui Avaient Jamais Été Écrites': Madame de Thémines's Letter as Proto-Psychological Fiction in La *Princesse de Clèves*." *The French Review*, vol. 91, no. 3, 2018, pp. 56–69.

Kudish, Adele. "'Emotions so Compounded of Pleasure and Pain': Affective Contradiction in Austen's *Persuasion*." *The Explicator*, vol. 74, no. 2, 2016, pp. 120–24.

Kudish, Adele. "Lost 'in a Sort of Wilderness': The Epistemology of Love in Richardson's *The History of Sir Charles Grandison*." *Studies in Philology*, vol. 114, no. 2, 2017, pp. 426–45.

Kuhns, Richard. "Interpretative Method for a Tale by Boccaccio: An Enchanted Pear Tree in Argos (*Decameron* 7.9)." *New Literary History*, vol. 30, no. 4, 1999, pp. 721–36.

Kukkonen, Karin. *A Prehistory of Cognitive Poetics: Neoclassicism and the Novel*. Oxford University Press, 2017.

Küpper, Joachim. "The Secret Life of Classical and Arabic Medical Texts in Petrarch's Canzoniere." *Petrarch and Boccaccio: The Unity of Knowledge in the Pre-Modern World*. Edited by Igor Candido, De Gruyter, 2018.

Lafayette, Marie-Madeleine. *La Princesse de Clèves*. Edited by Peter H. Nurse, Harrap, 1970.

Lafayette, Marie-Madeleine. *La Princesse de Clèves et Autres Romans*. Edited by Bernard Pinguad, Folio Classique, 1972.

Lafayette, Marie-Madeleine. *The Princess of Clèves*. Edited by John D. Lyons. Translated by John D. Lyons, Norton Critical Editions, 1994.

Lafayette, Marie-Madeleine. *Zayde: A Spanish Romance*. Translated by Nicholas D. Paige, University of Chicago Press, 2006.

LaGuardia, David. "The Voice of the Patriarch in the Heptaméron I: 10." *Neophilologus*, vol. 81, no. 4, 1997, pp. 501–13.

Landry, François. "Entre Noblesse et Bourgeoisie: 'Armance' Ou Le Désir sans Traduction." *Romantisme*, vol. 17–18, 1977, pp. 228–42.

Landry, Olivia. "Jewish Joke Telling in Muttersprache Mameloschn: Performing Queer Intervention on the German Stage." *Women & Performance: A Journal of Feminist Theory*, vol. 26, no. 1, 2016, pp. 36–54.

Lanham, Richard. *A Handlist of Rhetorical Terms*. 2nd ed., University of Chicago Press, 1991.

La Rochefoucauld, Francois de. *Collected Maxims and Other Reflections.* Translated by E. H. Blackmore et al., Oxford World's Classics, 2007.

La Rochefoucauld, Francois de. *Maximes.* GF Flammarion, 1977.

Lee, Wendy Anne. *Failures of Feeling: Insensibility and the Novel.* Stanford University Press, 2018.

Levarie Smarr, Janet. *Boccaccio and Fiammetta, The Narrator as Lover.* University of Illinois Press, 1986.

Lewis, C. S. *The Allegory of Love: A Study in Medieval Tradition.* Oxford University Press, 1958.

Lo, Louis. *Male Jealousy: Literature and Film.* Continuum Literary Studies, 2008.

Lorenz, Hendrik. "Ancient Theories of Soul." *The Stanford Encyclopedia of Philosophy*, edited by Edward N. Zalta, 2009, https://plato.stanford.edu/entries/ancient-soul/.

Lovejoy, A. O. *Reflections on Human Nature.* Johns Hopkins University Press, 1964.

Lyons, John D. *Before Imagination: Embodied Thought from Montaigne to Rousseau.* Stanford University Press, 2005.

Lyons, John D. "From Fortune to Randomness in Seventeenth-Century Literature." *French Studies*, vol. 65, no. 2, 2011, pp. 156–73.

Lyons, John D. "Mlle de Chartres at the Jeweller's Shop: Knowledge and Commerce in *La Princesse de Clèves*." *Seventeenth-Century French Studies*, vol. 27, 2005, pp. 117–26.

Lyotard, Jean-François. "The Sublime and the Avant-Garde." *The Bloomsbury Anthology of Aesthetics.* Edited by Joseph Tanke and Colin McQuillian, Bloomsbury, 2012.

Mackey, Louis. "Anatomical Curiosities: Northrop Frye's Theory of Criticism." *Texas Studies in Literature and Language*, vol. 23, no. 3, 1981, pp. 442–69.

Mäkelä, Maria. "Exceptionality or Exemplarity?: The Emergence of the Schematized Mind in the Seventeenth- and Eighteenth-Century Novel." *Poetics Today*, vol. 39, no. 1, 2018, pp. 17–39.

Marguerite de Navarre. *L'Heptaméron.* Edited by Nicole Cauzaron, Folio Classique, 2000.

Marguerite de Navarre. *The Heptameron.* Translated by P. A. Chilton, Penguin Books, 1984.

McCarthy, Conor, editor. *Love, Sex, and Marriage in the Middle Ages: A Sourcebook.* Routledge, 2004.

McKeon, Michael. *The Origins of the English Novel.* Johns Hopkins University Press, 2002.

McKeon, Michael, editor. *Theory of the Novel: A Historical Approach.* Johns Hopkins University Press.

McKillop, A. D. "On Sir Charles Grandison." *Samuel Richardson: A Collection of Critical Essays.* Edited by John Carroll, Prentice-Hall, 1969, pp. 124–38.

McMurran, Mary Helen. *The Spread of Novels: Translation and Prose Fiction in the Eighteenth Century.* Princeton University Press, 2010.

Meister, Jan Christoph. "Narratology." *The Living Handbook of Narratology*. Edited by Peter et al, Hühn, http://www.lhn.uni-hamburg.de/article/narratology.

Mellon, Lorna. "Death and the End of Testimony: Trauma Theory in Shakespeare's Hamlet." *Journal of the Wooden O Symposium*, vol. 6, 2006, pp. 116–23.

Meyer Spacks, Patricia. "The Grand Misleader: Self-Love and Self-Division in Clarissa." *Studies in the Literary Imagination*, vol. 28, no. 1, 1995, pp. 7–21.

Meyer Spacks, Patricia. *Novel Beginnings: Experiments in Eighteenth-Century English Fiction*. Yale University Press, 2006.

Migiel, Marilyn. "Boccaccio and Women." *The Cambridge Companion to Boccaccio*. Edited by Guyda Armstrong et al., Cambridge University Press, 2015, pp. 171–84.

Milner, Stephen J. "Boccaccio's Decameron and the Semiotics of the Everyday." *The Cambridge Companion to Boccaccio*. Edited by Guyda Armstrong et al., Cambridge University Press, 2015, pp. 83–100.

Milowicki, Edward, and Rawdon Wilson. "Ovid's Shadow: Character and Characterization in Early Modern Literature." *Neohelicon*, vol. 22, no. 1, 1995, pp. 9–47.

Moler, Kenneth L. *Jane Austen's Art of Allusion*. University of Nebraska Press, 1968.

Molina, Alvaro. "Glass Characters and Glass Fictions: The Poetics of 'El Curioso Impertinente' and 'El Licenciado Vidriera.'" *Mester*, vol. 25, no. 1, 1996, pp. 5–29.

Montaigne, Michel de. *Essais de Michel de Montaigne, in Three Volumes*. Edited by Emmanuel Naya et al., Folio Classique, 2009.

Moravia, Sergio. "From Homme Machine to Homme Sensible: Changing Eighteenth-Century Models of Man's Image." *Journal of the History of Ideas*, vol. 39, no. 1, 1978, pp. 45–60.

Moriarty, Michael. *Early Modern French Thought: The Age of Suspicion*. Oxford University Press, 2003.

Mouillaud, G. "Stendhal et Le Mode Irréel à Propos de l'impuissance Dans *Armance*." *MLN*, vol. 83, no. 4, 1968, pp. 524–42.

Munro, James. "Richardson, Marivaux, and the French Romance Tradition." *The Modern Language Review*, vol. 70, 1975, pp. 752–59.

Ngai, Sianne. *Ugly Feelings*. Harvard University Press, 2005.

Nichols, Stephen G. "Example versus Historia: Montaigne, Eriugena, and Dante." *Unruly Examples, On the Rhetoric of Exemplarity*. Edited by Alexander Gelley, Stanford University Press, 1995.

Nicole, Pierre. *Essais de Morale*. Vol. 6, Paris: G. Despretz, 1782.

Nussbaum, Martha C. *Love's Knowledge: Essays on Philosophy and Literature*. Oxford University Press, 1990.

O'Keefe, Charles. "A Function of Narrative Uncertainty in Stendhal's *Armance*." *The French Review*, vol. 50, no. 4, 1977, pp. 579–85.

Olson, Greta. "Reconsidering Unreliability: Fallible and Untrustworthy Narrators." *Narrative*, vol. 11, no. 1, 2003, pp. 93–109.

Ovid. *Metamorphoses*. Translated by Frank Justus Miller. Revised by G. P. Goold, Loeb Classical Library, 1984.

Paige, Nicholas D. *Before Fiction: The Ancien Régime of the Novel*. University of Pennsylvania Press, 2011.

Pascal, Blaise. *Pensées and Other Writings*. Translated by Honor Levi, Oxford University Press, 1995.

Pérez, Ashley Hope. "Into the Dark Triangle of Desire: Rivalry, Resistance, and Repression in 'El Curioso Impertinente.'" *Cervantes: Bulletin of the Cervantes Society of America*, vol. 31, no. 1, 2011, pp. 83–107.

Peterson, Jean. "The Future of (Close) Reading." *Early Modern Culture*, vol. 12, 2017, pp. 47–53.

Peterson, Nora Martin. "Competing Codes and Involuntary Confessions of the Flesh in La Princesse de Clèves." *The Romantic Review*, vol. 103, nos. 1–2, 2012, pp. 233–53.

Peterson, Nora Martin. *Involuntary Confessions of the Flesh in Early Modern France*. University of Delaware Press, 2016.

Pinch, Adela. *Strange Fits of Passion: Epistemologies of Emotion, Hume to Austen*. Stanford University Press, 1996.

Pingaud, Bernard. *Mme de La Fayette Par Elle-Même*. Paris: Éditions du Seuil, 1959.

Plato. *Phaedrus*. Translated by Alexander Nehemas and Paul Woodruff, Hackett Publishing Company, 1995.

Polachek, Dora E. "Scatology, Sexuality, and the Logic of Laughter in Marguerite de Navarre's *Heptaméron*." *Medieval Feminist Forum: A Journal of Gender and Sexuality*, vol. 33, no. 1, 2002, pp. 30–42.

Pons, Alain. "Sprezzatura." *The Dictionary of Untranslatables*. Edited by Barbara Cassin and Emily Apter. Translated by Steven Rendall, Princeton University Press, 2014.

Preston, John. "The Silence of the Novel." *The Modern Language Review*, vol. 74, no. 2, 1979, pp. 257–67.

Proust, Marcel. *À l'ombre des jeunes oilles en oleures*. Edited by Pierre-Louis Rey. Folio Classique, 1988.

Proust, Marcel. *Sodome et Gomorrhe*. Edited by Antoine Compagnon. Folio Classique, 1989.

Proust, Marcel. *In Search of Lost Time: Soddom and Gomorah*. Translated by C. K. Scott Moncrieff et al., The Modern Library, 1999.

Quint, David. *Cervantes's Novel of Modern Times: A New Reading of* Don Quijote. Princeton University Press, 2003.

Radiguet, Raymond. *Le Bal du comte d'Orgel*. Folio, 2002.

Reid, Martine. "Correspondences: Stendhal En Toutes Lettres." *Modern Critical Views: Stendhal*. Edited by Harold Bloom, Chelsea House Publishers, 1989.

Rendall, Steven. "Force and Language: 'Heptameron' 10." *Comparative Literature*, vol. 60, no. 1, 2008, pp. 74–80.

Richardson, Samuel. *Clarissa, or the History of a Young Lady; In Four Volumes*. Dent, 1976.

Richardson, Samuel. *Clarissa, or the History of a Young Lady*. Penguin Books, 2004.

Richardson, Samuel. *The History of Sir Charles Grandison*. Edited by Jocelyn Harris, Oxford University Press, 1972.

Richardson, Samuel. *The History of Sir Charles Grandison*. Edited by William Lyon Phelps, vol. 1, London: Croscup & Sterling Company, 1901.

Richardson, Samuel. *Moral and Instructive Sentiments, Maxims, Cautions, and Reflections, Contained in the Histories of PAMELA, CLARISSA, and Sir CHARLES GRANDISON*. London: Samuel Richardson, 1755.

Richetti, John. *The English Novel in History: 1700 to 1780*. Routledge, 1999.

Rikhardsdottir, Sif. "Medieval Emotionality: The Feeling Subject in Medieval Literature." *Comparative Literature*, vol. 69, no. 1, 2017, pp. 74–90.

Riskin, Jessica. *Science in the Age of Sensibility: The Sentimental Empiricists of the French Enlightenment*. University of Chicago Press, 2002.

Rivero, Albert J. "Representing Clementina: 'Unnatural' Romance and the Ending of *Grandison*." *New Essays on Samuel Richardson*. Edited by Albert J. Rivero, St. Martin's Press, 1996, pp. 209–25.

Ronchetti, Alessia. "Boccaccio between Naples and Florence, or the Desire to Become Two: Gendering the Author's Past in the *Elegia di Madonna Fiammetta*." *Italian Studies*, vol. 72, no. 2, 2017, pp. 205–17.

Rudler, Gustave. *La Jeunesse de Benjamin Constant 1767–1794: Le Disciple Du Xviiie Siècle Utilitarisme et Pessimism Mme de Carrière*. Paris: Librairie Armand Colin, 1909.

Saiber, Arielle. *Giordano Bruno and the Geometry of Language*. Routledge, 2005.

Sainte-Beuve, Charles. *Les Consolations*. Brussels: Société Belge de Librairie, 1837.

Saintsbury, George. *Letters from Sir Charles Grandison*. London: George Allen, 1904.

Sappho. *If Not, Winter: Fragments of Sappho*. Translated by Anne Carson, Vintage Books, 2002.

Schiffman, Zackary S. "Montaigne and the Rise of Skepticism in Early Modern Europe: A Reappraisal." *Journal of the History of Ideas*, vol. 45, no. 4, 1984, pp. 499–516.

Scordilis Brownlee, Marina. *The Severed Word: Ovid's Heroides and the Novela Sentimental*. Princeton University Press, 1990.

Sears, Theresa Ann. *Clio, Eros, Thanatos: The "Novela Sentimental" in Context*. Peter Lang, 2001.

Shakespeare, William. *Macbeth*: Folger Shakespeare Library. Washington Square Press, 2004.

Shattuck, Roger. *Forbidden Knowledge: From Prometheus to Pornography*. St. Martin's Press, 1996.

Shattuck, Roger. *Proust's Way: A Field Guide to In Search of Lost Time*. W. W. Norton, 2000.

Shoemaker, Peter. "Lafayette's Confidence Game: Plausibility and Private Confession in *La Princesse de Clèves* and *Zaide*." *French Forum*, vol. 27, no. 1, 2002, pp. 45–58.

Singer, Alan. *The Self-Deceiving Muse: Notice and Knowledge in the Work of Art*. Penn State University Press, 2010.

Smith, Adam. *Theory of Moral Sentiments*. University of Chicago Press, 2002.

Spinoza, Baruch. *Spinoza: Ethics: Proved in Geometrical Order*. Edited by Matthew J. Kisner. Translated by Michael Silverthorne and Matthew J. Kisner, Cambridge University Press, 2018.

Stanton, Domna. "The Ideal of 'repos' in Seventeenth-Century French Literature." *L'Esprit Créateur*, vol. 15, 1975, pp. 79–104.

Stendhal. *Armance*. Edited by Armand Hoog, Gallimard (Folio Classique), 1975.

Stendhal. *Armance*. Translated by C. K. Scott Moncrieff, Soho Book Company, 1986.

Symonds, John Addington. *Giovanni Boccaccio as Man and Author*. AMS Press (Reprint of 1895 John C. Nimmo edition), 1968.

Talbot, Emile J. *Stendhal Revisited*. Twaine Publishers, 1993.

Tanner, Tony. "In Between: *Persuasion*." *Jane Austen*, Harvard University Press, 1986, pp. 208–49.

Tilmouth, Christopher. *Passion's Triumph over Reason: A History of the Moral Imagination from Spenser to Rochester*. Oxford University Press, 2007.

Todd, Janet. *Sensibility: An Introduction*. Methuen, 1986.

Todd, Sarah J. "Heroides and (Anti-)Heroines: Gendered Discourse in Boccaccio's *Elegia Di Madonna Fiammetta*." *Hortulus*, vol. 8, no. 1, 2012, pp. 77–97.

Todorov, Tzvetan. "Reading as Construction." *Essentials of the Theory of Fiction*. Edited by J. Hoffman and Patrick D. Murphy, Duke University Press, 2005, pp. 140–53.

Valenza, Robin. "How Literature Becomes Knowledge: A Case Study." *ELH (English Literary History)*, vol. 76, no. 1, 2009, pp. 215–45.

Vance, Jacob. "Humanist Polemics, Christian Morals: A Hypothesis on Marguerite de Navarre's 'Heptaméron' and the Problem of Self-Love." *MLN*, vol. 120, no. 1, 2005, pp. S181–95.

Vermillion, Mary. "*Clarissa* and the Marriage Act." *Eighteenth-Century Fiction*, vol. 9, no. 4, 1997, pp. 395–414.

Virtue, Nancy E. "Ce qui doit augmenter le cœur aux dames: Telling the Story of Rape in Marguerite de Navarre's *Heptaméron*." *Romance Quarterly*, vol. 44, no. 2, 1997, pp. 67–79.

Vranjes, Vlasta. "Jane Austen, Lord Hardwicke's Marriage Act, and the National Courtship Plot." *Clio*, vol. 43, no. 2, 2014, pp. 197–223.

Waley, Pamela. "The Nurse in Boccaccio's Fiammetta: Source and Invention." *Neophilologus*, vol. 56, no. 2, 1972, pp. 164–74.

Wardropper, Bruce W. "The Pertinence of El curioso impertinente." *PMLA*, vol. 72, no. 4, 1957, pp. 587–600.

Watt, Ian. *The Rise of the Novel: Studies in Defoe, Richardson, and Fielding*. University of California Press, 2001.

Wiesmann, Marc-Andre. "Rolandine's lict de reseul: An Arachnological Reading of a Tale by Marguerite de Navarre." *The Sixteenth Century Journal*, vol. 31, no. 2, 2000, pp. 433–52.

Wiltshire, John. "*Mansfield Park, Emma, Persuasion.*" *The Cambridge Companion to Jane Austen*. Edited by Edward Copeland and Juliet McMaster, Cambridge University Press, 1997.

Wölfflin, Heinrich. *Renaissance and Baroque*. Translated by Kathrin Simon, Cornell University Press, 1979.

Wood, Michael. *Stendhal*. Cornell University Press, 1971.

Zak, Gur. "Boccaccio's *Fiammetta* and the Consolation of Literature." *MLN*, vol. 131, no. 1, 2016, pp. 1–19.

Zigarovich, Jolene. "Courting Death: Necrophilia in Samuel Richardson's *Clarissa*." *Studies in the Novel*, vol. 32, no. 2, 2000, pp. 112–28.

Zunshine, Lisa. *Why We Read Fiction: Theory of Mind and the Novel*. The Ohio State University Press, 2006.

# Index

Abélard and Héloise 178 n.21
Académie française, dictionary of the 1 n.3, 110
Aciman, André 15, 20, 170 n.4, 195; on "Curioso" 96–7; on psychological fiction 14–15; on the "recursive matrix" 17
adynaton 113. *See also* indescribability
affect 8, 17, 20, 28–9, 32; affective environment of *Armance* 174; in "Curioso" 88; in *Grandison* 148; in *La Princesse de Clèves* 104, 107–9, 112, 114. *See also* cataleptic impressions; involuntary confessions; sublime
affective contradictions 105–6, 108, 159, 168, 176
Albers, Irene 46 n.34, 193
Allaire, Gloria 49 n.42
Alliston, April 12, 161
Amoss, Benjamin 174
Amour. *See* Cupid
analytical fiction, definition of 14–29, 32–4
anatomy form 11–12
Andreas Capellanus: *De Amore* 37 n.8, 44
Andrei, Filippo 38 n.10
Ansgar Kelly, Henry 44 n.25
anti-humanism 4–5, 13, 192. *see also* Renaissance humanism
anti-romanticism: in *Clarissa* and *Grandison* 8, 33, 127–8, 144–5, 148 n.14, 150; in *Don Quixote* 85; in the *Elegia* 44, 60; *Grandison*'s compared with *La Princesse de Clèves*'s 151–5; in the *Heptaméron* 71; *Persuasion* and 165; Venus's in the *Roman de la Rose* 57. *See also* romanticism
Apuleius: *The Golden Ass* 46 n.32, 84; Psyche in 7, 35–6, 46, 58, 87
Ariosto, Ludovico: *Orlando Furioso* 75 n.36, 86, 89 n.65, 139. *See also* lovers' test theme

Aristotle 36 n.3, 59, 84; *peripeteia* (recognition) and *anagnorisis* (reversal) 16, 34, 45, 94, 120, 126, 134, 168; *Poetics* 10, 14 n.24, 28, 101 n.2
art (deception): affectation and 20 n.32; in the *Elegia* 44; of love, in the *Roman de la Rose* 54; Lovelace's description of women as the "plaguy sex" 140; Pygmalion's 24; versus nature in *Clarissa* 133; versus nature in *Persuasion* 172
Augustine of Hippo: Augustinian theology 4, 15, 21; *City of God* 5 n.13; *Confessions* 183 n.38
Austen, Jane: *Emma* 9, 18–9, 194; *Mansfield Park* 171; *Persuasion* 29; chapter 5 summary 8–9; chapter text 158–73; Anne Elliot as an outsider/observer in her own family 160–1; character growth in 163–5; class tensions in 158–9, 172; definitions of "persuasion" 162–3; intimacy and affective contradiction in 165–9, 171–3; mindreading in 170; redirected love in 169–70; social and economic changes in England in 158–9

Backscheider, Paula R. 130
Baker, Mary J. 4 n.11
Balzac, Honoré de 27, 31
Baragwanath, Emily 2
Barolini, Teodolinda 45, 48 n.39
Baroque 17, 83, 101–3
Barr, Rebecca Anne 145
Barthes, Roland 25, 27, 31
Beebee, Thomas O. 129 n.3
Beecher, Donald A. and Massimo Ciavolella 59
*bienséance* (propriety, etiquette) 43, 125, 164, 182
bildungsroman 3, 21, 164
Binhammer, Katherine 194 n.4

Boccaccio, Giovanni: *Decameron* 2 n.4, 45; Pyrrhonean skepticism in 13; proclaimed therapeutic properties of 46, 193; sex in 65; *Elegia*: chapter 1 summary 7; chapter text 35–61; cyclical representation of time in 39–41; desire in 2 n.4, 16; exempla in 48–9; failures of language in 48; free will in 57–8; genre of 38; love at first sight in 25; rape accusation in 58–9; self-deception in 43–5; storytelling in 51–3; tension between words and deeds in 45–7, 51; unreliable narrator of 41–3
Boethius: *Consolation of Philosophy* 11, 59
Booth, Wayne 42
Bourget, Paul 14
Bradshaigh, Lady Dorothy 143
Branca, Vittore 38 n.9
Braun, George M. 54
Bray, Joe 145, 148
Brock, Theresa 64 n.2
Brody, Annalise 40 n.16, 46 n.34, 57
Brooks, Peter: on the *portrait morale* 15; on realism 31; on worldliness 12 n.21, 25, 31 n.48, 34, 127
Brownstein, Rachel 171
Burckhardt, Jacob 38 n.9
Burke, Edmund 21–2, 28. *See also* sublime
Burns, E. Jane 49
Burton, Robert: *Anatomy of Melancholy* 11
Bynum, Caroline 45 n.29

Calabrese, Michael A. 38 n.9, 49, 52, 58–9
Callahan, Anne 130
Caluori, Damian 13 n.23
Calvinism 5 n.13
Campbell, John 4 n.10, 103, 105, 110, 114, 130
Caruth, Cathy 28
Caruthers, Peter 6 n.15
Castelvecchi, Stefano 11
Castiglione, Baldassare: *Il Cortegiano* 20 n.32
Castle, Terry 133
cataleptic impressions (Martha Nussbaum) 9, 17, 18, 104, 114, 182
catharsis (purgation) 28

Causa-Steindler, Mariangela 36 n.2, 49 n.42
Cervantes, Miguel de: *Don Quixote*: ending of 98–100; influence of Pyrrhonean skepticism on 13; reality in 84; "Curioso": chapter 2 summary 7–8; chapter text 83–100; narratorial interventions in 90, 95; philosophical argumentation in 89–90; playacting in 95–6; radical uncertainty of 85, 96 n.87; "The Glass Graduate" 83; *Novelas ejemplares* 83
Chang, Leah 104, 114
Chapman, Raymond 10, 11
Chatman, Seymour 3 n.9, 27
*chiaroscuro* 101 n.2
Chico, Tita 145, 148 n.15, 151
Chilton, P. A. 64–5, 71–2
Cholakian, Patricia Francis 69, 73 n.27, 76
Cicero, Marcus Tullius 13 n.22
close reading 4, 7 n.16
Cohen, J. M. 85 n.54, 56
Cohen, Margaret 29, 31
Cohn, Dorrit 6, 26–7
Coleridge, Samuel Taylor 159
comparative approach 3, 155
Constant, Benjamin 157
Counter, Andrew 177
counter-exemplarity: in the *Elegia* 51; Florida in the *Heptaméron* 79; in *La Princesse de Clèves* 114; of passionate love 20 n.32. *See also* exemplarity
*courtoisie* (courtly love) 19–21, 44, 56, 57 n.73, 71–2, 130, 152. *See also* Andreas Capellanus; *serviteur*
Croce, Benedetto 11
Culler, Jonathan: on close reading 7 n.16; on genre 10–11; on indescribability trope 27
Cupid (Amour, god of love) 35–6, 46, 54–7, 87
cyclicality: in *Clarissa* 132–3, 135, 139–40; in the *Elegia* 39–41; 47; as a feature of analytical fiction 5–7, 15, 21, 24, 94; in the *Heptaméron* 66, 79; in *La Princesse de Clèves* 106, 122, 125; in *Persuasion* 166. *See also* narrative *durée*; time

Dallas, Dorothy 103 n.3
Dällenbach, Lucien 2 n.7
Dante, Alighieri: *Commedia* 36 n.5, 48 n.39
Dawson, Lesel 60
daydream (*songe*) 103, 112 n.28, 123–4
De Armas, Frederick A. 87
De Armas Wilson, Diane 85 n.56
death: in *Armance* 187, 189; in *Clarissa* 132–5, 194; as a cure for analytical fiction's recursivity 16; in "Curioso" 96 n.87, 98–9; *Fiammetta* and 41, 43 n.22, 49, 58; in the *Heptaméron* 67, 75, 82; in *La Princesse de Clèves* 106, 107–8, 110, 113, 123, 126; metamorphosis and 23; in *Persuasion* 169; the sublime and 22
*dédoublement* (doubling) 21, 148
Defoe, Daniel: *Robinson Crusoe* 9 n.17, 29–30; *Moll Flanders* 43
DeJean, Joan 111, 113
Delers, Olivier 29, 30 n.45
Deleuze, Gilles and Félix Guattari 111
deliberation: in *Armance* 186; in "Curioso" 89; in the *Heptaméron* 63–4, 66, 69, 71, 76, 78, 80; in *Grandison* 145; inconsequentialism of 8; in *La Princesse de Clèves* 111–12, 117
de Mourgues, Odette 5–6
Derrida, Jacques 11, 42 n.21
Descartes, René 1, 45 n.29, 50
Diderot, Denis 128
dilation. *See* narrative *durée*
Dion, Céline 18
disnarration (Gerald Prince) 59
dissimulation: in analytical fiction in general 7; in *Armance* 174, 182, 187–8; in *Clarissa* 140; in "Curioso" 88, 96; in the *Elegia* 44, 51–3; in the *Heptaméron* 63, 65–9, 71, 73, 77, 79–80; in *Grandison* 150–1, 152; in *La Princesse de Clèves* 104, 108 n.15, 110, 112 n.29, 114–16; in *Persuasion* 160
Doody, Margaret Anne 36, 37, 41
Douthwaite, Julia V. 103
dream visions 53–4
Duncombe, William 143
Duras, Claire de: *Olivier ou le secret* 173 n.6

Eagleton, Terry 130 n.4, 131 n.5, 133
Easton, Celia A. 194
Eaves, T. C. Duncan and Ben D. Kimpel 129
Echlin, Lady Elizabeth 143
Edel, Leon 14
Edwards, Thomas 141–2
ellipsis 7, 13, 16, 108, 111, 112–13, 186
El Saffar, Ruth 91, 94
emotions: historically constructed 59 n.78. *See also* passions
empiricism 32, 83, 86, 87, 97–8, 101, 125
epistemological certainty 85
epistemology 2, 24, 83, 102, 115, 132; in Cervantes 83; and control in *Grandison* 141–6; of failed love 3, 4, 6–7, 21, 60, 100, 136, 142, 155; in the *Elegia* 38, 50, 60; of failure 191; and secrets 148; and the unreliable narrator 43
exemplarity 27, 38; in *Clarissa* and *Grandison* 131; in the *Elegia* 48–9, 60; exemplary value versus fixed meaning 111; in *La Princesse de Clèves* 114. *See also* counter-exemplarity

Fabre, Jean 4 n.10, 15, 21, 30
fallible narrator 41–3. *See also* unreliable narrator; untrustworthy narrator
Faret, Nicolas: *L'honnête homme, ou, L'art de plaire a la cour* 20 n.32
Febvre, Lucien 75
Felman, Shoshana 186
feminist interpretations 192; of "Curioso" 96; of the *Elegia* 38; of the *Heptaméron* 64, 65
Ferguson, Frances 9 n.17, 132, 193–4
fictive discourse (E. Jane Burns) 49
Flaubert, Gustave: *Madame Bovary* 33
Fleming, John V. 54
Fontenelle, Bernard le Bovier 70
forms of fiction (Northrop Frye) 11–12
fortune 57 n.73, 58–60, 97
Foucault, Michel 102
Fox, Cora 22
François, Anne-Lise: choice of primary texts 10; on *La Princesse de Clèves* 113, 120 n.38, 122, 125; on *Mansfield Park* 171–2; on *Persuasion* 168

Freccero, Carla 68, 76, 80, 81
free indirect discourse 111, 170
Frelick, Nancy 65, 77
French Revolution 174, 176, 189
Friedman, Emily 148 n.14
Frye, Northrop: *Anatomy of Criticism* 3 n.9, 11–12, 14

Garcia Lopez, Jorge 87, 89, 94
Garrett, Matthew 29, 31
Gaylin, Ann Elizabeth 158
gaze: in *Armance* 178, 180–1; in "Curioso" 90–2; in the *Elegia* 40; in the *Heptaméron* 66; love at first sight 25; in *La Princesse de Clèves* 102, 109 n.19, 114, 119–20; in *Persuasion* 161–2. *See also* spying
Genette, Gérard 11, 173 n.6
genre: theory of 10–11; analytical fiction as sub-3–5, 7, 9–14, 28, 155; novella 10; the novel 13–14, 29–33; classical forms 14; *portrait morale* 15; documentary texts 30 n.46
Gide, André 2 n.7, 173 n.6, 186
Gilby, Emma 21, 27–8
Ginsburg, Warren 38 n.9
Ginzburg, Lydia 30
Girard, René 88
Glatigny, Michel 124
God/gods: absence of in the *Elegia* 50, 51–2, 58; Christianity in the *Heptaméron* 82; divine intervention in the Pygmalion myth 23; grace in Augustine 5 n.13; in *The Golden Ass* 35–6; Juno 57 n.73; as justification for rape in the *Heptaméron* 72; lack of in most analytical fiction 6; Panfilo conflated with Cupid in the *Elegia* 52. *See also* Cupid; Venus
Goethe, Johann Wolfgang von 9 n.17; *Elective Affinities* 10
gossip 43 n.22, 91, 98–9, 107–8, 177
gothic novel 3
Gottfried Von Strassburg 49 n.42
Gracián, Baltasar: *The Art of Worldly Wisdom* 16
Gratian: *Decretum Gratiani* 4 n.11
Gravdal, Kathryn 65 n.3
Gray, Floyd 64, 66 n.6, 68, 77–8, 79

Green, Robert 15
Greene, Mildred Sarah E. 129
Guillaume de Lorris and Jean de Meun: *Le Roman de la Rose* 7, 53–7, 72; Cupid in 54–7; Danger or Dangier in 54–7; Venus in 54–7

Hagedorn, Suzanne 48–9, 51
Halberstam, Judith (Jack) 191 n.1
Hamlin, Cyrus 11
Hardwicke's Marriage Act 144 n.12
Harris, Jocelyn 142 n.11, 159 n.2, 167
Harvey, Elizabeth 52 n.57
Hawthorne, Nathaniel 9 n.17
Hebrew Bible, *Jeremiah* 2
Heckerling, Amy: *Clueless* 9, 18–19, 26, 194
Heinrichs, Katherine 38 n.9, 56
Hemmings, F. W. J. 157, 173 n.5, 176 n.15, 179
Herodotus 2
*historia verdadera* (true history) 84, 87 n.59
Hodgson, Richard 104, 115
Hogg, James: *The Private Memoirs and Confession of a Justified Sinner* 11–2
Hollander, Robert 36 n.4, 43, 48, 57 n.72
Horace, *Ars Poetica* 42, 79, 144

Immerwahr, Raymond 85 n.56
implied author 42, 53, 134
indescribability 7, 25–8; in *Armance* 174, in the *Elegia* 50–1; in the *Heptaméron* 78–9; in *La Princesse de Clèves* 105, 112–13
indifference, feigned 16–17, 19, 43, 69, 73, 79, 104, 136 n.8, 160, 179
infidelity 17, 139; in the *Elegia* 43 n.22, 53; in the *Heptaméron* 65; in *Grandison* 144, in *La Princesse de Clèves* 110, 115–16, 121, 122, 153
insight (*pénétration*): André Aciman and Peter Brooks on 15; in *Armance* 179, 180–1; in *Clarissa* 128, 133; in "Curioso" 94, 97; in the *Elegia* 58; failed, as a feature of analytical fiction 2, 4, 5, 15–16, 17, 21, 24, 40, 93, 192; in the *Heptaméron* 73; in *Grandison*

148; in *La Princesse de Clèves* 30, 104, 105, 119; La Rochefoucauld on 2; in *Persuasion* 167, 170–1
interpolated stories 3, 76 n.40, 83–6, 87, 106–8, 144. *See also* exemplarity, counter-exemplarity
interruptions: in *Don Quixote* 83–7, 90, 112, 134, 160, 173 n.6; in the *Heptaméron* 66, 73
intertextuality 10, 13, 155, 166–7
intimacy: in *Armance* 175, 192; in *Clarissa* 133; definition 16–17, in "Curioso" 93, 193; in the *Elegia* 40; in the *Heptaméron* 66, 68, 73–4; in *La Princesse de Clèves* 118, 123, 124; in *Persuasion* 157, 158, 159, 166–9; in the *Roman de la Rose* 54
involuntary confessions (Nora Martin Peterson) 67, 69, 77, 104
irony 9, 195; in *Armance* 183, 189; in the *Elegia* 38, 44; in the *Heptaméron* 64, 66, 76; in *Grandison* 147, 149; as inherent in analytical fiction 2, 14, 32; in *La Princesse de Clèves* 8, 112, 113, 116; narrative 42; and Northrop Frye 11 n.20; in Ovid's *Metamorphoses* 22–4; in *Persuasion* 159

Jakobson, Roman 31 n.48
James, Henry 14
Jansenism 5 n.13, 15, 125
jealousy 6–7, 17–18, 44, 71, 168; in *Armance* 180–1, 185, 189 character in *Le Roman de la Rose* 54, 56–7; in *Clarissa* 139; in "Curioso" 86, 93–6, 99; dissimulation and 175; in the *Heptaméron* 68–72; in *La Princesse de Clèves* 109–10, 112, 116–17, 119, 122; in *Persuasion* 158, 162–3; romantic love and 145–6, 150–2;
je ne sais quoi 27, 149–50
Johnson, Barbara 7
Johnson, Claudia L. 165
Johnson, Samuel 32 n.50, 141
Jones, Wendy 144 n.12, 155 n.23
Joyce, James 31

Kahler, Erich 19 n.31, 133, 141
Kamuf, Peggy 118
Kant, Immanuel 27

Kaplan, David 75 n.36
Kaps, Helen Karen 103
Kelly, Henry Ansgar 44 n.25
knowledge, Augustinian idea of 5; Cartesian 1, 34; control over in Richardson's novels 128, 133–4, 140, 145; dilated 21, 24, 61, 86, 144; empirical 32 n.51, 86–7, 97, 101–2; historical 2, 83; impressionistic 113–14; impossibility of attaining 66, 85, 89 n.67, 121–2, 162; inhibition of 6; intimacy and 16; metaphors for 36, 140; metaphoric fiction and 31 n.48, 34; misrepresentation of 150; Monsieur de Clèves's sagacity at extracting 108; narrator's 157; ontology and 24, 86, 89; progress of 16–17; realism and 30; relationship between feeling and 6, 32; Richardson's "enlarging" of 141; search for 32, 174, 195; sensory 1, 32; shared cultural 27; successful 170, 182; suspended between ignorance and 23–4, 117; as an unstable entity 148; verbs that aim to produce 25. *See also* self-knowledge
Koehler, Martha J. 144, 150
Koppisch, Michael S. 103
Kriesel, James C. 60, 193
Krueger, Alison E. 86, 88 n.64, 89
Kudish, Adele 76 n.40
Kuhns, Richard 13
Kukkonen, Karin 133
Küpper, Joachim 36 n.3

Laclos, Pierre Choderlos de: *Dangerous Liaisons* 9 n.17, 29
Lafayette, Marie-Madeleine de: *La Princesse de Cleves*: chapter 3 summary 8; chapter text 101–26: affective contradictions in 105–6; affective descriptions in 104–5, 109–11; appearances versus reality in 101, 136; avowal scene 121–2; cabinet scene 109 n.19, 112–13, 123–4; critiques of 29–30, 120; description of the court in 22 n.36; ending of 125–6; genre of 14 n.24; importance of visual sense in 103; infidelity in 115–16, ironic structure

of 108; jealousy in 17; limits of mind reading in 105–8; misreading in 108, 122, 124; portrait scene 119–20; signs and 115–119; trope of indescribability in 26–8, 112–14; *Zayde* 31
LaGuardia, David 66 n.5, 68, 70, 77, 78
Landry, François 177
Landry, Olivia 191 n.1
Lanham, Richard 113
La Rochefoucauld, François de: *Maximes* 2, 3, 5, 15, 16, 21, 128
Lee, Wendy Anne 28 n.44
letters: Anna's about Hickman (*Clarissa* and *Grandison*) 135; Camila's to Anselmo in "Curioso" 92; in *Clarissa* and *Grandison* 128–54; *Epistulae Heroidum* 36 n.5; Fiammetta's unwritten to Panfilo 51; frankness in (*Clarissa* and *Grandison*) 145, 148; forged letter in *Armance* 187–8; Frederick's to Anne in *Persuasion* 171; in the *Heptaméron* 66–7, 76, 79; knowledge is controlled by in (*Clarissa* and *Grandison*) 140, 145; Madame de Thémines's in *La Princesse de Clèves* compared with Marcel's in *À l'ombre des jeunes filles en fleurs* 76 n.40; Octave's to Armance in *Armance* 184, 186–8; Richardson's to his friends 129 n.3, 143; self-knowledge in 147–50; therapeutic nature of writing 191. *See also* writing as therapy
Levarie Smarr, Janet 42, 43, 48, 57 n.72
Lewis, C. S. 57
Locke, John 15, 30, 32
Longinus 21, 28
Lorenz, Hendrik 36 n.3
Lovejoy, A. O. 2
lovers' test theme (David Kaplan) 63, 75, 86–9, 92–4, 137–40
lovesickness: in *Armance* 176; in the *Elegia* 36, 45, 46 n.34, 50, 193
Lukacs, Georg 31
Lyons, John D. 27, 30, 59, 73, 101 n.1, 103
Lyotard, Jean-François 22, 27, 28

McCarthy, Conor 44 n.25
Mackey, Louis 11 n.20
McKeon, Michael 3 n.9, 83–4, 87 n.59, 102

McKillop, A. D. 143
McMurran, Mary Helen 10, 12–13, 127
Madariaga, Salvador de 85 n.56
Mäkelä, Maria 27
Mandeville, Bernard 16
Marguerite de Navarre: the *Heptaméron*: chapter 2 summary 7–8; chapter text 63–82; attempted rape in 65, 75, 77, 79, 82; counterintuitive behavior in characters 54, 66–7, 69, 75, 81; cyclicality of the plot of 97; dissimulation in 69, 71, 73, 77, 79; indescribability trope in 26, 78–9; intertextuality in 10; outer frame's gender tensions 64–5; self-harm in 79–80, 96
Marivaux, Pierre de 129 n.3
marriage: as a cover 67, 87, 91, 110 n.22; characters' ambivalence toward 127–8, 144–5, 154, 178–80; forced 72, 131; foreign 130; opposition between courtly love and 19–20, 44 n.25, 104; for practical reasons 151–3, 155 n.23, 162; refusal of 132 n.6, 160, 185–8; subject to parental intervention 19, 130, 144 n.12, 162 n.3; sublimated into spiritual 82 nn.51–2, 193; successful or happy examples of 135, 151, 166; unhappy state of 105, 116, 135
marriage plot novel 3, 9, 16, 85, 151, 154, 159, 189
Marxist framing of novel theory 29
Medea myth 46 n.32, 49
Meister, Jan Christoph 12
melancholy. *See* lovesickness
Mellon, Lorna 28–9
Menippean satire 11, 12
Mérimée, Prosper 188
metaphoric action (Roman Jakobson; Peter Brooks) 31 n.48
Meyer Spacks, Patricia 31, 134, 136
Migiel, Marilyn 42
Milner, Stephen J. 43 n.22, 46 n.34, 52 n.57
Milowicki, Edward and Rawdon Wilson 22
*mise en abyme* 2, 51, 94, 102, 104
Moler, Kenneth L. 162, 172
Molina, Alvaro 83–4, 88
*Mondanité. See* worldliness

Montaigne, Michel de 1–3, 13, 16, 21, 22, 41 n.18, 69, 92, 116, 128; "Apology for Raymond Sebond" 1; "On Presumption" 1–2; on Boccaccio 2; "Cannibals" 63
*moralisme* 15, 21, 128. *See also* mores
Moravia, Sergio 32 n.49
mores 27, 115
Moriarty, Michael 4, 21
Mouillaud, G. 173 n.6, 181 n.33
movement: in Baroque painting 101 n.2, 103; of the passions 21, 28, 109–11; physical 28, 136, 149
Munro, James 129
Murphy, Brittany 18

Nabokov, Vladimir 85 n.56; *Lolita* 33
narration, limitations of 6, 25–6, 157, 195
narrative *durée* 7, 12, 21, 22–5; in *La Princesse de Clèves* 120. *See also* cyclicality; in the *Roman de la Rose* compared with the *Elegia di madonna Fiammetta* 56; time
narratology 12
national literary canon 12, 127, 155
Ngai, Sianne 28
Nichols, Stephen G. 59
Nicole, Pierre 15–16, 128
novel, theory of the 13–14, 29–33. *See also* genre
novel of adventure 3
novella 7–8, 10, 48 n.39, 193
Nünning, Ansgar 42
Nurse, Peter H. 111
Nussbaum, Martha 17, 104, 114

O'Keefe, Charles 173 n.6, 174, 175, 177
Olson, Greta 42–3
opacity of mind (Peter Caruthers) 6
Ovid (Publius Ovidius Naso) 44; Actaeon 24; Daphne 24; *Epistulae Heroidum* 36 n.5, 38 n.9; Galatea 24; Lovelace's comparison of himself to 140; *Metamorphoses* 22–4; *Pamphilus de amore* 58; Pygmalion myth 22–4

Pabst, Walter 36 n.2
Paige, Nicholas D. 14 n.24, 31
Painter, William: *The Palace of Pleasure* 10
Paolo and Francesca 48 n.39
Pascal, Blaise 3, 5 n.13, 21
passions 5, 16, 114; of the soul (Pascal), 3
Pérez, Ashley Hope 87–8, 94, 96, 99
*peri hypsous*. *See* sublime
*peripeteia*. *See* Aristotle
persuasion: definition of 162–3
Pessimism: in *Armance* 189; Biblical 5 n.13; in *Clarissa* and *Grandison* 155; in the *Elegia* 60; in the *Heptaméron* 66; in *La Princesse de Clèves* 8, 116, 127; in Ovid 22; as worldview of analytical fiction 2, 4, 6, 33, 34, 40, 192, 194
Peterson, Jean 7 n.16
Peterson, Nora Martin 67, 69, 77, 104
Petrarch 36
*Phaedra* (Seneca) 59
*Phaedrus*. *See* Plato
picaresque novel 3
Pinch, Adela 159, 163
Pingaud, Bernard 15, 17, 34
Plato 36 n.3, 59; *Phaedrus* 38 n.10, 48
platonic love 20, 71
Polachek, Dora 10 n.18
Pons, Alain 20 n.32
Preston, John 173 n.6
presumption 1–2
Prévost, Antoine François (Abbé) 128, 129 n.3
Prince, Gerald 59
Proust, Marcel 10, 18; *À l'ombre des jeunes filles en fleurs* 76 n.40; *Sodome et Gomorrhe* 20–1
Psyche (character). *See* Apuleius
psychoanalysis 6, 15, 28–9
psychological novel: as a separate tradition from the analytical novel 9 n.17, 29–31. *See also* realism
psychomachia 38, 54
Puckett, Kent 12
Pyrrhonean skepticism. *See* skepticism

Quint, David 88, 100

Radiguet, Raymond: *Le Bal du comte d'Orgel* 14–15
rape 4, 9, 192; in *Clarissa* 132, 134, 140; in the *Elegia* 58–60; attempted in

*Grandison* 142, 194; attempted in the *Heptaméron* 65, 75, 77, 79, 82
rationalism 1, 5, 98,125
the reader 2, 11, 32–3; didacticism and, in *Grandison* 142; and the *Heptaméron* 65, 79; indescribability and 26–7, 79, 112–13; and knowledge in *Don Quixote* 96, 98; narrative irony and 42–3; satire and 83; and sublimity 21
realism 29–31, 33, 123, 159, 180; in the *Heptaméron* 77. *See also* psychological novel
reality effect (Roland Barthes) 31
recessive action (Anne-Lise François) 10
Reid, Martine 184 n.39
Renaissance humanism 4, 5, 13. *See also* anti-humanism
Rendall, Steven 65, 77
*repos*: in *La Princesse de Clèves* 124–6; in *Clarissa* 135; in *Armance* 189
Restoration (French) 158, 174, 189
Richardson, Samuel: French literature's influence on 129; chapter 4 summary 8; chapter text 127–55; similarities between *Clarissa* and *Grandison* and *La Princesse de Clèves* 127–31; *Clarissa* 131–41; Anna Howe, character in 129, 135–8, 148 n.14, 149; Denis Diderot on 128; dissimulation in 140; imagination in 134, 137; John Belford, character in 131–2, 135, 137, 139; Lovelace's misreading of Clarissa in 134, 139; lover's test theme in 139; quest for knowledge in 132, 133; rape in 132, 134, 140; reliance on physiognomic signs in 137–8; repeating structures of the narrative 133; *Grandison* 141–55; affective environment of 148; attempted rape in 142, 194; Charlotte Grandison, character in 33, 142, 144, 146–8, 154; Clementina della Poretta's abstention from love in 8, 150–5, 166; Clementina as a foreigner and a foil for Harriet 130, 142–4; deliberation in 145; frankness as a virtue in 128, 145, 148; Harriet's anti-romanticism 144–5, 148 n.14, 150; Harriet's jealousy of Clementina 146; irony in 147, 149; Lucy Selby, character in 142,

144–51, 154; the novel as example of parental persuasion 162 n.3; reference to *La Princesse de Clèves* in 150–5; withdrawal from society 153; *Pamela* 9 n.17, 127, 135, 142; *Moral and Instructive Sentiments* 152 n.17
Richetti, John 133
Rikhardsdottir, Sif 59 n.78
Riskin, Jessica 32 n.51
Rivero, Albert J. 144
Robbe-Grillet, Alain 31
*roman d'analyse*. *See* analytical fiction
*roman d'apprentissage*. *See* bildungsroman
romantic comedy 19
romanticism 19–20, 44, 57, 71, 165, 189. *See also* anti-romanticism
Ronchetti, Alessia 36, 38 n.9, 40 n.14, 46, 48, 52
Rousseau, Jean-Jacques: *Julie, ou la nouvelle Héloïse* 9 n.17; *Confessions* 183 n.38
Rudd, Paul 18
Rudler, Gustave 157 n.1

Saiber, Arielle 113
Sainte-Beuve, Charles Augustin: *Les Consolations* 14; *Volupté* 14
Saintsbury, George 130 n.4, 143
salons 31 n.48, 130–1
Sánchez, Francisco 13, 88 n.64
Sappho 20–1, 36, 59
Sartre, Jean-Paul: *Huis Clos* 34
Schiffman, Zachary S. 13
Schlegel, Friedrich 10–11
Schneiderman, Jason 113 n.30
Schnell, Rüdiger 59 n.78
Scordilis Brownlee, Maria 36 n.4
Scudéry, Madeleine de 12 n.21, 103 n.3
Sears, Theresa Ann 134–5
self-deception 1–3, 6, 15, 18, 34, 165; in *Armance* 174, 183, 186; in *Clarissa* 128, 129, 137; in "Curioso" 100, 192; in the *Elegia* 43–4; in *Grandison* 145, 147, 150, 155 n.23; in Montaigne, referring to Ovid 21; in *La Princesse de Clèves* 108, 116, 121, 126; in *Persuasion* 162, 170; the self-deceiver (Alan Singer) in literature 33
self-governance 5–6, 13, 100, 166

self-knowledge 15, 24; in *Armance* 181, 183, 189; in *Clarissa* 134; in *Clueless* 19; in "Curioso" 99; dilation of 21; in the *Elegia of madonna Fiammetta* 45; in *Grandison* 144, 148, 154, 155; in the *Heptaméron* 74; impossibility of, in general 5, 6, 9, 17, 22, 27, 34, 165, 191; and narrative refusal 27; Pierre Nicole on 15–16; in *La Princesse de Clèves* 105, 114, 121; verbs associated with 25
self-love (*amour propre*) 5–6, 128 n.2, 184 n.41, 134, 139
Seneca the Younger (Lucius Annaeus Seneca) 15, 36 n.5, 60; *Phaedra* 59
sensibility 32–3, 127
sentimental fiction 32–3, 135
*serviteur* 71, 74
Sévigné, Madame de (Marie de Rabutin-Chantal) 15, 129
Sextus Empiricus 13. *See also* skepticism
Shakespeare, William: *Hamlet* 10, 94; *Macbeth* 35, 81; *The Merchant of Venice* 75; *Othello* 159
Shattuck, Roger 2 n.5, 21, 29
Shikibu, Murasaki: *The Tale of Genji* 10
Shoemaker, Peter 107
silence 9; in *Armance* 173–90; in "Curioso" 90–1, 93; in the *Heptaméron* 82, in *Grandison* 151; in *La Princesse de Clèves* 113, 121; in *Persuasion* 160, 163, 167, 169; and the sublime 22
Silverstone, Alicia 18–19
Singer, Alan 33
skepticism 7, 12, 43, 104, 194; and in *Clarissa* 89 n.65; Descartes 1; in *Don Quixote* 85, 87, 97; narrative 13; in *Persuasion* 164, 166; Pyrrhonean *vs.* Academic 13
Smith, Adam 32
social class: aristocracy in Restoration France 177, 188–9; Don Quixote's 100; growth of the middle class in *Persuasion* 158–60; in relation to marriage laws in England and improper marriage in Richardson 144, 172; and the novel of worldliness (Peter Brooks) 12 n.21
soul error (Roger Shattuck) 2, 41, 69, 92
Spanish inquisition 84

Spinoza, Baruch 105
*sprezzatura* 20 n.32
spying 90, 103, 105, 112, 119, 121–3, 137, 161. *See also* gaze
Stanton, Domna 125
Stendhal (Marie-Henri Beyle), *Armance*: chapter 5 summary 8–9; chapter text 173–90; abstention from love in 179–80; affective environment of 174; ambivalence about marriage in 178–80, 185–7; death in 187, 189; dissimulation in 174, 182, 187–8; impotence in 173 n.6, 174, 178, 186; letters in 184, 187–8; political background of 174, 176; search for knowledge as a theme in 174; self-deception in 180–3; the significance of the gaze in 180–1; Stendhal's preface to 173
Sterne, Laurence 11, 33
Stoicism 17, 37, 104, 114, 125
sublime (*peri hypsous*) 21–2; Burke 21–2, 28; Kant 27; Longinus 28
Symonds, John Addington 38 n.9

Talbot, Emile J. 182 n.36
Tanner, Tony 162, 164
Testing. *See* lovers' test theme
Thackerey, William Makepeace: *Vanity Fair* 26–7
Thucydides 2
Tilmouth, Christopher 5
time: narrative movement forward versus recursive movement 21, 33, 104, 112 n.28, 126; stagnation of 104. *See also* cyclicality; narrative *durée*
Todd, Janet 32, 159
Todd, Sarah J. 53
Todorov, Tzvetan 174
transhistorical literature 3, 13
Tristan and Isolde myth 44, 49
*Tristano Panciatichiano* (anon.) 49 n.42
*trompe l'oeil* 101 n.2
Troyes, Chrétien de 49 n.42

unreliable narrator 7, 42–3, 45, 82, 153 n.18
untrustworthy narrator: Fiammetta as 42–3

Valenza, Robin 25, 133
Valincour, Jean-Baptiste-Henri de 120

Vance, Jacob 64–5, 71, 77
Velásquez, Diego 102
ventriloquism (Elizabeth Harvey): accusations of in Boccaccio 52. in Ovid 23; in *The Golden Ass* 35 6; as a metaphor for love 70
Venus (goddess of love): in the *Elegia* 37, 39, 44, 50, 53–4, 60, 92, 154; in the *Roman de la Rose* 54–7
Vermillion, Mary 144 n.12
Virgil (Publius Vergilius Maro): *The Aeneid* 38 n.9
Virtue, Nancy E. 65
virtue: balance between passion and 154–5; in chivalric love 70–1, 77; Christian 43; construction of ideals of 44; in *Clarissa* 138, 140; in "Curioso" 86–7, 95; *Grandison*'s effect on the reader 141–2; in *La Princesse de Clèves* 153; in *Persuasion* 172; vice and 15; women's 65–6, 75
Vranjes, Vlasta 164

Waley, Pamela 38 n.9
Warburton, William 129 n.3
Wardropper, Bruce 85 n.56
Watt, Ian: *The Rise of the Novel* 29–30, 31 n.48
Weber, Max 29
Wiesmann, Marc-André 78
Wiltshire, John 167
withdrawal from society: *in La Princesse de Clèves* and *Clarissa* 128, 130, 141; *in La Princesse de Clèves* and *Grandison* 153
Wölfflin, Heinrich 101 n.2
Wood, Michael 173 n.5, 176
worldliness (Peter Brooks) 25, 31 n.48, 34, 127
writing as therapy 46–7, 51, 191. *See also* letters

Zak, Gur 37, 46 n.34, 48
Zigarovich, Jolene 133 n.7, 194
Zunshine, Lisa 107 n.11, 140

www.ingramcontent.com/pod-product-compliance
Lightning Source LLC
Chambersburg PA
CBHW052039300426
44117CB00012B/1886